CREATIVE LIVES AND WORKS

From Antiquity to Ethnography

From Antiquity to Ethnography: Keith Thomas, Brian Harrison and Peter Burke is the first time a collection of these interviews is being published as a book. They have been conducted by one of England's leading social anthropologists and historians, Professor Alan Macfarlane.

Filmed over a period of several years, the three conversations in this volume are part of the series *Creative Lives and Works*. These transcriptions form a part a larger set of interviews that cut across various disciplines, from the social sciences and the sciences to the performing and visual arts. The current volume is on three of Britain's foremost social and cultural historians.

The study of historical traditions, social mores and practices come alive in these conversations. We also learn about the painstaking nature of notetaking which the subject demands. The three conversations in this volume reflect how interconnected the disciplines of history and anthropology/ethnography are. Keith Thomas brings in his vast knowledge of historical sources combined with rich ethnography. Brian Harrison candidly describes his childhood trauma and his meticulous system of card indexing with equal ease. Peter Burke paints his canvas by combining linguist prowess with the interdisciplinary aspects of history and anthropology.

The book will be of enormous value not just to those interested in the subject of History, Culture Studies and Ethnography but also to those with an avid interest in Comparative Studies and Literature.

Alan Macfarlane was born in Shillong, India, in 1941 and educated at the Dragon School, Sedbergh School, Oxford and London Universities where he received two Master's degrees and two doctorates. He is the author of over forty books, including *The Origins of English Individualism* (1978) and *Letters to Lily: On How the World Works* (2005). He has worked in England, Nepal, Japan and China as both an historian and anthropologist. He was elected to the British Academy in 1986 and is now Emeritus Professor of Anthropology at the University of Cambridge and a Life Fellow of King's College, Cambridge. Professor Macfarlane received the Huxley Memorial Medal, the highest honour of the Royal Anthropological Institute in 2012.

CREATIVE LIVES AND WORKS

From Antiquity to Ethnography
Keith Thomas, Brian Harrison and Peter Burke

In conversation with
Alan Macfarlane

Edited by
Radha Béteille

Routledge
Taylor & Francis Group
LONDON AND NEW YORK

SOCIAL
SCIENCE
PRESS

First published 2022
by Routledge
2 Park Square, Milton Park, Abingdon, Oxon OX14 4RN

and by Routledge
605 Third Avenue, New York, NY 10158

Routledge is an imprint of the Taylor & Francis Group, an informa business

© 2022 Social Science Press

The right of Alan Macfarlane to be identified as author of this work has been asserted in accordance with sections 77 and 78 of the Copyright, Designs and Patents Act 1988.

Print edition not for sale in South Asia (India, Sri Lanka, Nepal, Bangladesh, Pakistan or Bhutan)

British Library Cataloguing-in-Publication Data
A catalogue record for this book is available from the British Library

Library of Congress Cataloging-in-Publication Data
A catalog record for this book has been requested

ISBN: 9781032158952 (hbk)
ISBN: 9781003246152 (ebk)

DOI: 10.4324/9781003246152

Typeset in Sabon
by Manmohan Kumar, New Delhi 110020

SOCIAL
SCIENCE
PRESS

Contents

Preface

ENCOUNTERS WITH THREE SOCIAL HISTORIANS

The three social and cultural historians in this volume are of special interest to me because they have been among the most formative teachers and mentors in my life. They are not only connected to me, but strongly connected to each other. All of them are products of Oxford University and both Brian Harrison and Peter Burke, like myself, were pupils of Keith Thomas.

Brian and Peter were also friends at Oxford. They were all between four and eight years older than me, the distance to an older brother, yet they had all had experience of the world through National Service in a way which I had not. So, they brought a sense of a wider world to my rather sheltered early upbringing. The reasons for my gratitude and admiration for their lives will become apparent in the interviews. I will try to explain in this introduction a little of how each of them helped to shape my academic life.

In any intellectual or creative walk of life one tends to have 'masters' or exemplars, people one both tries to emulate and perhaps to surpass, who teach, inspire and guide one. For me, the most important of these is the distinguished historian, Keith Thomas.

Keith was assigned as my supervisor when I settled down to do a D.Phil. at Oxford in 1963. I was quite over-awed by both his austere, schoolmasterly, manner, full of nervous energy and his immense erudition. His large room at St John's College seemed huge and stuffed with books.

In that year (1963) he published his article on 'History and Anthropology' in *Past and Present* which was a huge inspiration for me and which I have read and re-read many times. He also, in 1958, published an article for the same journal on 'Women and the Civil War Sects'. I think he must have decided to make a study of witchcraft and magic just before I met him, so when I read out my list of possible topics, though sex and myth also interested him, he suggested I tried the witchcraft topic.

It is difficult to convey the immense privilege and excitement of being the first (and for some time the only) D.Phil. student of someone of Keith's brilliance at a time when he was not encumbered by his later administrative burdens and was gathering materials and writing his most famous book, *Religion and the Decline of Magic* (1971).

I remember supervisions with both of us sitting on his sofa and sharing my chapter as he made both detailed and broad criticisms. I was fairly terrified as he was meticulous and fairly un-inhibited in his criticisms. I remember he became exasperated at times because I would argue each point. Yet there was a constant flow of suggestions and references and although he was writing a book on the same subject, I don't remember a single instance of conflict or difficulty in this. There is a very detailed account of our relationship in *Oxford Postgraduate*.

One of the most important influences was on style. Everything must be unpretentious, without jargon or complication, crystal clear like his own writing. This meant that one had to have things very organised in one's mind before, or as, one wrote. In a way, one always continues to write for one's first supervisor, so whenever my sentences become over-long or I tend to verbosity I hear his crisp, schoolmasterly, voice in my ear.

A second major influence, and one that was decisive on my later career, was on my choice of discipline. Keith was himself at the height of his interest in the relations between anthropology and history, so he encouraged me to become immersed in anthropology. On his suggestion, I went to lectures in the social anthropology department and met many of the distinguished anthropologists then at Oxford.

Keith's great reputation was a continuing asset. To have one of the most respected and energetic historians as one's patron and referee-writer throughout life accounts for a good deal of my subsequent career. I owe my first job to him. For when in 1970 I was writing up my Nepal Ph.D. I received a postcard from Keith (some 3 years after I had finished being formally supervised by him and after changing my subject) to say that there were some history research fellowships being advertised for King's College, Cambridge. I applied, he was a referee, and I got a Senior Research Fellowship at King's, where I have been since.

There can be no doubt that his references for my Readership and Professorship must have been very important.

As for the formal influence of his books and ideas, these were also considerable. Like many others, I was bowled over by the scope, energy and erudition of *Religion and the Decline of Magic*. I read and re-read it and still regard it as a great book.

The final influence is difficult to measure. To a certain extent one writes for a very small set of people, perhaps half a dozen. One continues to write for one's supervisors all one's life. Keith's great advantage in this respect was that he set such a high standard, acting as a voice in the back of my mind all the time, urging clarity, precision, scholarship. I sent him copies of all my books and he invariably sent me encouraging and positive comments, plus a detailed and meticulous list of mistakes. Altogether an impressive man and a very hard act to follow. My full debt to him as a supervisor is described in my book *Oxford Postgraduate* (2018).

BRIAN HARRISON

I first met Brian at the start of my second term as an undergraduate reading history at Oxford. I had failed the Latin part of my Preliminary Exam in the first term and if I failed on the re-take, I would lose my place at Oxford. The College arranged for me to be given some extra Latin from David McLellan, then doing a D.Phil. David became one of the great writers and editors of Karl Marx and shared a flat with Brian.

I noticed when I visited for lessons that Brian had an impressive array of large folders and when he showed them to me, I found that they contained an amazing number of summaries and extracts from books and lectures which he had made as an undergraduate. I asked if I could borrow them, which he kindly allowed, and I proceeded to re-type many of them. Whether this helped or hindered in my understanding of history, I am not sure, but it was both a generous act and gave my confidence a boost.

I also noticed that Brian had several filing cabinets filled with small cards which had short quotations and cross-references to his files. This gave me the idea to do the same thing. During my last year as an undergraduate I extracted hundreds of quotations, facts and statistics onto little cards and learnt these off by heart. I deployed many of them in my examinations. Again, I do not know whether this improved my performance, but again I was learning something about work organization and this method of cross-indexing has become a central theme in my life.

We kept in touch through my undergraduate years and when I came back to do a D.Phil. Brian was immediately supportive and able to give me advice as he had by then become a Research Fellow at St Antony's College. A few days after I arrived to do my postgraduate degree, still unsure whether it would be a two-year M.Litt. or a three-year D.Phil., I consulted Brian and he wrote as follows, a wise and encouraging note which also made me feel special with an offer of dinner at his College and talks about research methods, and the flattering suggestion that I should write an article for a history journal.

I did go for the discussion about methods, and there he explained more fully the philosophy of 'one fact one card' which he had partly derived from the work of Beatrice Webb. I used this extensively hereafter, not only for writing theses and books but as the basis of complex research projects of a historical and anthropological kind throughout my life. Out of this emerged a continuing fascination with information retrieval which lay behind many years of work with computer scientists to device better methods of multi-media data retrieval. None of this would have happened, without my chance encounter with Brian.

Later in life we kept in touch and I heard of his various impressive achievements, including editing and contributing three chapters to a multi-volume history of Oxford University, and contributing two volumes to a new history of England, and becoming the editor of the New Dictionary of National Biography. His interest was precisely in the sociological questions about everyday life which interested me. As I wrote in a letter to him in the last months of my doctorate, *All the problems you are studying for the C19 I am tackling for the C16 – which makes for interesting comparisons.*

His materials were mainly historical, but he was also an early pioneer in oral history, based on recorded interviews with college servants and others. This also overlapped with my interest in preserving the past through interviews, as in the series represented in this book.

He was, and is, immensely driven and hardworking, as the following letter to my mother in May 1965, after I had nervously invited him to a meal I cooked during my second year as a doctoral student: '... *my "70-hours-work-a-week" friend* [Brian Harrison] *at Nuffield came to supper. He's very nice. He doesn't seem to have suffered from food-poisoning which is lucky as the frustration would have driven him mad!*

Having a chance to interview him, a particularly frank and self-aware session, with a visit to his garage where his more than one hundred thousand small cards had found a resting place, perhaps helped to lay the last ghost of my long-past apprehension and relief about the effects of my cooking!

PETER BURKE

I first met Peter Burke in January 1971. In the previous October, when I was still writing my anthropology Ph.D. in Yorkshire and felt out of the academic circle, he wrote me a nice letter inviting me to give a talk on witches at the Renaissance club. I gave the talk and greatly enjoyed meeting him and we have remained friends since. He was then a Lecturer at Sussex and I already knew of his links to Keith Thomas. I had also already started to read his books before we met and immediately found some of the qualities in his writing which have influenced me greatly.

His canvas is very broad, asking deep and wide questions and looking across sweeps of time and comparing different parts of Europe. He is a superb linguist and has read much of the original and secondary material available in most major European languages. He has travelled extensively and has friends all over Europe. He loves the variety and particularly the Mediterranean and its contrasts with Holland and the north. Later his love of southern Catholic culture was extended to a deep interest in South America, strengthened by his marriage to the Brazilian academic Maria Lúcia Pallares whose world there he often visited.

He is interested in everything, from dreams and fantasies to art and literature. And he writes about all these things in an absolutely clear and attractive way. The depth of thought is concealed by the simplicity of style. He reminds me of one of his heroes, Montaigne, and like Montaigne he is a brilliant essayist.

He particularly interested me because he moved outside conventional historical approaches and knew a good deal about the neighbouring social sciences, particularly anthropology and sociology. He was interested in the methodology of history, drawing extensively on the French Annales school of Marc Bloch and Lucien Febvre and translating work from that tradition. So the questions I was beginning to ask were exactly the same as those earlier pioneered by Peter.

When I was asked to convene a series of seminars combining some of the most interesting anthropologists, sociologists and historians in Europe in 1977, I asked Peter to be the Chairman of the first session, which we filmed, on Carnival. His excellent direction of the event and interventions, which can be seen in the filmed recording of the event (https://sms.cam.ac.uk/collection/2679146) helped make it a really special occasion.

One thing I increasingly came to admire was not only his productivity, for he seemed to be producing a book every year or two, and always interesting and challenging, but also the way he ranged over many different subjects. Each was very different from the last. His vast curiosity, encyclopaedic knowledge and mastery of method allowed him to escape from the usual narrowing tendency of historians. His talk in the frequent conversations we had over the years, especially when he came to Cambridge as a Fellow of Emmanuel College and University Lecturer in January 1979, was as lively and delightful as his writing.

Even our young children enjoyed his company and were particularly amused by finding an adult who seemed to maintain his child-like innocence, confessing that he could not drive and could not ride a bicycle and was completely without pretension, but full of bird-like interest in all around him. He influenced me generally, but also in particular ways. For example, as I approached retirement, I read an article he had written for the well-known French sociologist Pierre Bourdieu. Bourdieu had expressed extreme puzzlement about how Cambridge Colleges worked, and Peter had written an article for Bourdieu's journal (in French), to explain the mystery of one of the world's great anomalies. He did it in the form of a slightly tongue-in-cheek anthropologist and it was both charming and insightful. When published in English, Peter discretely hid his name behind that of a seventeenth century iconoclast. It gave me encouragement and inspiration and I incorporated ideas from it in my book *Reflections on Cambridge* (2009).

Peter is a continuing inspiration and friend, highly productive into his eighties and always incredibly efficient and courteous. He completes this trilogy of remarkable thinkers without whose guidance and example I would have led a far less interesting and fruitful life.

Transcriber's Note

The transformation of videographed speeches into the written word has been a riveting experience. Transcriptions, while retaining the essence of a conversation, lend a new dimension to the oral transmission, opening them up to a wider readership, including those with diminished auditory functions. This collection of transcripts lucidly captures the engaging interactions between Alan Macfarlane, one of Britain's foremost social anthropologists, and three eminent social historians — Keith Thomas, Brian Harrison and Peter Burke. In fact, the intellectual discourses in these interviews on history and historiography draw in the reader as a participant. And, while offering a different order of internal cohesiveness, accentuates the readers' ability to retain information, in this case, knowledge and scholarship.

Here, it must however be noted that not being a subject expert has been somewhat limiting. Besides, I have had to acquaint myself with speech patterns, accents, diction and intonations in areas that I was unfamiliar with when I began.

Furthermore, the transcribing of oral transmission leaves little room to represent facial expressions and non-verbalized sounds such as chuckles, laughs, sighs and for that matter exclamations, as well as pauses and idiosyncrasies in actual speech. Thus, I have taken the liberty to replace them with closely corresponding punctuations, so as not to alter the meaning or import of what is being said. Discrepancies in speech patterns have been isolated and addressed. Any misrepresentation of words and phrases, is entirely inadvertent.

The trust and generosity of Professor Macfarlane in sharing his wealth of scholarship with Social Science Press cannot be adequately expressed in words.

– Radha Béteille

Introduction
Alan Macfarlane

There have been many autobiographical accounts of the creative process in science as well as in the arts, humanities and social sciences. Yet these tend to concentrate on one level, and within that one aspect, the cerebral, intellectual working of a single thinker's mind. If we are to investigate further the connections between the levels of civilization, institution, network and individual, and the fifth dimension of chance or random variation, we need to supplement these accounts, in particular by letting scientists and others talk in a relaxed way about what they think has been important in their lives and works. Over the years I have been collecting such data and here I would like to describe how this happened and what opportunities it opens up for further understanding of the springs of creativity.

***

There is a puzzle as to why I have spent so much time and effort (and expense) on interviewing (on film) a large number of academics and others over the years. No-one else has done this as far as I am aware and it has few tangible rewards except the occasional gratitude of one's colleagues. Why and how did this project build up over the years to a point where I now have about 250 lengthy interviews, almost all of them on the web?

One factor is clearly my anthropological training and the experience of anthropological fieldwork. Although some social historians of the recent past began to become interested in oral history and the tape-recording of memories from the late 1960s, for example

Paul Thompson, Brian Harrison and others, on the whole historians deal with dead people who cannot be interviewed. Certainly, as a 17th century historian I was not interested in interviews.

Anthropologists on the other hand deal with the living and the 'life history' or in-depth study of one or two 'informants' naturally leads into the use of recording devices – again usually tape-recorders, but also sometimes film cameras, to record interviews. So, from my first fieldwork in 1968–70 in Nepal, I was aware of the potential of interviews. Alongside the interviews with intellectuals described below, I have made in-depth interviews with my anthropological subjects, in particular a ten-part interview with Dilmaya Gurung in 1992. I also taped and filmed members of my family talking about their lives, especially my grandmother in 1978.

My interest in biographical details as a source of social history was also stimulated by the accident of moving through a number of different intellectual landscapes in my early years. My grandmother's stories of Burma and India and then my mother's vivid autobiographical writings in her letters and when she visited me from India were early influences which led to an interest in listening to older people talking about their lives. So, when I became an undergraduate and then a graduate at Oxford (1960–66) I spent some time listening to elderly academics, particularly my history tutor Lady Rosalind Clay with her deep immersion in the world of Oxford life through her father A.L. Smith (Master of Balliol), Sir Henry Clay her husband and links to the Mitchison an Mitford families. She seemed to know personally many of the people whose books I was reading – Namier, Tawney, Trevelyan, Hill, Habakkuk, and she told me about their lives and personalities. I also began to hear about the folklore and gossip of historians from my other teachers – Harry Pitt, Keith Thomas and others.

The world of the historians was brought into relief by being on the edge of another group of academics, the social anthropologists. As I did my D.Phil. on witchcraft I began to meet the older members of the distinguished school of anthropologists, the Lienhardts, John Beattie and above all E.E. Evans-Pritchard. This was a particularly intense and gossip-connected tribe and I heard their stories of the great feuds and friendships and how they had survived their fieldwork. The interest in biography was also strengthened by my early apprenticeship in history at Oxford where I was taught how important it was to study not only the works but also the lives of great historians – Gibbon, Macaulay, Tocqueville, Bede and others. This led me much later in my life to write detailed studies of other major figures in books on Montesquieu, Adam Smith, De Tocqueville, Maitland, Fukuzawa and others which put a strong emphasis on the biography as well as the ideas.

As a social historian I wanted to get inside the mentality as well as the social structure of the past. As an undergraduate I had discovered that letters (Pastons, Stonors) and diaries (Pepys, Kilvert) were wonderful sources for social history. So, my first book was a study of the life of one individual *The Family Life of Ralph Josselin*, based on the diary of a 17th century clergyman. Henceforth I collected letters, autobiographies, diaries, travellers' journals and made a great deal of use of this biographical material in a number of my books.

The early experience of eves-dropping on what appeared to be a disappearing world of a certain academic endeavour in the pre-war world of Oxford history and anthropology, was reinforced by moving to the London School of Economics for two years, where giants of the post-Malinowski generation, Raymond Firth, Isaac Schapera, Lucy Mair, were on the point of retiring. Then when I moved to the School of Oriental and African Studies (SOAS) I met another group of giants from a previous age, particularly Adrian Mayer and Christoph von Fürer-Haimendorf who became my supervisor.

When I moved as a research fellow to Cambridge in 1971, I encountered again several oral worlds which intrigued me. There were a new set of older anthropologists, Meyer Fortes, Audrey Richards, G.I. Jones, Edmund Leach, S.J. Tambiah, Jack Goody among them. And there were a group set of historians, in particular Peter Laslett and Tony Wrigley. A third world was that of King's College, where memories of the Bloomsbury era lingered on with Dadie Rylands, Peter Avery, Christopher Morris, Richard Braithwaite and others.

With six or seven sets of oral history washing through my life by the age of thirty it would have been a rather insensitive and myopic young scholar who did not realize that he was experiencing something special and perhaps something that should be recorded for posterity. I did not want to write a conventional history of academic disciplines, yet I had a sense that there were webs of ideas and connections which were carried by elderly individuals which should be recorded. They should be treated with the same respect and desire to save and document as was accorded to small oral cultures around the world whose myths, legends, rituals and folklore was carefully recorded by anthropologists.

It was perhaps a jumble of such motives, combined with friendship with the Director of the Cambridge University Audio-Visual Unit, Martin Gienke, which led to the first experiment to record academics on film. I had been asked to organize a series of seminars in history and anthropology in 1976–77 for the Economic and Social Research Council and this I knew would be a chance to gather together some of the leading thinkers in both fields. If they were coming for several days to Cambridge, might it not be an idea to film them, both as an archive for future generations and to show to students and colleagues who could not come to the meetings? So, I organized the seminars and two were filmed. Amongst those attending were many younger scholars who would become well known – Maurice Bloch, Raphael Samuel, Keith Thomas, Keith Hopkins, Peter Burke, and a number of more senior figures in their prime such as E.P. Thompson, Edmund Leach, Maurice Godelier, Jack Goody, Arnaldo Momigliano and Ernest Gellner.

I had assumed that this experiment, which is up on the web would be repeated by others as the technology became better. Yet, to my knowledge, it has hardly ever been duplicated. One of the few instances when something similar was done was again an idea I had. When making a six-part series for Channel 4 on the history of the world over the last 10,000 years, we assembled five leading historians and they talked for two days about various aspects of the past. The whole was filmed and is also up on the web.

The next step was probably influenced by this early filming attempt. Jack Goody had been involved in the filmed seminar and five years later, with the help of the Cambridge linguist Stephen Levinson, he arranged three seminars where Meyer Fortes, Audrey Richards and M.N. Srinivas would be filmed talking about their lives and work. Jack Goody then retired, but continued to take an interest in the project and interviewed several others for me, including John Barnes and Jean La Fontaine.

In 1982 a portable video camera which took low-band U-matic was available and so I founded the Rivers Video Project with several of my Ph.D. students, to experiment with the use of film in teaching and research in anthropology. Among the early projects were several biographical and archival films, including a film of Brian Hodgson and a long interview in June 1983 of my supervisor Christoph von Fürer-Haimendorf. The group also filmed my undergraduate lectures and some of the students made a film as part of their course on T.R. Malthus.

Now that I had started to film interviews, I could see the way in which my early interest in the gossip and interconnections of what was in effect a small tribe of British social anthropologists could be turned into a permanent record. The first interviews tended to be done by someone who knew the subject well – Goody in the cases above, Jean La Fontaine interviewing Lucy Mair, Caroline Humphrey interviewing Owen Lattimore. But gradually this faded away and I did nearly all the interviews and all the filming. About ten of the interviews were however done by friends and colleagues abroad and sent to me.

At first the focus was almost exclusively on anthropologists – with some sociologists who were also anthropologists such as André Béteille, John Barnes, Ronald Dore. Later it was extended to others in the general area of social sciences, more sociologists and some historians.

The filming continued to be done for the next ten or fifteen years on low-band u-Matic and the tapes were stored away. It was not easy or necessary to edit them, but nor was it easy to show them, so very few were ever shown to students or colleagues. I looked at the collection as an archival collection, a time capsule of a vanishing world, which might be interesting in a hundred years time. That was assuming that it would be possible to play them. Already twenty years after they were made the tapes of the ESCR seminars were unplayable in Cambridge and had to be saved by the National Film Council.

Then a set of interconnected technological changes occurred which affected many of my projects. The internet and high-speed broadband made it possible to send films across the world. Large external hard discs and new compression techniques made it possible to store and edit the films. The arrival of a Digital repository in Cambridge in 2004 made it possible to put up the interviews we had done until that date in June of that year, an idea first suggested by Mark Turin.

This development, which meant that the material could be appreciated by many more people, and the arrival of better cameras for the filming, meant that I began to increase the number of my interviews. By 2004 I had done about thirty interviews, by 2006 there were about 70 interviews and lectures. I described my project in relation to the Arts, Humanities and Social Sciences to some colleagues in King's College. The scientists Patrick Bateson and Herbert Huppert were excited by the idea and asked whether I could extend the filming to cover the natural and physical sciences.

I was surprised that very few people or organizations appeared to be doing the in-depth 'lives and works' kind of interviews I had undertaken for the immensely larger fields of the sciences. (Two sites which did have interviews on were that at globetrotter.berkeley and the Vega project at Sussex initiated by Harry Kroto). I was also hesitant about my ability to interview in fields about which I knew nothing. But they urged me to try and introduced me to a number of distinguished scientists. Shortly afterwards Gabriel Horn became an active advisor on the project as well.

I started gingerly with the scientists, filming Dan McKenzie with whom I shared a room in King's, the co-discoverer of tectonic plates and continental drift. It went well and I greatly enjoyed it. Pat

Bateson then interviewed Gabriel Horn and I filmed another session with them talking about their partnership, and I interviewed Pat Bateson himself. So, I was now sufficiently confident to interview other scientists. Having broadened it beyond arts and social sciences, there was all the world which lay between, such as economics, psychology, philosophy and so on. There were also other interesting people I wanted to film – the Vice Chancellor Alison Richard, the ex-Cabinet Secretary Richard Wilson, the musician John Rutter, the sculptor Anthony Gormley.

In fact, the series broadened out not only into politicians and civil servants, but into many other fields. There are interviews on the performing and visual arts, crafts and skills (pottery, gardening, sculpture), law, journalism, literary criticism, business, exploration publishing, the military, filmmaking, classics, archaeology, architecture and linguistics. Whenever I heard of or met someone who seemed to have made a creative contribution to the world, whether they were a road sweeper or a College butler, up to some of the most distinguished thinkers in the world, I would try to interview them. It is a wide spread.

So, from May 2007 when the first scientists were filmed, until September 2009 when I formally retired as Professor, I filmed something like another 80 interviews and the total now stands at about 200 films.

As far as I know this archive is unique and as a number of the major figures are dead and others are getting very old, so the interviewing cannot now be done. There are some small projects, sometimes influenced by our experiments, in Germany, the London School of Economics and elsewhere. Yet on the whole there is nothing quite like this.

***

Naturally the way in which I have done the interviews reflects both my own interests and my experience of what works. My central aim has been to let the speakers tell their own story, present themselves as they wish to do, without threatening or probing or adversarial questioning. Yet in doing so, and with a roughly chronological approach, I have been particularly interested in the question of what accidents, historical contingencies, or personal traits have influenced the subjects and sent them towards a particular career. In particular, what they do has contributed to their more creative and sometimes inspired work and innovation in their various fields.

From the very start of my interest in the oral history of my seniors and contemporaries, I have been keen to learn what I should do to make me as good an anthropologist and historian as possible. What are the craft skills and what are the ways of thinking and ordering one's life which will make maximize the chance of making a serious contribution to our knowledge of the world? This early interest was heightened when I found myself in the incredibly privileged surroundings of Cambridge for forty years, surrounded by the ghosts of Newton, Darwin, Rutherford and many others.

The following describes the topics I have tried to cover in my interviews. On the surface, the interviews are almost unstructured and I avoid referring to a written questionnaire as this can distract from the spontaneity of the occasion. I encourage the interviewee to talk about whatever they would like. My role is similar to a psychiatrist's, that is to say to let the subject narrate their life, in particular in relation to the obstacles and encouragements to creativity and discovery. We tend to cover the following:

when and where born
ancestry – going back as far as they like, including occupation and temperament and possible effects of grand-parents, parents and siblings
first memories and hobbies as a child
first and subsequent schools, with important teachers, hobbies, subjects which gripped them, sports and games, music, special books
university and those who taught and studied with them and interests there
first research, supervisors, mentors, influences

jobs and career and travels through life, work abroad
colleagues, friends and network of workers, partners and children
methods of working and thinking
major achievements and problem-solving during life, how they
occurred, including especially important bursts of activity
administrative tasks
teaching and supervising of students
effects of their work environment (laboratories, departments,
Colleges etc)
philosophy and religion
political views and activities
advice for a young person starting out in their field
specifically ask if there is anything which they would like to have
talked about and I have omitted to ask about

Yet if the subject does not want to follow this order, or to answer all of these, or to add further subjects, that is fine. What I want the viewer to see is the inside of a life, told in a conversational and personal way.

***

The interviews are an intimate probing of personal experience, usually by a complete stranger who is holding a potentially threatening video camera. The subjects know that this may be seen by almost anyone in the world – friends, students, competitors, and enemies, now and in the future. This could be intimidating, especially to older subjects and for those who share a widespread reserve and distaste for talking about themselves.

I have therefore developed a number of techniques for putting the subjects at their ease. These have contributed, I believe, to the rather startlingly honest and trusting conversations which I have managed to have with a wide range of near strangers. It is worth briefly summarizing these since they could be helpful for others who help to extend this project.

1. It is important to have a fairly small and unostentatious camera that does not dominate or frighten the subject. The less intrusive the microphone the better – which is one reason why I have given up using lapel microphones. I place the camera on my knees and do not use a tripod, which can again be intimidating.

2. The room in which the interview is done is important. I avoid formal settings if possible – lecture theatres, 'offices', and seminar rooms. A room with gentle furnishings. an easy chair for both interviewee and interviewer, books and pictures and objects in the background, a pleasant view all helps. And of course, absolute silence and absence of telephones, mobiles, computers and interruptions is essential. I do not sit too close, or too far away. I sit at the same level, as I would do in any normal relaxed conversation between friends.

3. I try to develop the sheep-dog technique. When gently moving a flock of sheep to its destination, a good sheep dog is mostly silent and still. Each time the sheep move in a satisfactory direction, the dog creeps forward. And then sinks onto the grass and waits attentively. It does not bark, just guides. So, if possible, I try to help the interviewee along, but only interrupt when they need encouragement or direction. I never shut them off (though I occasionally warn them if the conversation is getting into the realms of damaging speech and check that they are aware of this), but try to bring them to subjects as they are needed.

4. I always try to show interest, however little I know, or even care about the subject being discussed. What is being said is often important to the subject and has a depth which I, or others, may only realize later. They deserve serious attention and respect for what is often a summary of a life. Of course, I may verbally disagree a little, or query things, but I try always to do so in the pursuit of a common goal of understanding. Curiosity is the most important attribute.

5. It is important for there to be no sense of rush. If I want an hour of film, I allow 90 minutes, which gives time for general conversation, a cup of tea etc.

6. I used to prepare carefully for the interviews. With people in my own subjects, this was possible. With scientists, beyond reading a brief life in an encyclopaedia, I cannot really prepare. It seems to work as well without preparation.

7. I used to think that it would be good if the 'subjects' prepared themselves in some detail, and when they asked me, I would advise this. In fact, I have found that spontaneity, even if it leads to some confusion, forgetting of names etc., is better and I advise people not to think about the interview – just that it will be chronological and they can say what they like (though they can look at one or two of the earlier interviews on the web if they would like to do so).

8. The fact that there is no commercial side to the endeavour has an effect. That I am doing it without specific pay for the job and not as part of a well-funded project, is usually obvious and helps. That all the materials are freely available on the web, can be downloaded for free anywhere in the world and used in teaching and research, all adds to the trust and spirit of altruistic collaboration.

9. The absence of any bureaucracy is important. We enter into an implicit contract. I have no paper for them to sign, assigning copyright, intellectual property rights etc. It is all agreed verbally and informally in the act itself. And hence the bond of friendship is not broken.

10. One of the things that has developed over the years and has greatly increased the interest and usability of the interviews is the possibility of putting up a summary with some time codes to help viewers navigate to an area that particularly interests them. The summaries are often very detailed and the development of the web has again made them more interesting and reliable since one can check names, theories, and connections. It is an art form in itself, combining considerable synthetic skills, a jigsaw ability and great concentration. It is not easy, but the website gives many examples of highly professional examples which have won high praise from the interview subjects who are often amazed at how accurate and complete they are. The

obvious comprehension shown in the summary further adds to the sense of trust.

11. Before the interview it is important to explain that anything that is said can be retracted or glossed later. People should not censor themselves too much. Candour and a relaxed flow of ideas are important and trying to avoid things detracts from this. I explain that while filming – before or after saying something – the interviewee can easily say 'this is not for public dissemination', 'this is confidential' or whatever. Any such passage is then excised from the version that becomes publicly available – but the original tapes are kept for posterity. I also explain that we will send them the full summary which needs to be checked for accuracy (especially names and technical terms), interpretations of statements, and also gives the person a chance to withdraw any section or passage if they wish. They may, as has sometimes happened, feel that they want to add something – some more autobiography, a clearer exposition of something technical. It is not difficult to put this into the summary either in square brackets or as an appendix.

12. The duration of time people can concentrate varies. Most people can manage an hour, and then, with a break, another hour. When the tape ends, I allow a few minutes for revival – but it is important not to lose the momentum. Some people prefer to do an hour, go away and come back some days later. This is alright, but can lead to repetition. But for older subjects (and many of mine are in their later eighties and older) it may be necessary. The older subjects also often feel more comfortable in their own homes amongst their books and belongings. This often gives an added dimension to the interviews.

If the subjects do reveal things which should be kept private for some years or even decades, these are edited out of the versions that go on the web, but the original tapes and full interviews will be preserved for posterity. Meanwhile the edited versions are put up on DSpace at Cambridge and on other websites, including YouTube, and now increasingly on websites all over the world – Scandinavia,

America, China and elsewhere. The value of the interviews is enormously enhanced by the excellent and thorough summaries which Sarah Harrison has made of them all, taking much more time and skill to do than the interviews themselves. What has been created, through a set of accidents, is a resource for the study of a number of academic disciplines, from anthropology to molecular biology, from history to astronomy, from sociology to mathematics. It also provides rich material for the study of British academic life and institutions in the twentieth century. Furthermore, for those interested in the conditions of creativity and discovery, it is a unique archive.

The project has developed as a result of a set of accidents and through the help and support of many people, in particular Sarah Harrison, Mark Turin, Jack Goody, Gerry Martin and many others. This project to publish the full interviews of selected individuals was the idea of Esha Béteille, whose support and advice have been indispensable. I would particularly like to thank Radha Béteille who it has been a great pleasure to work with. Her transcripts and editing have been extraordinarily well done and I am deeply impressed and grateful for her contribution. Institutions such as Cambridge University (DSpace and the Streaming Media Service in particular) and King's College, as well as the British Academy, the Leverhulme Trust, the Firebird Foundation and others have also made all this possible. It is hoped that others will take the task on through the 21st century.

PART one

Keith Thomas.

St. John's College
Oxford
Telephone 47671/2

13 Nov

It looks as if I may be supervising you after all! Could you call in sometime — next Monday (18th) at 12.15 would suit me.

KVT.

A card which changed my life, when Keith invited me to meet him as a potential D.Phil. supervisor.

Photographs courtesy Alan Macfarlane.

Keith Thomas

Sir Keith Vivian Thomas, CH, FBA, FRHistS, FLSW (b. 1933) is a Welsh historian of the early modern world based at Oxford University. From 1986 to 2000, he was President of Corpus Christi College, Oxford. He was a Fellow of All Souls College, Oxford, from 1955 until 1957, when he was elected Fellow of St John's College. He was Reader in Modern History in the University of Oxford 1978–85, and Professor of Modern History in 1986, in which year he became President of Corpus Christi College. He retired in 2000, at the statutory age of 67, and the following year he was once more elected Fellow of All Souls College; he is now an Honorary Fellow. He served for some time as Pro-Vice-Chancellor of the University and a Delegate of the University Press. He chaired the Supervisory Committee of the Oxford Dictionary of National Biography *between 1994 and 2002 and was an editor, with J.S. Weiner, of the* Oxford Paperback University Series (OPUS) *and the editor of* Past Masters, *both published by Oxford University Press.*

He was a member of the Economic and Social Research Council 1985–90, of the Reviewing Committee on Exports of Works of Art 1990–93, and of the Royal Commission on Historical Manuscripts 1992–2002. From 1991 until 1998, he was a Trustee of the National Gallery and from 1999 to 2008 a Trustee of the British Museum. Between 1997 and 2002 he was Chairman of the British Library Advisory Committee for Arts, Humanities, and Social Sciences.

He was elected a Fellow of the Royal Historical Society in 1970 (Vice-President 1980–84) and a Fellow of the British Academy in 1979 (President 1993–97). In 1983, he was elected a Foreign Honorary Member of the American Academy of Arts and Sciences; in 1993, he was elected to the Academia Europaea; and in 2009

*he was made an Hon. Member of the Japan Academy. He is also a
Founding Fellow of the Learned Society of Wales*

*He is an Honorary Fellow of Balliol (1984), St John's (1986),
Corpus Christi (2000) and All Souls (2015) Colleges, Oxford, of
Cardiff University (1995) and of the Warburg Institute, London
(2008). He has been awarded honorary doctorates by the University
of Kent (DLitt 1983), University of Wales (DLitt 1987), Williams
College (LLD 1988), University of Sheffield (LittD 1992), University
of Cambridge (LittD 1995), University of Hull (DLitt 1995),
University of Leicester (DLitt 1996), University of Sussex (DLitt
1996), Oglethorpe University (LLD 1996), University of Warwick
(DLitt 1998), Columbia University (LittD 2007), and Uppsala
University (PhD 2014).*

*Portraits of Sir Keith Thomas hang at Corpus Christi College,
Oxford, and the British Academy and National Portrait Gallery,
London.*

He is best known as the author of Religion and the Decline of
Magic: Studies in Popular Beliefs in Sixteenth- and Seventeenth-
Century England *(First published, 1971),* Man and the Natural
World: Changing Attitudes in England, 1500–1800 *(First published,
1983),* The Ends of Life: Roads to Fulfilment in Early Modern
England *(First published, 2009) and* In Pursuit of Civility: Manners
and Civilization in Early Modern England *(First published, 2018).*[1]

I

Alan Macfarlane (AM): It's a great pleasure and honour to have a chance to talk to Keith Thomas who I've known for some years now. Keith, when and where were you born?

Keith Thomas (KT): I was born in Wales, in a village called Wick in the Vale of Glamorgan in January 1933.

AM: People like to go back a generation or two, but some go back to the Norman Conquest,[2] in one case, Sir John Gurdon.[3] Most people just go back to their grandparents or people they knew. Can you tell me something about your parentage?

KT: If your name is Thomas, the problem with what they call nominal recognition is very difficult. I can't trace it. I haven't attempted really, to trace the family back very far. But essentially my father was a farmer and his father was a farmer and his father, I think, began as a farm labourer and became a farmer, all in this small area, the Vale of Glamorgan. My mother's father was a schoolmaster who came from a farming family a little north of the Vale. But he had married a Scottish woman who came from Glasgow and who was a schoolteacher. They'd met, I think, when they were teaching together.

I know little about my Scottish ancestors. Their surname was Moodie, although I believe their original name was Macfie. One of them had been a sea captain and they lived in the Isle of Bute. At the age of four, my mother took me up to Scotland and we went to the great Empire Exhibition in Glasgow,[4] which I remember very well. And then on to the Isle of Bute, where it rained all the time, even during our visit to Ettrick Bay. Two maiden aunts of my mother, sisters of my grandmother, lived there in Rothesay. When they died, that was the end of the Scottish connection. My family, otherwise, were all Welsh and all farmers.

This interview was conducted by Alan Macfarlane on 22 June 2012. The transcription for this interview has been provided by Rittika Dhar, for this volume. These interviews are available for viewing on:
https://www.sms.cam.ac.uk/media/1402073
https://www.youtube.com/watch?v=aazqSnw2Q08
https://www.youtube.com/watch?v=N7N1bpffEIU

AM: Did you know either of your grandparents well?

KT: My father's father, who was a farmer, I used to meet when my father went on Mondays to the market in Bridgend. For some obscure reason they met outside the bank. I was then a very little boy and my grandfather, who had a moustache, used to kiss me when we said goodbye. He had a very distinctive smell, which I now recognize as whisky; market day was an occasion of mild conviviality. My father's mother died when he was about 12. He was one of seven children, six boys and a girl. The six boys were brought up in conditions of extreme austerity with flannel shirts, no underclothes and a pretty basic diet. My grandfather ate very well, but the boys didn't. The result of the consequent savings was that he was able to set up each of the six boys on a tenant farm of their own, which, by the standards of the day, was a notable achievement.

AM: Tell me something about your parents.

KT: Well, my father was a very intelligent man with quite an acute, energetic mind, but he left school at about 13 to work on his father's farm. My mother was a university graduate, from the University of Cardiff, where she did a lot of acting and emerged with an undistinguished degree in English, but a great love of literature. After graduating, she was appointed head of the village school in Marcross, near Wick. It was a tiny school, with, I suppose, about 30 or 40 pupils. My father grew up nearby and that was where they met. As a graduate, my mother always saw herself as the educated part of the marriage and my father had a slight inferiority complex about that—somewhat unjustified in my view because I think he was actually rather more intelligent than she was, though less literary. After their marriage, there followed a somewhat painful period of self-education on his part. I remember in the house there were volumes of Carlyle's *History of the French Revolution*⁵ which my mother had given him as prescribed reading. I don't think he got very far with that. He never became a very bookish person, but he took a knowledgeable and intelligent interest in world affairs.

He was also a very good farmer. He began on a small tenant farm in Wick, but when I was about two, he and my mother moved ten miles or so east to rent a rather bigger farm of 250 acres in

Llancarfan, in the Vale of Glamorgan. It had originally belonged to the Church, but when the Welsh Church was disendowed by Lloyd George, the land went to the University of Wales. So, we were the University's tenants and our landlord was the Principal of University College, Aberystwyth. He used to make an annual visitation, something I was reminded of years later, when, as a Fellows of St John's College, Oxford, I used to accompany the Bursar on a yearly inspection of the College's farms. But when I lwas a boy we were on the receiving end. I remember my mother being so bold as to ask if we could have a bath installed. The rather pompous Principal of the University College of Aberystwyth replied that he had always thought a hip bath was quite adequate. Equipping our farmhouse with mod cons was a slow business. I remember when the water was put in and when, much later, electricity was installed. My early reading was by the light of a paraffin lamp.

After very difficult times for farmers in the 1930s, there came the War. Agriculture was a protected activity. It was a good time for farmers and my father prospered. Living as we did, only a few miles from St. Athans aerodrome, we grew used to nightly air raids, but, although they did great damage to nearby Cardiff, they made little mark on the countryside, despite the decoy lights which were turned on in the fields at night in order to attract the bombs intended for the aerodrome. We children used to go out in the morning to collect the empty shells of the incendiary bombs which had fallen in the night. Throughout the 1940s, my father, who was of a cautious disposition, remained content with his 250 acres, to which, had I met the normal expectations of a farmer's eldest son, I would in due course have succeeded.

AM: You had siblings then?
KT: Yes, I had and have a younger brother and I had two sisters, the younger of whom died at the age of nine. The other one played hockey for Wales, married a farmer and was widowed, but has children and grandchildren. My brother left school at the first opportunity and joined my father on the farm. This was partly in reaction to the way I'd turned out. From an early stage, I was very bookish and completely hopeless on the farm. My mother greatly

encouraged me in that direction. She was a very reluctant convert to agricultural life, though she worked extremely hard, running the house and cooking meals unaided for an unpredictable number of farm workers. She fed me with books and encouraged my academic ambitions. My father, I think, regarded my exodus from the farming world to become a town-dweller as rather disappointing. Only when I became a Fellow of All Souls, a position which had a rather greater social cachet then than now, did he regard me as having redeemed myself. My brother, Tony, by contrast, saw that I was my mother's favourite and duly reacted by joining my father on the farm, which he then built up enormously. He was bolder by temperament than my father, and was prepared to borrow large sums of money from the bank to buy a great deal of land, something which my father would never have done. Tony's good fortune was that the 60s and 70s were a time of high inflation, which made it much easier for him to pay back the loans. He is now by far the largest landowner in the Vale of Glamorgan. He and his son, my nephew, farm three and a half thousand acres or something like that. He began this process by buying from the University of Wales the farm on which we had grown up, a bold step which my father, quite wrongly, regarded as a disastrous one.

AM: You mentioned bookishness, you also mentioned paraffin lamps and it's evident that you're myopic, short-sighted, with glasses. Is there any connection between these things? In other words, James Campbell[6] was quite interesting to meet also but he was actually born myopic and diagnosed very early. At what point did you start wearing glasses?

KT: Well, I think it wasn't till I was about ten or eleven. I grew up in a rural world where anybody caught reading was immediately told they were ruining their eyes. You know more about myopia than I do. I don't know whether mine was a result of early reading or not.

AM: Were you doing a lot of lamplight reading early on?

KT: I suppose so, yes. I can't remember when I couldn't read and in the winter much of it would have been by lamplight, though my mother always sent us children to bed very early

AM: And what sort of works, other than Thomas Carlyle, were you reading?

KT: Well, I didn't read the works of Thomas Carlyle. My mother was pretty good about knowing what you should read after about the age of nine. I devoured works like *The Wind in the Willows*[7], *Treasure Island*,[8] and other classic children's stories. I then went on to a lot of popular history. I remember Marshall's *Our Island Story*[9] and *The Boys' Book of Heroes*,[10] that kind of thing. I was very hot on heroes. Even in the Vale of Glamorgan, the imperial background was quite important. In school, there was this great map of the world on the wall with a great chunk of it pink. And one had no doubt at all about our superiority to other nations. Indeed, when I was about 10, I won an essay prize given by a body called The Royal Empire Society, or something like that. The prescribed title was: 'The British Empire is the greatest force for good the world has ever seen', or something like that. I remember saying that the Empire had eliminated yaws, though I hadn't the faintest idea what yaws was.

AM: There was no plan to send you off to map your own adventure?

KT: No, though I do remember my father saying, 'Well, he's not a great help on the farm'. There was a lunatic idea that I might become a naval officer, which would have been a first for someone as short-sighted as I was, though, come to think of it, Nelson was blind in one eye.

AM: Having nature and the natural world and animals and so on, is it right to picture you as a little boy who was bookish but was also spending your time hunting for birds' eggs and things like that?

KT: Absolutely. We ran free, loose in the fields, and I recall that there was hardly any traffic on the roads. I spent an enormous amount of time out of doors, making huts in the woods and, I'm afraid, stealing birds' eggs. There were very few children in the village. My chief companion, apart from my brother, who was two years younger, a large gap at that stage, was a boy called Billy Tucker. He was the son of a farm labourer who worked for my father. Billy was very much better at climbing than I was, so it was he who would go up the trees to get the eggs. We always left one egg in the nest, believing that birds couldn't count. On one occasion, however, we found a jay's nest, a rarity, but containing only two eggs. We couldn't each have an egg and leave one in the nest. 'What shall I do?', Billy called down from the tree. 'Take them both!', I said, which he did, to the accompaniment of much squawking by the mother bird, which was flying around the nest. I still feel ashamed about that.

Billy, I should add, was barely literate, but an extraordinary child of nature, who could catch rabbits with his bare hands. We spent a lot of time together, camping in the woods or playing in the river, fishing for eels and trout and so on. I had an idyllic childhood in many ways.

AM: One's always trying to go and see links. Do you think all this natural interest and so on fed into your later works?

KT: Well, I suppose so. But I reacted against all this very strongly when I became a teenager and began studying quite seriously. Like all farmers' children, I was regarded as part of the labour force at busy times of year. The school holidays always saw a most terrible battle between my father and me. There was I, claiming to be working, when all I was doing was sitting on a deck chair, reading a book, and there was all this corn waiting to be stooked and carried. Leaving the countryside was liberation for me at the time. I suppose there was a vague sort of nostalgia about my return to it years later in a literary way and my earlier experience of the country certainly left its mark. Unlike many town-dwellers, I knew the difference between ash and oak or wheat and barley and I could identify a lot of birds. I used to compete in the Young Farmers Club in tractor driving, which is ironic, since I have never tried to drive a car. The other competition I used to enter was wildflower identification, I was rather good at that, nut it was supposed to be something for girls.

AM: What was your first memory? Apart from sort of waving overhead trees above your pram, what actual event?

KT: In terms of public life, I remember the egg-and-spoon race in the village sports to celebrate the coronation of George VI. Later on, I have a very clear memory of listening to the speech by Neville Chamberlain in September 1939 telling the nation that we were at war.

AM: You were six then?

KT: Yes. I remember being disappointed that Mr Chamberlain didn't say, 'I declare war', which is what we boys used to say. I also expected fighting to break out instantly on the road outside. Those are my memories of public events. Much more intense is my memory of starting school, the village school, when I was four.

AM: Is this the one your mother was teaching in?

KT: No. She taught in Marcross school, near Wick, before I was born. She'd married and given up teaching before we moved to Llancarfan. The school there, which I attended, was the same sort of village school as the one she'd taught in. There was a board on the wall, with a number chalked on it, indicating how many pupils there were; it was usually between 46 and 48. There were three classes.

AM: Were there any teachers that you remember or that had any particular influence?

KT: I remember all the teachers. The infants' class was taught by Miss Griffiths and the middle class by Miss Thomas. The headmaster, who taught the top class, was Mr Davies. I think I was already a prize exhibit there, partly because it was a very little school in a very little village, where everyone knew that my mother had been a teacher. That created an atmosphere of awe. I was handled with kid gloves, I suspect, and indeed I peaked there, with my greatest scholastic achievement, which was to have got 150 out of 150 for mental arithmetic in what we called `the scholarship exam', but is known nowadays as the eleven-plus. As a result, I passed top of the county and went to Barry County School, or Barry County Grammar school, as it later became. That, initially, was a pretty traumatic step, because it meant going from a cosy rural haven into a busy urban seaport, as Barry still was then. Some of the children from the dock area were distinctly rough. In the school, there were A forms, B forms and C forms; and, as far as I was concerned, boys in the C forms were best avoided. I started badly by losing my cap on my very first day and having it held up by the headmaster at the morning assembly. I developed a bad stammer, no doubt in a nervous reaction to this new experience; and for that I was duly mocked. Worse still, it was about this time that I was prescribed spectacles and had to suffer innumerable taunts about 'four eyes', and people in glass houses not throwing stones.

AM: Were you a day boy?

KT: Yes, but so was everyone else. We were all day boys. Travelling from Llancarfan to Barry and back each day was quite a business. I had to be up in time to leave the house at 8 o'clock, when a friend of the family who worked in Rhoose (where Cardiff airport now is) picked me up in his car and dropped me there, where I caught a bus to Barry. The 'country boys', as we were called, were a little minority who were allowed to leave school about 10 minutes early in order to catch what was the only bus home. In the middle of the last lesson of the afternoon, there was the great ordeal of having to interrupt the lesson by holding up my hand and asking, 'Please sir, can I go now?' This was often a matter of great irritation to the teacher. The bus took me from Barry to Aberthaw, where I would get off and walk home up a hill for about a mile and half. It was a tedious walk, particularly as I usually carried a heavy satchel. On one occasion I was pleased to accept the offer of a lift from a young man in a car. He invited me to look at some photographs in the glove compartment, which he said might interest me. One glance was enough and I prudently asked to be let out, as we had reached my home, which, of course, we hadn't.

AM: This seems to be a rather special school because it produced a number of historians, Habakkuk[11] and so on. What was special about it?

KT: I think the first part of the answer is that the Glamorgan grammar schools were culturally very important. Very few boys were sent away to English public schools. There were two Welsh public schools, Brecon and Llandovery, but the pupils who went there were usually middle-class children who had failed the eleven-plus. The grammar schools shovelled up most of the talent.

Barry had had a very distinguished headmaster between the two wars called Major Edgar Jones. And it was during his time that Hrothgar Habakkuk and Glyn Daniel,[12] a famous Cambridge archaeologist, were pupils there. I think the tradition of producing academics continued until the school went comprehensive. Barry provided three Oxbridge professors of economic history: Habakkuk; David Joslin,[13] who got the Cambridge chair, but died young; and Martin Daunton,[14] who also became Master of Trinity Hall. Looking back on it, I can see that some of the teachers at Barry were better than the others, but there were some very good people there. I was fortunate in having an excellent history master. I think that behind the great majority of academics, you will usually find a particular schoolmaster or mistress. That was certainly what happened in my case.

AM: What's his name?

KT: His name was Teifion Phillips[15] and he was, I suppose, still a young man at the time, though he didn't seem young to me. He'd come from Swansea. He was Leftish, a pillar of the local Labour Party and intellectually ambitious for his pupils. The prescribed textbook we used was M.M. Reese's *Tudors and Stuarts,* but he leavened that with other suggestions. I remember he lent me a copy of the *Modern Quarterly,* a Communist journal, in which I first encountered the name of Christopher Hill as the author of an article on 'The English Revolution 1640'. I'd always thought the Revolution was in 1688.

AM: You read this before you went for your interview at Oxford?

KT: Yes, but not in that spirit. I'd read it long before then. Teifion also introduced me to Tawney's[16] *Religion and the Rise of Capitalism,* which was a very influential book as far as I was concerned. There was a boy from Barry in the previous year who had sat the Balliol scholarship exam and got an exhibition. He was David Rees, who became a monk and died recently. I hadn't intended to do history in the sixth form. But luck and chance play a large part in people's lives, I remember the day in school, when we had to say what subjects we wanted to do for Highers, as it was called. It's A levels now. I had settled on English, French and Latin, which would have been a disastrous combination, so far as Oxford was concerned, because Latin would have been no use without Greek, and French no use without another modern language. English would have been risky, because literary appreciation ca dangerously subjective. I was on the way to the room where we had to register our choices, when I was intercepted by Teifion Phillips, who said, 'You're going to do history, aren't you?' I've always been a complete feather in the wind, so I said, 'Yes, of course'.

AM: You're saying you've been a feather in the wind .... doesn't fit with what I know of Keith.

KT: It doesn't? Well, I do have a tendency to believe the last thing I've read.

AM: I don't believe that either.

KT: Well perhaps Teifion put some more rational arguments to me too. Anyway, I changed my choices and settled on English, History and Latin, a much better combination. I liked my English and Latin masters and Teifion's Sixth-Form History teaching was very good indeed. In my first year in the Sixth, he suggested that I should try for Oxford. The headmaster was very much against that, arguing, along with the tacit suggestion that Oxford was not for the likes of us, that it was too soon. I got hold of a copy of the Oxford University Gazette and looked at the list of all the awards on offer. I was tempted by something called the Bracegirdle Exhibition at St. Catherine's, because I rather liked the name. But in the end, I settled for Balliol, chiefly because David Rees was there already. So, I sat the scholarship exam for the Balliol group of colleges in a crowded Keble Hall, and was viva-ed by the Balliol History tutors. I learned long afterwards that they were much taken by me, because when I was asked where I went on my holidays. I replied, quite truthfully, that we didn't go anywhere, but had to stay at home because the cows had to be milked. After that, they clearly felt that they had to rescue this poor deprived boy and they gave me their top scholarship, the Brackenbury.

AM: The school, which is at times very important, just one or two questions about that. Were there any particular hobbies you had then, music, acting, politics?

KT: One of my great regrets and something I've been trying to make up for in later years is that in my childhood there was no music at home, save for the passages from 'No, no, Nanette', which my father liked singing. He also enjoyed singing hymns. His favourite was 'The day thou gave us, Lord, is ended', which I thought unnecessarily pessimistic. For most of my time in school, there was not much music either, apart from hymn-singing, and an annual concert by a trio from Cardiff University. When I was in the sixth form, the school appointed a music teacher for the first time. He gave a few lessons to sixth-formers and I can still remember the three records he played to us. They were Rossini's overture to *William Tell,* Mendelssohn's *Fingal's Cave* and Saint-Saëns's *Danse Macabre.* This was my first introduction to classical music, and I liked it. But it was years later that my wife introduced me to the rest of the canon.

Otherwise, I played cricket at school and wasn't hopeless at it. I captained the 2nd XI and enjoyed it very much. And I read novels, of course.

AM: Were you an actor?

KT: Yes, I was an actor. I even out-auditioned someone for a part in a school play who subsequently became a moderately famous professional actor. His name is Keith Baxter and he played Prince Hal in the Orson Welles[17] film, *Chimes at Midnight.* As a schoolboy, I loved play-reading, acting and debating. The school had a Literary and Debating society ('Lit and Deb'), of which I was an active member.

AM: You touched on music which you discovered, was that at Oxford or after that?

KT: I think that was really after I got married. Valerie, my wife, is very fond of music. She listens to music on the radio in the day and plays recorded music in the evening. So, I've learned a lot from her.

AM: Is there any particular music?

KT: I think my tastes are pretty conventional, that's to say Bach,[18] Mozart,[19] Beethoven,[20] Schubert,[21] Brahms. I also like Elgar and Stravinsky,[22] but I'm afraid I'm not very much into contemporary music.

AM: Some people use music in a very intellectual way. They either write to music or listen to the music and then write or others just use it to relax from thinking.

KT: I hate the idea of background music. I'm thoroughly against that. Partly because I think it doesn't help the work and it certainly doesn't help the music. If I listen to music, I prefer to hear it on its own.

AM: You never played anything?

KT: No. I have got no manual dexterity whatsoever.

AM: The other thing is, I didn't ask about your parents in the English or Scottish religious sort of place. Did your parents have any religious leanings?

KT: They were Anglican or, to be precise, Church of England in Wales, which is something slightly different. My father was a churchwarden. My mother lost any faith she might previously have had after the death of my younger sister, Rosemary. She died quite suddenly when she was nine. I was abroad, in Jamaica, doing National Service in the army when she died, and I was desperately upset. It was an even more was a terrible experience for my mother. The local vicar seems to have behaved insensitively. I don't know the circumstances. as I wasn't there. But the result was that thereafter she went completely off religion of any kind whatsoever and became an uncompromising unbeliever. Far from driving her into religion, as often happens in such circumstances, Rosemary's death had the opposite effect. My father remained a regular churchgoer, partly, but not entirely, for social reasons. I was brought up to be C of E in Wales. That, of course, was in itself a statement, because, in Wales, the division between church and chapel was a crucial and indeed political one. In those days, Church meant Conservative and Chapel meant Liberal or Labour. It was basically a class difference. I was confirmed when I was about thirteen and even taught for time in a Sunday School. Later, when I was in the Army, I went to church quite often and when I was in Balliol, I went to chapel occasionally. Thereafter, I gradually stopped doing even that, save for weddings, funerals and memorial services, all of which I regard as important and necessary. I'd prefer a non-theistic funeral service, but I've not yet discovered a satisfactory one.

AM: If you were forced to tick one of the boxes of agnostic, atheist or believer, what would you tick?

KT: I suppose I'm an atheist really. Having said that, I should add that I have a considerable affection for church architecture, church music, the Authorised Version of the Bible, and the Book of Common Prayer. I subscribe to the upkeep of sundry churches. I would hate to see them go. One of my favourite buildings, which the late philosopher Jerry Cohen told me was also one of his, is Cholsey Church, which you see as you're going from Didcot to London on the train.

AM: Have you ever been there?

KT: No, it would spoil it if I went there. But its silhouette is enchanting.

AM: And the rituals? For instance, when you were President of Corpus, did you...?

KT: Did I go to chapel? Very seldom. Funerals, memorial services and carol concerts apart, I only went if there was a particularly notable visiting preacher.

AM: Were you not obliged to attend?

KT: No, there was no statutory obligation and the chaplains tolerated my absence. I'm sure he regretted it, but they were too polite to say so. It is very unfortunate that, although a secular outlook seems to me to be the only one which makes any sense intellectually, it is extremely deficient when it comes to providing unifying rituals. The point about the Anglican church service, as originally devised, was that, in principle, all the members of the parish were gathered there together. Nowadays there is no such occasion when that happens. I lament that, just as I lament the absence of a satisfying secular ritual of burial. I dislike taking part in a funeral which holds out the totally unconvincing prospect of the resurrection of the dead.

AM: I often ask, particularly scientists, that everyone knows is very ardently secular, in other words, there's Richard Dawkins, about their religious persuasion.

KT: I have no desire to disabuse other people of what gives them comfort, even if I happen to think it's a spurious sort of comfort. I am not offended by people going to church or the knowledge that these often wonderful buildings are used for religious purposes. And

I greatly respect most of the Christian ethic. I'm less respectful of the ethics of some other religions.

AM: When you talked about the intellectually secular world anyone can support and yet deficient, it's one of the subthemes in your *Religion and the Decline of Magic.* You discovered the loss of belief or there wasn't much anyway. Do you think that, in any way, is linked to your own movement from some belief to no belief?

KT: By the time I embarked on that book, I was not moving to a state of no belief. I had already got there and was quite settled in it. I suppose it could be said, and critics certainly have said, that it meant that I did less than justice to the religious belief of people in the past, for example, in the 15th century. I remember one reviewer saying that I had no sense of the numinous. I'm never been absolutely sure what 'numinous' means, though I agree with that reviewer that I have no direct experience of it. But my book wasn't intended to be an atheist or agnostic tract. It was just an objective account of how people thought at the time.

AM: Were you surprised? One of the things that surprised other people was how limited and garbled the beliefs of ordinary Englishman in 15th, 16th, 17th centuries were.

KT: No, not at all. I wasn't surprised at all, because I suspect that if you interviewed people coming out of church today and said, let's just run through the ten commandments, they might not do too well either!

AM: Let's move on then to Balliol. When did you do your national service? Before?

KT: I got my scholarship at Balliol when I was just 17 and the College expected people to come up after they'd done their national service. That was my saving really. If I'd gone up at 17, I would have sunk without trace. In those days, an Oxford scholarship automatically qualified you for a state scholarship, i.e., financial support at the University. So, I didn't need to be studying for Highers anymore and I spent my last two terms in school enjoyably reading around. Nevertheless, today, without either A Levels or a PhD, I feel something of an impostor, particularly when encountering somebody like you, who has got, not one, but *two* doctorates! I certainly wouldn't get away with a record like mine if I was trying to become an academic today.

I went to the Army to do what was originally supposed to be eighteen months of National Service, but in the autumn of 1950 was turned into two years. That experience began with another trauma. I was assigned to the infantry, initially the Welch regiment, and was posted to Dering Lines, Brecon. I can't pass the Brecon Beacons now without recalling those days. I found the first couple of weeks in a barrack room pretty ghastly. Not so much the military routine, as the company of the unregenerate. Although I'd always thought of Barry as quite rough, I didn't know what rough really was. The nonstop obscenity of the barrack room wouldn't bother me now, but it bothered me quite a lot then. After basic training, I was, by great good fortune, transferred to the Royal Welch Fusiliers (the RWF). If I'd stayed in the Welch Regiment I should have gone to the war in Korea and might well not be sitting here now. Instead, I was sent to Jamaica, where I became a corporal in the orderly room, a sort of spider in the middle of the battalion's administrative web. My time there was by no means disagreeable. I played cricket most afternoons and, when on leave, my friends and I explored the island.

AM: I'd love for you to tell me something about Jamaica because Sarah and I remember doing research on Jamaica. We discovered my family was one of the biggest families in Jamaica two and a half centuries ago.

KT: Where were they?

AM: Oh, she'd tell you, I mean, all over. The first white child born in Jamaica was my 12th generation grandfather, James, in 1656.

KT: That's very early because the English only went there in 1655.

AM: Yes, exactly. Straightaway, the first child, a white child. And they had these huge estates, we have their family papers and slave books and some of them continued intermarrying with all the top Jamaican families for centuries and didn't really leave till the late 19th century. So, we're doing a lot of work on Jamaica. Tell me what it was like to be there?

KT: The camp was Up Park Camp which is just outside Kingston. The first thing to say about it is that its surroundings were very beautiful, with a marvellous view of the Blue Mountains on one side and the sea on the other. The climate was delightful: warm, not too hot, and never cold. Kingston itself was a rather seedy place. It had a large red-light area, which was very popular with some of my fellow-soldiers, though getting VD was a military offence. The poverty was pretty obvious, but one had the possibly misleading impression of a rather cheerful population. Of course, it was far from being a total pastoral fantasy, but there was, as far as I could see, relatively little political discontent, though there certainly was some. We wouldn't have been there if there wasn't. The Army's role was to police British rule in the Caribbean. Periodically, the RWF sent out companies to Grenada, Antigua, and British Guyana to deal with what used to be euphemistically called 'labour problems'.

I was very struck by the beauty of the Jamaican hinterland. When we had a fortnight's leave, my friends and I made an expedition to the Cockpit Country, where we fell into the hands of the Maroons, the descendants of escaped slaves, who still lived there in a sort of state within a state. They claimed that, under a Treaty made with them in 1730 or thereabouts, outsiders were not permitted to go there. We were arrested by them and subjected to a sort of mock trial, in which we argued with our captors as to whether or not we were in breach of the Treaty. The 'trial' went on into the evening, in a barn illuminated by paraffin lanterns. But as neither we nor our captors really knew what exactly the Treaty said, all ended amicably when we bought some beer for our interrogators.

It was a privilege to have spent nearly eighteen months in Jamaica. The landscape was ravishingly beautiful, though there were slums in the towns. The social setup was very unsatisfactory, with, on the one hand, a great deal of poverty and, on the other, rich American villas and luxury hotels on the North coast. We soldiers lived on Army food, of course. It made no concessions to local cuisine, and was exactly what we would have been given to eat if we'd been back in Brecon. But the cricket was good. We had the chance of playing on Kingston's famous ground Sabina Park and, on one occasion, we also played against the famous Test bowler, Alfred Valentine. Unfortunately, play was interrupted by a thunderstorm. It flooded the pitch, but, undaunted, the locals poured petrol over the wicket and set fire to it. A huge black cloud arose, over what was a more than usually rapid drying wicket.

AM: Were there, any vestiges of a long history of slavery, was it casteish? Did it have a complex caste system?

KT: I didn't know Jamaican society well enough to answer that. What I could see at a glance was that there was an incredible ethnic mix, so that it would have been possible, if you assembled enough people, to line them up and go from the whitest of whites to the blackest of blacks, with a barely discernible difference between any two next to each other in the line. And white professional people spoke with a strong Jamaican accent. No doubt there were all sorts of subtle distinctions of which I was unaware. We were in camp for most of the time and didn't encounter Jamaican society at close quarters. When I was let out for weekend leave, I used to stay with some British family friends who taught at the University.

AM: You know another impression Sarah's got is that as the slaves had no incentive to work very hard, they would drag as much as possible for obvious reasons. There was a generally laid-back, relaxed mañana mañana sort of atmosphere.

KT: There were no slaves in my day, of course. But there was still a laid-back style. One was very conscious of that when one went into the Jamaican countryside. People were not bothered, never in a hurry. At the same time, however, there was a great deal of violent crime and violent punishment. The lower classes regularly carried machetes. The only time we were issued with live ammunition was when there was a very spectacular hurricane, which, among other things, blew down the walls of the prison. We were sent out to try and recapture the prisoners, some of whom were under sentence of death. To my relief, we totally failed to recapture anyone. They were hanging people there all the time. Sometime after I'd returned to the UK, the man who'd been the battalion's cricket coach, a former Test player, was hanged for murdering his wife's lover.

AM: Let's come back to England then. Balliol, we missed the interview. Is that something you look back to? The first encounter with Christopher Hill.

KT: I remember, as people do, my entrance interview very well. We waited in a room, which I think belonged to somebody called Hugh Leech, whom I never met. He was a lecturer there. I remember it chiefly because on the table there were the two very handsome volumes of Sir Maurice Powicke's[23] *Henry III and the Lord Edward.* There were a number of people at the interview and I was not entirely clear as to who was who. But the Master, Sir David Lindsay Keir,[24] was there, and so was Christopher Hill, but not Dick Southern,[25] who would become one of my tutors, but was then, I think, on sick leave. Also present were Hugh Stretton, a brilliant young Australian, who'd been offered his tutorial fellowship when he was still an undergraduate,[26] and A.B. Rodger, who'd been a Fellow since the 1920s. The story which Stretton used to tell subsequently was that, when I was asked what I did in the holidays, I replied in a thick Welsh accent that I never had any holidays, because there was always work to be done on the farm. Otherwise, the interview went quite well. Teifion Phillips had warned me that it was prudent to have an answer ready. should I be asked what I'd been reading lately. I had duly read D.B. Quinn's[27] *Raleigh and the British Empire,* which was a volume in the *Teach Yourself History* series. I was asked about it by Christopher Hill, who, as it happened, greatly approved of Quinn. So that went alright. I also remember Keir asking me what sort of history I liked best. I said social history. So, he asked what the main developments were in the social history of my period and I said the rise of the middle class. As you see, my social history was not particularly sophisticated. However, when I was sitting later that night in a very gloomy room, which I was sharing with someone called Keith Thompson (you can see the principle on which the rooms were allotted), there was a knock on the door and in came Christopher Hill. He said to me, 'If we give you an award, you mustn't go on to do "bloody Highers", but should concentrate on improving your languages'. I was cheered by this advice, but amazed that he should use a word like 'bloody'. Anyway, on the

Monday morning, I got a letter from Christopher, in a small brown envelope. Written on a little piece of paper, it said, 'May I be one of the first to congratulate you on the Brackenbury scholarship which we propose to award you?'

AM: Were you still in the college then when you got this letter or at home?

KT: No, I was at home. It arrived on the Monday after my return from a week doing the written exam in Keble Hall, a very daunting experience, as there seemed to be hundreds of candidates there.

AM: So, there was a written exam other than the interview.

KT: Oh yes, it took the best part of a week. There was an Essay paper, a General paper, two History papers and as many language papers as you could do.

AM: So, you started. Were there any of your classmates or contemporaries at Balliol who you've kept in touch with or worked with or want to talk about?

KT: The contemporaries who became well known included Raphael Samuel,[28] who was in my year and was still a communist at that time. We used to have breakfast at the same table in Balliol hall every morning. On one occasion he appeared late, wearing a dark suit and a black tie, and had obviously been weeping. `What on earth's the matter?', we asked. Choking back his tears, he said, 'Uncle Joe is dead', and rushed out of the hall. Very different was another friend, Peter Brooke, who went on to become President of the Union and a Conservative Cabinet minister for Northern Ireland. We are still in touch with each other, but only a few of my Balliol friends, alas, are still alive.

AM: Samuel's personal beliefs and style is very different from yours, by observation. Does your interest overlap obviously and do you have a high regard for him?

KT: Yes, indeed, though he was chaotic and would come for his tutorials laden with sheets and sheets of paper. He never finished his essays, and used to drop little bits of them all over the floor. After leaving Oxford, he taught at Ruskin College and went on to become a distinguished historian.

AM: His hair was like that as well.

KT: He had a year out, so we didn't take Schools in the same year, because he had to go off and cool down a little bit. He was very precocious. I remember having coffee in his room after lunch and while he was making the coffee, I was glancing vaguely at his books. One of them I saw was Adam Smith's[29] *Wealth of Nations*, which was a set book for prelims. The inscription inside was 'To Raphael on his eighth birthday'. He was a good deal more precocious than I was and two years younger. He was a communist then. I wasn't, but I was very interested. I went to a few meetings and even became an officer of something called the Oxford University Past and Present Society, which hitherto had been known as the Oxford University Karl Marx History Society. Another well-known contemporary of mine was the Canadian political philosopher Charles (Chuck) Taylor.[30]

AM: The philosopher.

KT: Yes, he was very genial. I had a number of very good friends as an undergraduate.

AM: Another person who I'm not very sure was the absolute same year, whom I've interviewed recently which was Lord Bingham, Tom Bingham.[31] He was born in the same year as you, but he may not have done the national service, he may have been a year ahead or behind you.

KT: He was, I think, two years behind me.

AM: The curious thing is, in his interview, he said, 'I came up to read history but I discovered after a while I wasn't good enough to read history so I read law'. In your case, certainly in an interview with you it says you came up ready to be a lawyer. You discovered you weren't good enough and you became a historian.

KT: No, I didn't discover I wasn't good enough. I applied, offering history to read law. I was going to be a barrister. I was interviewed by the Balliol law don, who was Theo Tylor.[32] The interview didn't go very well and I felt that there was something strange about this man, but I was too stupid to work out what it was, which was, of course, that he was totally blind. Somebody told me about it afterwards.

Anyway, I then went on to be interviewed by the historians and they said, 'We see you want to read law. You don't want to read law, do you?' Being my usual feather in the wind, I said 'No, of course not.' So that put an end to my legal career, though I've retained an interest in the law and enjoy reading the law reports in the newspapers.

Incidentally, that's rubbish about Tom Bingham not being good enough to do history. In fact, as well as getting a First in History, he won the Gibbs prize, the top prize in the University for third-year historians.

AM: You'd be quite a good barrister.

KT: I don't know about that, but I wouldn't have minded having a try.

AM: There seemed a crossover at that point, big numbers behind you.

KT: Yes, Maurice Keen[33], Tom Bingham, John Keegan, Peter Brooke and others. I knew the four of them very well, of course and liked them very much, but they were not in my year and that made quite a difference in those days. I belonged to a debating society in Balliol, a rather pretentious one, called the Arnold Society. You couldn't just join, but had to be elected. The members wore little red corduroy bow ties. In my time there was a tremendous split in the Arnold Society. It was essentially a social split. The smart set of socially more sophisticated members, including Tom and Maurice, hived off and formed the Brackenbury Society. I stayed with the Arnold Society. When all the *dramatis personae* had gone down, the two societies reunited and became the Arnold and Brackenbury Society. I don't know whether it still exists.

AM: Which of the teachers you mentioned, who really influenced you as an undergraduate in their teaching?

KT: As an undergraduate, Christopher Hill undoubtedly, though I had interesting relations with the others, particularly Dick Southern, whom I got to know very much better later, because he became President of St John's when I was Fellow there. I saw a lot of him then and both admired and liked him very much. As a tutor, I'd found him rather remote. He threw you in at the deep end. I had done no medieval history previously, but the weekly essays he set for English

I, the examination paper on English History up to 1307, were all on Latin sources for the period. The first essay was on Asser's *Life of Alfred*.[34] The next was on the *Regularis Concordia*,[35] which, you will remember, was a monastic agreement of 973 about the rules for English Benedictine houses. The next was on Domesday book and the last one on Walter Daniel's *Life of Ailred of Rievaulx*.[36] As a result, I had acquired some rarified knowledge, but hadn't the faintest idea about the general outlines of the period. In my third year I went back to Dick and asked if I could write four essays for him, but this time on topics of my choice. So, we did mainline topics, like the Norman Conquest and the Baron's Revolt, and when I took Schools, English I was my best paper.

On the modern end, we had Hugh Stretton. He was easily the intellectually most sophisticated of my tutors, and was famous for setting such essay questions as, 'Which is the better portrait of Mr Asquith, the one in the Hall or the one in the Senior Common Room?' (One portrayed a Victorian senator and the other, an Edwardian drunk.) All the Balliol tutors expressed the greatest contempt for 'Schools', the University's final examination. The only time I saw Christopher Hill lose his temper was when my tutorial companion complained about an essay topic Christopher had proposed, on the grounds that the subject wouldn't come up in Schools (the final examination). Christopher got very cross indeed and said, 'You are here to study history, not to do Schools'. Balliol's attitude to the University's exams was one of total insouciance.

AM: Balliol was the place. Everything was ranked against Balliol.
KT: At the Freshmen's dinner, we were addressed by Sir David Lindsay Keir,[37] who impressed upon us that we hadn't come to Oxford: we'd come to Balliol. There was a great said about Balliol men's `tranquil consciousness of effortless superiority'. It was heady wine, but it gave people tremendous intellectual self-confidence, particularly in History, as Balliol was a college from which a large proportion of the leading historians had come. So, the Balliol History Society (the Devorguilla) was able to persuade real grandees, like Namier, Toynbee[38], Tawney and G.D.H. Cole, to come to speak to them.

AM: They came to talk at the history society?

KT: Yes, they did, though I missed Tawney, who came before my time. These outstanding people reinforced the feeling that Balliol was the centre of it all. Christopher Hill was a fanatical Balliol man. Despite his strongly left-wing his political views, membership of the College trumped everything. Essentially, you couldn't go far wrong with him if you were a Balliol man, regardless of your political opinions.

AM: That's interesting. Your picture of supervision with Christopher. I think I've read another account which was identical more or less, which doesn't conform to modern RAE [Research Assessment Exercise] requirements and supervisions.

KT: Christopher and Dick Southern would have sailed through any assessment of their research, which was, of course, of great distinction. But I suspect that their teaching would have been regarded as insufficiently didactic and rather too heady wine for the average undergraduate. Indeed, I'm fairly sure that some of the people who got thirds at Balliol would have got seconds at a less intellectually pretentious college.

AM: Christopher didn't tell you what to do and he didn't suggest any readings and he didn't make any comments?

KT: No, that's not fair. He expected you to choose your essay subject, but he would suggest some topics if you were at a loss. If you asked him, he'd also recommend books and articles for you to read. But having, on one occasion, suggested that I should read a pamphlet, of which, I discovered, there was only one surviving copy and that was in the Library of Trinity College, Dublin, he was cautious thereafter. He didn't offer many comments on the essays I read to him and I, being someone who can't bear pregnant silences, often found myself making the conversation. For example, I might go on to say what I'd have put in the essay if I'd had more time.

AM: How did that stimulate you?

KT: Well, I just had the feeling all the time that, for Christopher, nothing but the best would do. The chemistry of these tutorial encounters was very subtle. He was somebody whom I wanted to think well of what I did and, of course, he knew that. He was exceptionally well-read, in modern historical writing, as well as in the literature of the 17th century. He used to buy every monograph on his period, read it, and, at the back of the book, list the pages on which he wanted to make notes. Having made them, and rubbed out the scribbles at the back, he would, more often than not, sell the book to Thornton's bookshop across the road from Balliol. Browsers in the shop could always tell which books had come from Christopher by the ineffectively-erased notes at the back. His room in College was puzzling because, although it was lined with books and Marxist periodicals, there was never so much as a tiny piece of paper on his desk. It was absolutely clear. I don't know how he managed that.

AM: I used to go to his lectures too. He had a stammer, didn't he?
KT: Yes, he did, which was rather more obvious in the lectures.

AM: Did you go to his lectures?
KT: I went to some, but they were not particularly notable events for me. The lectures I remember were John Prestwich 's[39] on medieval history. They weren't very well delivered and he had a nervous tick of clearing his throat at the end of a sentence. We used to lay bets as to how many times during the lecture he would do that. But the content of the lectures was based entirely on primary sources and extremely original. He published very little and it was essential to go to his lectures to find out what he was up to. Habakkuk's lectures were similarly first-rate and also very well delivered. I was a great groupie of his, not least because, as I mentioned earlier, he, like me, had been to Barry County School. In general, however, Balliol tutors were pretty snooty about most of the lectures and there were very few courses which I followed to the end. Christopher would say that so-and-so's lectures might be worth going to and then add, 'Oh dear, I see that they are at 9.00am. No gentleman [we were all referred to as "gentlemen" in those days] could be expected to get to a lecture as early as that.'

AM: There were some famous lectures by Isaiah Berlin, A.J.P. Taylor.
KT: I never heard Isaiah Berlin lecture and to my shame was barely aware of his existence when I was an undergraduate. He became a

great friend and supporter when I went to All Souls. I didn't hear Alan Taylor lecture when I was an undergraduate, but, a few years later, I went to a lecture by him on the causes of the First World War. After ostentatiously pushing aside the lectern and pushing up his sleeves, to show he was not carrying any notes, he said that he wasn't going to talk about the causes of the War, but would discuss why there was peace before and afterwards. I thought there was too much showing off and I didn't fall under his spell. I thought rather better of Trevor-Roper's lectures. though, because of his attacks on Christopher Hill's interpretation of the English Civil War, he was *persona non grata* in Balliol. He read his lectures, which were, of course, eloquently written,

AM: They were good?

KT: Yes, though they were very narrative in structure. This made it harder for an undergraduate to grasp what was new or controversial about what he was saying. I'd been educated in Balliol to regard him as The Enemy, because of his attacks on Christopher Hill's interpretation of the English Civil War

AM: One event which overlaps with my last interview. You entered for the most prestigious history prize, the Gibbs Prize and shared it with James Campbell,[40] is that right?

KT: Yes, that's true. The two examiners were Betty Kemp, a modernist, and Lionel Butler, a medievalist, and they were divided as to whether the Prize should go to James or to me. Ironically, I was the medievalist's choice and, James was the modernist's choice. I had already written a University Prize essay, the Stanhope essay. The subject proposed in my year was 'Anthony Wood', a 17th-century Oxford antiquarian. All his manuscripts were in the Bodleian and written in a beautifully legible hand. I had a very enjoyable time working on them in Duke Humfrey's Library. It got me very interested in the antiquarian movement of the 17th century, a subject which I later contemplated as a possible subject for a D.Phil.

AM: You won that prize?

KT: Yes, I did. A stranger knocked on my door in Balliol one day, came in and informed me that a notice had just gone up saying that I had won the Stanhope Prize, and that he had also been a competitor. He asked if I had a copy of my essay and, if so, whether he could see it. I did and gave it to him. He scanned it for a few minutes, made some not entirely complimentary remarks about it and left. I discovered later that he was Theodore Zeldin, who would become well-known as a historian of France.

II

AM: You got a First and you ended your time as an undergraduate. Then what happened?

KT: By then, I was quite sure I wanted to be an academic. Visions of the bar receded. I got, or had got by the time I took Schools, what they called a senior scholarship at St. Antony's College, which was of course a pretty new college then. It was supposed to be for people working only on 20th-century history and politics. But Bill Deakin, the Warden of the college, believed in having one or two people who studied earlier periods, in order to give the College a more civilized tone! So, I went to St. Antony's as a Senior Scholar. I then set about the process of enrolling to do a DPhil, beginning with what was called a probation period, and. my supervisor was going to be John Cooper, J.P. Cooper.[41] He's never heard of these days, but he was a very formidable presence on the Oxford historical scene. He was a Fellow of Trinity and a severe critic of other people's work. Originally, I was going to do a thesis on Robert Cecil,[42] but Joel Hurstfield[43] wrote to say he was about to publish the definitive life of Robert Cecil. Of course, he never did, but it stopped me from doing that. Then, I was going to study the court of James I. The reason for that was that at this time, 1955, the really fashionable historical subject was the rise of the gentry and the social conflicts which had supposedly precipitated the Civil War. I planned to study the Jacobean court, I suppose rather in the way that Gerald Aylmer[44] was doing the court of Charles the First. But at that point, I sat the All Souls exam and was lucky enough to win an All Souls Fellowship. It was quickly indicated to me by my new college that it was rather *infra dig* for a Fellow of All Souls to be doing a DPhil. After all, you might end up by having your thesis examined by a Fellow of another college....

AM: Was it, at the time, a seven-year fellowship?

KT: Yes, it was two years without any commitment. After two years, you had to decide whether you were going to be an academic or go out into the world. In either case, it was for seven years. This was a big turning-point in my life. One day, I was a penniless graduate student and the next day, literally the next day, I was dining with cabinet ministers and judges and so forth. I promptly dropped the idea of doing a D.Phil. That wouldn't happen these days. Thereafter, my interest fluttered from one topic to another. First of all, I was going to do something on the antiquarian movement, going back to Anthony Wood,[45] I suppose. Then, having started on a study of religious toleration in the mid-17th century, I came across the argument, made in the 1640s, that people shouldn't be allowed to choose their own religion, because it would subvert the authority of their parents, as well as emancipate women, and goodness knows what else. That got me interested in the relationship between women and sectarianism and I published an article on 'Women and the Civil War Sects'.

AM: That was in *Past and Present*?

KT: Yes, that was in *Past and Present*, which was then a young and struggling journal. The editor, John Morris, sliced my piece. It had begun as a long article which was partly about the effect of toleration on the position of women and partly about its effect on the family. But he only wanted the women part. Thereafter, I concentrated on the history of women. Young fellows of All Souls were encouraged to give lectures and the first lectures I offered in Oxford were on women. I advertised them for Michaelmas 1957, as 'The relations between the sexes in England from the Reformation to the First World War'. It took a bit of nerve to do that, as I was a very innocent, unmarried and unpublished 24-year-old at the time and, of course, virtually nobody came.

AM: Well, not of course. Because now, everyone would come.

KT: Yes, perhaps. There was a correspondence in the *New York Review of Books* some years ago about why it was that so few people came to those lectures. Olwen Hufton[46] had suggested in an article that it was because I was well ahead of my time. But, in a robust rejoinder, Fiona McCarthy[47] said that people didn't come to my lectures because I was a totally obscure figure whom nobody had heard of. I'm sure she was right about my obscurity, but she was wrong about the reasons for the poor attendance. When, in the following term, I lectured in the hall of St John's on Aristotle,[48] Hobbes[49] and Rousseau,[50] the room was packed out because the subject was a compulsory part of the syllabus, and I had to move to the South Schools. I stayed with women's history for a bit and submitted one of my lectures, which was on the `double standard' of sexual morality, to the *Journal of the History of Ideas*. It wasn't really their sort of thing, but I couldn't think of anywhere else to send it and they published it. As a result, I was regarded by some as a sort of sex maniac. The generally cool reception with which my ventures into the history of women were received, I'm afraid, deterred me from going much further with the subject.

AM: Your reputation as a sex maniac was to my advantage. Because I told that story to Christopher and when he heard I was interested in sex and magic, he said you should go to see Keith Thomas. He knows more about sex than me.

KT: In those days, of course, half the books on sex you needed to ready were classified as φί (fie!) in Bodley and you needed special permission to read them. If that was given, you had to sit at a special desk, where everybody could see you.

AM: So, there wasn't any feminist agenda in your....

KT: Not initially. But through reading about the subject, I did quickly become a feminist. I was much influenced by Simone de Beauvoir's *The Second Sex*.[51] I took the view, which indeed I still hold, that men and women are completely malleable and that the characteristics they develop and the activities they follow are shaped by the culture in which they live; in a different culture, their roles could equally well be reversed.

AM: Do you read Margaret Mead?[52]

KT: I read Margaret Mead, yes.

AM: She has professed a strong difference between sex and temperament.

KT: Yes. I see that there are limitations to the malleability of male and female characteristics. Biological differences do have social consequences and gender is more than a purely cultural formation. But my views on women's potential were very radical at the time.

AM: You weren't doing a DPhil but you were going to work on history of women. Now, this was about early 60s?

KT: No, it was earlier than that. My two articles, on 'Women and Civil War Sects' and 'The Double Standard', were both written between 1955 and 1957, when I was in All Souls. In 1957, St John's advertised a tutorial fellowship in my period. I could have stayed at All Souls for another five years, but the prospect of a permanent post was too enticing and I decided to apply for it. When I asked Christopher Hill to write me a reference, he exclaimed with horror, 'St John's? St John's?' (I should explain that it wasn't then the top college that it is now.) I replied defensively that it was a very beautiful college. He retorted that he had thought that three years at Balliol would have taught me to put the soul before the body. I hadn't realized that Balliol had a soul, but I prudently kept silent. At the time of my application to St John's, I had published nothing and, of course, had no doctorate. But things were different in those days and the prestige of an All Souls Fellowship was considerable. So, at the age of 24, with nothing to show for myself, I was elected to what was, in effect, a job for life. I started at St John's in the autumn of 1957 and was very happy there for the next 29 years.

AM: You had a pretty punishing regime of teaching, didn't you? I mean, you had 12 supervisions a week and two lectures a week.

KT: Yes, though it was two sets of lectures for the year, not for each term I didn't mind that, as in those days there was no pressure to be publishing anything. The President once asked me what I was working on, but he didn't press the point. In fact, a majority of my St John's colleagues were FRSs or FBAs, and published a great deal, but they were self-motivated. I enjoyed the teaching very much. History in St John's was slightly rundown when I went there. But I was lucky to have some very brilliant pupils straight off. My first pupil was Peter Burke,[53] who was a bit of a challenge, because his essays took about four minutes to read (essays were read aloud in those days). By five past twelve, his contribution was finished, and he had, in concise form, said everything there was to be said about the subject. For a young tutor, the remaining 55 minutes were a yawning gap which took some filling. Then there was Brian Harrison[54] the next year and Prys Morgan.[55]

AM: Tell me something about Brian because he had a huge influence on my life later on.

KT: Brian Harrison?[56] Did he?

AM: Well, he did lend me all his undergraduate notes while I was reading history. So, I basically retyped all his notes to help me. And also, his 'one fact one card' method, he was assiduous, abstracts on small cards, as you know and he had these filing cabinets and that had a huge influence on me for more than 20 years.

KT: I didn't know that.

AM: Along the years, he was probably the most influential person. Because David McLellan,[57] whom he shared rooms with, got me through my Latin examinations, so that's how I met Brian. Tell me something about Brian.

KT: Well, Brian was the year after Peter Burke and he was the exact opposite, that is to say, his essays would have lasted forever. He too didn't leave me much to say, but, fortunately, most of the hour was happily taken up by the essay. He was an amazingly diligent student who regularly turned in capacious and very well-written essays; he was a model for other people.

AM: An older student, he'd done national service. Well, both of them had, hadn't they?

KT: Yes, they both had. They were younger than me, but not that much younger. Brian, of course, became a 19th- and 20th-century historian, but, as an undergraduate, he did the Italian Renaissance special subject. So, I didn't see as much of him as I would have liked. I've followed all his work since and very impressive it is.

AM: Did he play a part in your election as Master of Corpus?

KT: President of Corpus, yes. Oh certainly. It was he who approached me in the first place and yes, he orchestrated that, I'm quite sure.

AM: You said you enjoyed teaching very much. Did you enjoy both the supervision and the lecturing?

KT: I liked giving lectures, but I hated the time preparing them and I'm afraid that I settled down into an annual performance of the same eight lectures on the set authors for the 'Political Thought' paper, namely, Aristotle, Hobbes and Rousseau.

AM: Which I came to.

KT: Yes, and you got a First Class mark on that paper, as my ancient mark book reminds me, though I wasn't the one who marked your paper. I used to revise the lectures each year, so they came to resemble the famous boat which remained the same boat, even though every bit of it had been repaired and replaced. Despite all my revisions, the lectures remained the same lectures and I gave them to large audiences for 20-odd years. I also gave a special subject class, which counted as a lecture course, and in that way, I fulfilled my lecturing stint. But I also taught over a wide range, which involved a great deal of reading and keeping up. Most of my time was devoted to that, but I found it very rewarding.

AM: Do you have any kind of philosophy of undergraduate supervision, any practices?

KT: Well, I think they've all been prohibited now. The first thing to go was the convention that people read their essays. Next, undergraduates nowadays are handed typed reading lists, preferably with the page numbers of the books and the library shelf mark. to save them the trouble of looking it up. Whereas the reading lists I gave were oral and sometime rather vague. I'd say there's good article on such and such in *Past & Present* for around 1964 or was it 1965? Now, it is all very much more precise. It's also much clearer what the syllabus is. It wasn't at all clear in my time. You knew that a paper was on, say, English (as it was then) History, 1307–1688, but it was left to the examiners to decide what aspects of that period would be asked about.

AM: Do you think it's improved as a result of much more formal guidance?

KT: No, I don't. I think the teaching is technically more efficient, so far as exam results are concerned, though how much is the result of grade inflation, I wouldn't know. The proportion of firsts is quite extraordinary by comparison with what it used to be. That's primarily because the criteria for entry to the University are much more stringent academically than they used to be. But I think it leads to less intellectual initiative.

AM: You weren't forced or even asked whether you were doing something else but did you start to?

KT: Yes. I had a special subject class, Commonwealth and Protectorate, with John Cooper.

AM: Were you terrified? Because he always terrified me.

KT: Yes, he had an unfortunate manner and a short fuse. I wasn't terrified, though. But the class was a demanding exercise in competitive cooking. John Cooper and I spoke in alternate weeks and delivered what were essentially research monographs, with one's colleague as the main audience. That's how I came to write about the Levellers. Previously, I had edited the *Oxford Magazine*, the don's newspaper, in 1961, when I reviewed Evans-Pritchard's[58] pamphlet on 'History and Anthropology' or was it 'Anthropology and History'? I wrote an enthusiastic piece, which Lawrence Stone[59] asked me to expand for a seminar he was running, and arranged for me to publish in *Past and Present*. But I was still pottering along with the Levellers and other 17th-century topics with no particular direction. It was when I was pursuing the Levellers, for one of those classes with John Cooper, that I found that there was a manuscript in Bodley relating to the Leveller Richard Overton.[60] I ordered it up, only to discover that the manuscript was a letter pinned inside one of the astrologer William Lilly's casebooks, asking Lilly whether he thought it was a good idea for him, Overton, to continue being a Leveller. This, of course, awakened me to the importance of astrology. I began to study the casebooks of Lilly and others. I soon discovered that one of the problems which people took to Lilly was their conviction that they had been bewitched. That was how I got launched on *Religion and the Decline of Magic*.

AM: These two streams, Evans-Pritchard and did you read any of his stuff on witchcraft at that time?

KT: Yes. For the purpose of writing the article on history and anthropology, I read quite a lot. In fact, when I sent an offprint of my article to E.P., I got a sardonic note back. He said, 'You seem to have read more anthropological works than I have. I find them very ill-written.'

AM: Did you meet him?

KT: Yes. He'd been a colleague at All Souls. I knew him, but we weren't close. I found him rather cynical and I suspected him of playing his younger colleagues in Anthropology against each other. But I haunted the Institute of Social Anthropology and gave papers there. So, I knew the Lienhardts[61] and Rodney Needham,[62] Peter Rivière[63] and John Beattie.[64]

AM: You didn't go to any lectures?

KT: I used to go sometimes to the weekly seminar.

AM: So you started on...this was...?

KT: In the mid-60s.

AM: You were already working on this obviously when I met you in '63, so you'd begun. Tell me, since we've come to *Religion and the Decline of Magic*, tell me the theme of book for the more general...I mean, it's a huge book so pick one or two bits for a general audience or interest in your work. What was the question behind the book or the questions?

KT: Well, I'm not sure it started that way. It was essentially a descriptive book. The first part I wrote were the chapters on the astrological casebooks of William Lilly[65] and others in Bodley. This was an aspect of 17th-century life with which I was totally unacquainted. It became quite clear that it was an important one. Lilly and his colleagues had over 2,000 cases a year, with people from all places in the social scale coming to him for help or advice on a very wide range of problems. I suppose the first question I asked was why people went to astrologers and what was it that made astrological practice so popular. To answer that question, I drew a certain amount by analogy from accounts of what African diviners did and why they did it. A common problem of Lilly's clients was that of whether or not they were bewitched. Although a good deal had been written on it, I thought that witchcraft remained a seriously understudied subject, despite being a major preoccupation in the early modern period. Since it wasn't a preoccupation of the

20th century, why was it one in the 16th and 17th? That question quickly brought up the issue of the relationship of these practices to the orthodox religion of the day. I came to the view that 17th-century religion had been purged of a good number of its 'magical' elements, but that they had been very conspicuous in the later middle ages, when people turned to religious remedies for practical help in daily life, an activity which Protestants would strongly repudiate. Of course, some Catholic intellectuals also rejected it, but the Protestants made it a bigger issue. So, that was what the book was about.

AM: And the central thesis, which is partly that there was this vacuum created by the climate, the magical element in Catholicism, which was at the time filled by or that was behind some of the excesses of witchcraft and then it faded away into science and technology and so on and so on. Do you still think that's a reasonable overarching framework? Or have you rethought it?

KT: Well, the first criticism of the book which anybody made was that there was more witchcraft in the 18th and 19th centuries than I had allowed for. In reply to that, I persist in thinking that there was a very big difference between the status of village magic in the 19th century and that which prevailed three or four hundred years earlier. The 'educated' classes of Hanoverian and Victorian England dismissed the whole idea as rubbish and that represents a big change. A lot of the functions which had been discharged by the cunning men in the 16th century were now performed by other agencies, like the police, who tracked down stolen goods, or medical doctors, who cured sick people, or a whole range of consultants, who gave advice on personal matters, such as psychiatrists, psychotherapists, and marriage-guidance counsellors. These advisors have taken over the role of cunning men and they deal with very similar problems.

AM: One of the difficulties which neither of these types have certainly solved is that there seems to be a kind of gap, that is to say, the functional substitutes for these people occurs a hundred years after the decline of the witchcraft prosecutions and the belief of witchcraft among the educated. There is some improvement in medicine or insurance or firefighting, of course, but not terribly much in the late 17th and early 18th centuries, when the witchcraft beliefs among the educated declined. They seem to have anticipated, as it were, the effective means which weren't yet quite available.

KT: Yes, that's certainly true and it is indeed a problem. The 18th century anticipated the modern secular world in lots of ways, though it lacked its technological resources. The Hanoverian aristocracy were essentially pagan, as the mausolea they built demonstrate. As you say, it's difficult to explain.

AM: I'm always interested in how people work and two things that struck me with you, one was that when you read, you're notable in Bodley and you kind of sit with these huge piles of books around you and you were going through them extremely fast. You seem to have an ability to cut books and take out what you want very quickly. Is that true?

KT: Yes, I suppose that I do read very fast, and I have always read omnivorously. I believe that to understand a period you have to immerse yourself in all the sources available, of which, of course, there are usually rather a lot.

AM: But how do you combine that? Is it easy to read very fast if you know exactly there are three or four things you want to get out of a book or you know exactly what you read around it enough to know it duplicates a lot to what you've read already? Also, rather nicely, I don't know whether it's your phrase, but you've talked about reading against the grain, in other words, picking up things which were not, at the time, necessarily useful to what you're reading. And saving those as well. So that requires a deeper reading.

KT: Yes, I did make the point about reading against the grain. I'm a fast reader and can skim people's articles and books very quickly, only stopping when I come to a passage I want to ponder or make a note about, and then I'll read more slowly. I'm somehow programmed in such a way that a passage relating to one of the scores of different topics in which I'm interested will come out at me. I can't explain the process, but I don't think I miss many of the relevant bits in what I'm reading. Of course, this skill, if that's the word, is made well-nigh obsolete by the search facilities of 'Early English Books Online' (EEBO) and 'Eighteenth-Century Collections

Online' (ECCO). Anyone can, for example, type 'witchcraft' and immediately get a vast number of references to the word in the English printed literature for the 16th, 17th and 18th centuries. But such references are useless unless one knows their context and the circumstances in which the work from which they come was produced, and that often requires a more prolonged inquiry. Moreover, those who use only this method will miss the passages which refer to witchcraft without actually using the word. A study of, say, attitudes to poverty, will not get far if it is confined to sources that contain the word 'poverty'.

AM: To some extent, because another example you gave which is stuck in my mind, the sermon in which the preacher says that you mustn't be like British children who sail their paper boats on ponds. Now, with a search engine you wouldn't know to....
KT: Yes indeed. That's perfectly true and, of course, the search engine only picks up words. It doesn't pick up ideas.

AM: Yes, exactly. There is still some room for us.
KT: Fortunately.

AM: The other thing, which as you know is of mutual interest, the *Religion and the Decline of Magic* is vaguely, it has been likened Frazerian,[66] in a sense, or Christopher Hillian, if you like, in that it has a vast bibliographical apparatus and footnotes and so on and shares a vast reading as does your most recent book *The Ends of Life* (2009)]. How was it that you kept references? Christopher just used to write at the back of his books, pages and references, he knew it was in this book and then he could find the page. How did you index all this stuff?
KT: Well, it's not the past tense, it's still the method I use, I'm afraid. When I read anything, I make notes. If it's a book, I put the page number on the left hand side of each passage I copy out. If it's a manuscript, I put the folio number. So, if, for example, I've been reading a sermon by William Perkins,[67] published in 1605, I write 'Perkins 1605', and the page number opposite each of the passages I'd noted. Then, take out a pair of scissors and slice my notes into separate slips, each containing a single passage. Then I

file them away in different envelopes according to the topic they relate to.

AM: You don't write a heading in a notebook? A subheading of the topic, in other words?

KT: Well, I don't need to write that, because I can see they're all about adultery or whatever. Of course, this is potentially a terrible method, because by separating the passages from each other you've completely lost the context. To avoid that happening, I used for a time, until I found it too laborious and too wasteful of paper, to keep two copies, one the original set of notes unmutilated and the other the notes cut into little slips. I don't do that now. But if I get to the point of wanting to include a passage in a publication, I always go back and check it against the original, a time-consuming process, but, thanks to the internet, much less so than it used to be, when it often involved making a day trip to London.

AM: Because that was one of the main criticisms made about Christopher Hill.

KT: Yes, well, I think, Christopher was not always accurate in his footnotes and he quite often quoted something out of context. If I quote out of context, it's not on purpose. I'm highly self-conscious about the dangers of decontextualized citation.

AM: How do you deal with a problem which I have, because I don't know if Brian got this method from you, but anyway, Brian's method was little cards. And I found that my categories, the way I was placing all the material in envelopes, my interests in the categorization, were shifted over time so what I found, after about 20 years of this, was my systems weren't useful because I couldn't...I had to reconstruct my mental archaeology of say 20 years ago when I was reading to re-find things because they were in the wrong envelope.

KT: That's absolutely right. That certainly is a very serious problem of mine. My conceptual scheme, if I can call it that, doesn't always stand up very well these days. I try to keep the whole thing alive by looking periodically at my envelopes and taking things out of one and putting them in another. And, of course, there's a real problem when one particular passage relates to half a dozen of my topics. It's all highly imperfect.

AM: And the other problem, is that beyond about I reckon 20,000 slips or cards, the difficulty of filing stuff away because each time you have an extra thing the difficulty becomes exponentially greater. In that system, I found I was spending so much time thinking about what sub-category to file things under, I was just worn out and gave up by the end. Do you have large piles of unfiled slips?

KT: I'm afraid so. I have boxes of them and their contents stare up reproachfully at me every day. I'll get round to it sometime, I hope....

AM: Because I've got some of Frazer's[68] notebooks and he used a similar method. Though they haven't been torn up or anything obviously, towards the end he clearly ran out of energy.

KT: Yes, indeed. The great Awful Warning is Lord Acton.[69] Do you remember Charles Oman's description of his library after his death? `There were pigeonholed desks and cabinets with literally thousands of compartments, into each of which were sorted little white slips with references to some particular topic, so drawn up (so far as I could see) that no one but the compiler could easily make out the drift of the section.' I fear that my slip-filled envelopes are embarrassingly close to that account and my impenetrable handwriting makes the situation worse. But what is the alternative? Having a lot of research assistants, I suppose, but I've never had one.

AM: Well, let's move on. You taught at St. John's for how long?

KT: I went to St John's in 1957 and I was a tutor there until 1986, when I became a professor *ad hominem*. I held that title for only for nine months, which was something of a record at the time, and then went to Corpus. I was at St John's for 29 years.

AM: Anything else about that time at St John's which is worth recording?

KT: Well, it was in many ways my most productive period really. In the 1960s I achieved a certain notoriety, first with the *Past & Present* article on history and anthropology article and then with a polemical piece in the *TLS* [*Times Literary Supplement*].

AM: I remember you going away to write that. You went off to Wales. You were panicking about it and I remember a phone call from a public phone to you and you said, 'I can't do it. I can't work here. I've got to go away to Wales. I've got to write this article' and you disappeared for a few days and then you came back and you were relaxed again.

KT: Yes, well, I don't recall that now. The *TLS* article wasn't my idea. They ask me to write it. I don't know who put them up to it, but I think it was Moses Finley.[70] He came to see me and asked me to write about history and the social sciences. And somehow this turned into a great diatribe. 'The Tools and the Job'. This Churchillian title was the editor's idea, not mine. And, of course, what I said in the article made me very unpopular with a lot of distinguished people.

AM: It was a wonderful article and it had a great influence on many of us, including myself, but you've subsequently felt it was too black and white.

KT: Yes, it wasn't very subtle and I've become a pluralist about what historians should do. I'm happy for them to do almost anything and I think we need them all. They're all, so to speak, God's creatures. I even have more respect than I used to for the old-style, tough, EHR[71] type of medievalist.[72] We need them too. So, I'm much more ecumenical than I used to be.

AM: You were something of a convert to cliometrics and statistical methods.

KT: Yes. There's a Latin tag, *Video meliora, deterioraque sequor,* 'I see the better, but I follow the worse'. I've never been a cliometrician myself; and I'm fortunate or unfortunate enough to study a period where statistics won't take you very far. On the other hand, I think if you're writing about 20th-century history, statistics are important. When there is sufficient evidence to make quantitative statements with some precision, they are better than non-statistical ones. But I'm not at all quantitative in my own writing.

AM: You were really stressing how important it was.

KT: Yes. Well, it turned out to be perfectly prophetic in the sense that modern economic history is highly quantitative and rightly so.

AM: What were you attacked for or notorious for? Was it John Cooper?

KT: Yes, John Cooper was one of those people. Yes, he and Richard Cobb.[73] The hated the idea of the white-coated American technocrat historian. And they also thought, rightly, that I'd been insufficiently respectful to my predecessors.

AM: There was also a slight change, around this time which leads up to your second major book: a sort of shift, I think you describe it, from British social anthropology to more cultural anthropology.

KT: Yes, the other influence on me was the *Annales* school, not the *Annales* of hard quantitative history, but the *Annales* of Lucien Febvre[74] and what nowadays is called cultural history, though it wasn't called that then. I think Peter Burke was the first professor of cultural history. I just happened to find that kind of history temperamentally more sympathetic. I was not much interested in statistics about masses of people, but I was quite interested in what went on in individual heads. Indeed, I've become increasingly interested in the values, norms, tastes, and mental assumptions of the people of the past. I suppose that most of my work since 1971 was a sort of move towards an ethnography of a kind, but a very untheoretical and descriptive ethnography, of early modern England in all its different aspects.

AM: You mentioned Lucien Febvre, but not Marc Bloch.[75] If you had to go to a desert island with your favourite historians, historians you admire and who have influenced you, just two or three of them, who would you choose?

KT: That's quite difficult and I suppose I just don't think like that, really. It's like people asking what are your favourite novels.

AM: You don't have hero figures and models?

KT: I don't consciously have any models. No, not really. There were books at the time which I thought were marvellous. For example, I thought Leroy Ladurie's *Montaillou*[76] was a marvellous book. It was absolutely panned by the many medievalists, because of its cavalier use of the sources, but it struck me as an exemplary attempt at what historians of a vanished age ought to be trying to. I liked it very much.

AM: I talked to Patricia Williams who was a CUP [Cambridge University Press] person, I mean on CUP, and she was always wringing her hands that they turned it down, especially after you wrote such a....

KT: Yes, Penguin turned it down too. I wrote a report for both publishers and they both rejected it, as I understood because it was about an obscure 13th-14th century French village which no English reader was going to be interested in. And then, when it became a bestseller, Penguin at great expense bought it back in an abridged form.

AM: They were almost right. Whoever it was hadn't set it up very well. It might have sunk.

KT: Yes, I suppose so. But I thought it was a very good book. In answer to your earlier question, there are many historians whom I admire, but whom I don't even attempt to emulate, because I don't have their particular talents. For example, I think that Dick Southern was a very great historian and that Quentin Skinner[77] is a wonderfully fastidious writer; and there are lots of others.

AM: What about Maitland?[78]

KT: There was a passage in Maitland, I can't remember where it comes, in which he licks his lips as some wretched serf is sent to the gallows. It completely turned me off Maitland. I felt his sensibilities weren't mine. I know he is supposed to be the historian's historian, but, on the basis of that passage he's not for me.

AM: Because you said you were interested in law history or legal things.

KT: Yes, I greatly admire the work of John Baker, for example, or the late Brian Simpson.

AM: What about Braudel?[79]

KT: Well, I greatly respect him, but he's a bit of a geographical determinist. Tawney, I must say, was a deep influence on me and I admired him very much. I liked his eloquence. Marc Bloch I would certainly regard as a very great historian indeed.

AM: As you moved into this more cultural phase, about that time, you were asked to give the Trevelyan[80] lectures in Cambridge and you gave them and I came to those six lectures. What was the theme of the book that resulted from those lectures?

KT: I suppose the theme was the changing attitudes in England between 1500 and 1800 to the natural world. It included beliefs about man's place in nature, the treatment of animals, the classification of the natural world, tastes in landscape, ideas of conservation, and vegetarian inhibitions about cruelty to domestic animals. It had vaguely green implications, I suppose, though I wasn't particularly green myself. I just happened to have a bulging envelope called 'animals'.

AM: This was *Man and the Natural World*, the book? And again, reflecting back on it, do you think the central theme, this was probably somehow, some way linked to possibly one of the causes? The links to industrialization and urbanization and the separation of man, people, physically from the countryside and so on? That was certainly one of the themes in it. Do you still think this?

KT: Yes, I do and I think here my childhood background is relevant because when I came to live in the tow, I was very struck by the difference of the people in their attitudes to animals. For example, at the farm on which I grew up we had dogs who were indispensable when we had to round up sheep and cattle. They had names and we were very fond of them. But we would never allow a dog into the house, absolutely never. It would have seemed an obscenity. I also remember how we had horses, which were gradually replaced by tractors. They used to pull very heavy loads of hay or wheat or whatever. That was often quite difficult, because the carts, when loaded, would sink into the mud and the horse, however much it struggled and strained, wasn't strong enough to pull it. I was appalled to see somebody grab a pitchfork and beat the horse with, so as to get it to move. No doubt, you might have seen something like that happen with the London cabbies in the 19th century, but you wouldn't see it today. I came to believe that the different sensibilities of urban people derive from their being largely unaware of their material dependence on the countryside, which they value, not for its utility, but for its beauty.

AM: Well, we've only got about ten minutes and a lot of your life to cover. President of Corpus, you sort of implied this was intellectually a less productive period because you were busy running a college?

KT: Yes, I went to Corpus in 1986 and stayed there till I retired in 2000. During that period, I took on a great number of other responsibilities. I developed, unintentionally, a bit of a London life. First, I was put on the reviewing committee for the exportation of works of art. Then I became a Trustee, first of the National Gallery and, later, of the British Museum. I was also on the Historical Manuscripts Commission. Meanwhile in Oxford, I was a Delegate of the University Press for twenty years (1980–2000), twelve of them as Chairman of its Finance Committee, the equivalent of its Board. I was also President of the British Academy for four years in the 1990s. It's a wonder I got anything else done at all.

AM: Yes, and you took them very seriously. I remember you at your party when you left the Press, they said that you tended to read almost all the books that were submitted to be published. That's a vast library.

KT: No, I normally read only the prospectuses and readers' reports. I found them interesting and very educational. The other body I'm proud to have been associated with was the Supervisory Committee of the *Oxford Dictionary of National Biography*. It was published in 60 volumes in 2004.

AM: Earlier, there were also your own university commitments to look to in Oxford. And as a head of house, you'd also be on a lot of university committees.

KT: Yes, but to some extent they cancelled each other out, each one providing me with an alibi for not being present at the others. Most important, I had an excellent secretary in Corpus, Veronica Krailsheimer, who dealt very efficiently with telephone calls and unexpected visitors. I have a huge collection of the neatly-typed notes she used to leave me, recording what had happened during my absence from the office.

AM: Just one secretary with all those jobs.

KT: Yes, only one, but she was on top of them and I was cosseted. When I retired from Corpus, I hadn't been in a post office for 14 years.

AM: All these trusteeships and chairmanships, did you enjoy that kind of committee administrative work?

KT: The sad truth is that I did. Maybe not indiscriminately so, but they were all concerned with activities which I thought worthwhile. I also felt that I'd had quite a good time at St. John's, where I had to do very little in the way of administration, and that it was my turn to put something back. I also enjoyed the illusion of getting things done and seeing immediate results, by contrast with the glacier-like progress of writing a book. I liked the sociability of committees and I met all sorts of extremely interesting people.

AM: This is a problem of time, I am told, although it hasn't happened to me yet. But there's nothing to stop you from worrying about what you should be doing.

KT: No, I haven't found it a problem at all.

AM: Good, good. I've got two further particular questions. One is about your family, about Valerie and I have pictures of you sitting up with Valerie at night together so it was obviously a close relationship. She was a teacher?

KT: Yes, she taught in secondary schools. Most of her time was spent teaching she taught English Literature in the Oxford Girls High School (GPDST), where she had many distinguished pupils, who went on to write as many books as my pupils did. Hers was quite a demanding job. Teaching English, unlike, say, mathematics, involves an enormous amount of marking. So, she was sitting up late every evening, marking exercise books, when I was going to bed. But she has always found time to read everything I write and my work has been much the better for her criticisms and suggestions.

AM: Does she? And gives you valuable feedback?

KT: Yes indeed.

AM: You had some children?

KT: Yes, I have some children, two of them. They are both academics. My daughter, Emily, is a Professor of Latin in Cambridge, a Fellow of St John's and an FBA. My son, Edmund, is an Associate Professor of Roman architectural history in Durham University. And I have grandchildren.

AM: You've got grandchildren as well?

KT: Yes, three grandchildren.

AM: How delightful.

KT: Yes, absolutely. Two of them are exceedingly musical. One of them sang the opening solo in your King's Festival of Nine Lessons and Carols and went on to be the Organ Scholar at King's.

AM: Really? When was this?

KT: I think the solo was about 2005 or 2006.

AM: I must have heard it then. How nice. The other question is about your more recent work, you've just published another book. Again, what was the theme of this and what were you trying to do in this book?

KT: Well, what I was trying to do was to deliver the Ford lectures which I'd given in 2000. I had been asked to give them long before that, but, for various complicated reasons involving other people, they had to be postponed for some years. I wasn't quite sure what to give them on, but I had a good number of topics which I'd done some work, so I cobbled them together and called the book *The Ends of Life*. They are a series of studies in the values and objectives which people in the early modern period pursued, either consciously or unconsciously. There are extended discussions of military prowess as a form of masculine fulfilment, of work, again, as a source of fulfilment or a curse, and of material wealth and possessions, honour, reputation, friendship and posthumous fame. They are based on quite extensive reading and are meant to be a further contribution to my ethnography of early modern England.

AM: And now?

KT: I have to put together three volumes of essays, some of which have been published before and some not. I also gave some lectures in Jerusalem some years ago which have to be published. They are on civility and ideas of civilization in the early modern period.

AM: The three volumes, has it got a title yet or will they have separate titles?

KT: I think it's got an overall title of 'Approaching the Past', it's broken up into three separate themes.

AM: How wonderful. That's excellent. I've only got three or four minutes, but I often ask distinguished academics at the end to give a little bit of advice to starting scholars as if I were your PhD student or DPhil student coming to you and you were giving me my first supervision about how I should approach research and history and writing. Do you have any?

KT: The first thing I would say would be, 'Are you quite sure you really want to be an academic in this country, given the present state of the universities?' They have changed so much and are much more regulated from above and, as a result, much less satisfying. I enjoyed wonderful freedom when I was at St John's and I could go at my own pace. Nowadays, people are expected to lay eggs with great regularity and that means universities are not quite so obviously the home for the more questing spirit. So, first of all, I'd ask, 'Are you quite sure you want to do that?' After that, I'd say avoid all my mistakes: don't fritter your energies on lots of different topics, but stick to one thing and see it through.

AM: Stick to one thing?

KT: I mean I've never really specialized and specialization seems to be the fashion these days...

AM: But you've enjoyed it?

KT: Oh, very much. Absolutely. I wouldn't have wanted anything else, not even being a Naval Captain!

AM: You're more a fox that a hedgehog, would you say?

KT: Yes. Indubitably, yes. I don't know any single thing.

AM: But many great things. I think that's a very nice point to end. Thank you very much, my dear Keith.

KT: Thank you.

NOTES

1. Keith Thomas. 2021. Wikipedia. https://en.wikipedia.org/wiki/Keith_Thomas_(historian)

2. Norman Conquest, the military conquest of England by William, duke of Normandy, primarily effected by his decisive victory at the Battle of Hastings (14 October 1066) and resulting ultimately in profound

political, administrative, and social changes in the British Isles. https://www.
britannica.com/event/Norman-Conquest

3. Sir John Bertrand Gurdon, FRS, FMedSci, MAE (b. 1933) is an English
developmental biologist. He is best known for his pioneering research in
nuclear transplantation and cloning. He was awarded the Lasker Award in
2009. In 2012, he and Shinya Yamanaka were awarded the Nobel Prize for
Physiology or Medicine for the discovery that mature cells can be converted
to stem cells. https://en.wikipedia.org/wiki/John_Gurdon

4. Empire Exhibition, Scotland 1938 was an international exposition
held at Bellahouston Park in Glasgow, from May to December 1938. The
Exhibition offered a chance to showcase and boost the economy of Scotland,
and celebrate Empire trade and developments, recovering from the depression
of the 1930s. https://en.wikipedia.org/wiki/Empire_Exhibition,_Scotland

5. Carlyle, see Appendix.

6. James Campbell, see Appendix.

7. *The Wind in the Willows* is a children's book by Scottish novelist
Kenneth Grahame, first published in 1908. Alternatingly slow moving and
fast paced, it focuses on four anthropomorphised animals: Mole, Rat (a
European water vole), Toad, and Badger. They live in a pastoral version
of Edwardian England. https://en.wikipedia.org/wiki/The_Wind_in_the_
Willows

8. *Treasure Island* (originally *The Sea Cook: A Story for Boys*) is an
adventure novel by Scottish author Robert Louis Stevenson, narrating
a tale of 'buccaneers and buried gold'. https://en.wikipedia.org/wiki/
Treasure_Island

9. *Our Island Story: A Child's History of England*, published abroad
as *An Island Story: A Child's History of England*, is a book by Henrietta
Elizabeth Marshall, first published in 1905 in London by T.C. & E.C. Jack.
https://en.wikipedia.org/wiki/Our_Island_Story

10. *The Boy's Book of Heroes* by Helena Peake was published in 1923.

11. John Habakkuk, see Appendix.

12. Glyn Edmund Daniel (1914–86) was a Welsh scientist and
archaeologist who taught at Cambridge University, where he specialised
in the European Neolithic period. He was appointed Disney Professor of
Archaeology in 1974 and edited the academic journal *Antiquity* from 1958
to 1985. In addition to early efforts to popularise archaeological study
and antiquity on radio and television, he edited several popular studies of
the fields. He also published mysteries under the pseudonym Dilwyn Rees.
https://en.wikipedia.org/wiki/Glyn_Daniel

13. David Maelgwyn Joslin (1925–70) who had held the Chair of Economic History in the University of Cambridge since 1965 and had been, for the last two years, a co-editor of the Journal of Latin American Studies. He was educated at Barry County School, Glamorgan, and at St John's College, Cambridge. His undergraduate studies were interrupted from 1943–46 by service with the Royal Navy, first as an ordinary seaman and then as a Sub-Lieutenant. Returning to Cambridge in 1946 he did brilliantly in both parts of the Historical Tripos in 1947 and 1948, held the Strathcona Studentship at St John's College from 1949–51 and was then elected a Fellow of Pembroke College. He remained a Fellow of Pembroke till his death. http://bit.ly/3ofKcJD

14. Martin Daunton, see Appendix.

15. Teifion Phillips, see Appendix.

16. Richard Tawney, see Appendix.

17. George Orson Welles (1915–85) was an American actor, director, writer and producer who is remembered for his innovative work in radio, theatre and film. He is considered one of the greatest filmmakers of all time. https://en.wikipedia.org/wiki/Orson_Welles

18. Johann Sebastian Bach (1685–1750) was a German composer and musician of the Baroque period. https://en.wikipedia.org/wiki/Johann_Sebastian_Bach

19. Wolfgang Amadeus Mozart (1756–91) was a prolific and influential composer of the Classical period. He composed more than 600 works, many of which are acknowledged as pinnacles of symphonic, concertante, chamber, operatic, and choral music. https://en.wikipedia.org/wiki/Wolfgang_Amadeus_Mozart

20. Ludwig van Beethoven (1770–1827) was a German composer and pianist. Beethoven remains one of the most admired composers in the history of Western music; his works rank amongst the most performed of the classical music repertoire. https://en.wikipedia.org/wiki/Ludwig_van_Beethoven

21. Franz Peter Schubert (1797–1828) was an Austrian composer of the late Classical and early Romantic eras. Despite his short lifetime, Schubert left behind a vast oeuvre, including more than 600 secular vocal works (mainly lieder), seven complete symphonies, sacred music, operas, incidental music and a large body of piano and chamber music. https://en.wikipedia.org/wiki/Franz_Schubert

22. Igor Fyodorovich Stravinsky, ComSE (1882–1971) was a Russian-born composer, pianist, and conductor. He is widely considered one of

the most important and influential composers of the 20th century. https://en.wikipedia.org/wiki/Igor_Stravinsky

23. Sir Edward Coke, SL (1552–1634) was an English barrister, judge, and politician who is considered to be the greatest jurist of the Elizabethan and Jacobean eras. https://en.wikipedia.org/wiki/Edward_Coke

24. David Lindsay Keir, see Appendix.

25. Dick Southern, R.W. Southern, see Appendix.

26. Hugh Stretton, see Appendix.

27. D.B. Quinn, see Appendix.

28. Raph Samuel, see Appendix.

29. Adam Smith, FRSA (1723–90) was a Scottish economist, philosopher as well as a moral philosopher, a pioneer of political economy, and a key figure during the Scottish Enlightenment, also known as 'The Father of Economics' or 'The Father of Capitalism'. Smith wrote two classic works, *The Theory of Moral Sentiments* (1759) and *An Inquiry into the Nature and Causes of the Wealth of Nations* (1776). https://en.wikipedia.org/wiki/Adam_Smith

30. Charles Margrave Taylor, CC, GOQ, FRSC, FBA (b. 1931) is a Canadian philosopher from Montreal, Quebec, and professor emeritus at McGill University best known for his contributions to political philosophy, the philosophy of social science, the history of philosophy, and intellectual history. https://en.wikipedia.org/wiki/Charles_Taylor_(philosopher)

31. Thomas Henry Bingham, Baron Bingham of Cornhill, KG, PC, FBA (1933–2010) was an eminent British judge who was successively Master of the Rolls, Lord Chief Justice and Senior Law Lord. He was described as the greatest lawyer of his generation. https://en.wikipedia.org/wiki/Tom_Bingham,_Baron_Bingham_of_Cornhill

32. Sir Theodore Henry Tylor (1900–68) was a lawyer and international level chess player, despite being nearly blind. In 1965, he was knighted for his service to organisations for the blind. He was Fellow and Tutor in Jurisprudence at Balliol College, Oxford for almost forty years. https://en.wikipedia.org/wiki/Theodore_Tylor

33. Maurice Keen, see Appendix.

34. Asser, see Appendix.

35. The *Regularis Concordia* was the most important document of the English Benedictine Reform, sanctioned by the Council of Winchester in about 973. https://en.wikipedia.org/wiki/Regularis_Concordia_(Winchester)

36. Writing shortly after Aelred of Rievaulx died in 1167, Walter Daniel, his secretary and fellow monk, has created the picture of Aelred which

endures to this day. We come to know a man of 'charity and astonishing sanctity', an ailing abbot whose monks sat chatting around his bed. Only in passing do we glimpse the ambitious young steward at the court of King David of Scotland, the ecclesiastical diplomat and political counsellor who moved easily in royal and episcopal circles, or the canny property manager who guided his monasteries to prosperity. From Walter's pen we have a gentle, loving, ascetic abbot who offered spiritual guidance to his monks through conversation and to a wider audience through the treatises he composed, and who died a holy death. http://bit.ly/368lAeG

37. David Lindsay Keir, see Appendix.

38. Arnold Toynbee, see Appendix.

39. John Oswald Prestwich (1914–2003) was a Medieval historian who worked at Bletchley and studied the role of intelligence in earlier periods. As well as making a seminal contribution to the study of Anglo-Norman England, the Oxford historian John Prestwich worked at Bletchley and the Pentagon during the Second World War. Born in Leigh, Lancashire, in 1914, John Oswald Prestwich went to school at Sedbergh. Thereafter his life was spent very largely in Oxford: as an undergraduate at Hertford, a prize fellow of Magdalen, a tutorial fellow of Queen's from 1937 to 1981, and then in fruitful retirement in Old Headington. https://bit.ly/3fWSG6W

40. James Campbell, see Appendix.

41. J.P. Cooper, was a Fellow at Trinity College, Oxford and an expert on early modern history.

42. Robert Cecil, 1st Earl of Salisbury, KG, PC (1563–1612) was an English statesman noted for his direction of the government during the Union of the Crowns, as Tudor England gave way to Stuart rule (1603). Salisbury served as the Secretary of State of England (1596–1612) and Lord High Treasurer (1608–12), succeeding his father as Queen Elizabeth I's Lord Privy Seal and remaining in power during the first nine years of King James I's reign until his death. https://en.wikipedia.org/wiki/Robert_Cecil,_1st_Earl_of_Salisbury

43. Joel Hurstfield (1911–80) was a was a Professor at London University and an expert on Elizabethan England.

44. Gerald Aylmer, see Appendix.

45. Anthony Wood, see Appendix.

46. Olwen Hufton, see Appendix.

47. Fiona MacCarthy, see Appendix.

48. Aristotle, see Appendix.

49. Thomas Hobbes, see Appendix.

50. Rousseau, see Appendix.

51. Simone de Beauvoir, *The Second Sex*, see Appendix.

52. Margaret Mead (1901–78) was an American cultural anthropologist who featured frequently as an author and speaker in the mass media during the 1960s and 1970s. https://en.wikipedia.org/wiki/Margaret_Mead

53. Peter Burke, see Part II, page

54. Brain Harrison, see Part III, page

55. Prys Morgan, see Appendix.

56. Brian Harrison, see Part II, p. 61.

57. David McLellan, see Appendix.

58. Sir Edward Evan Evans-Pritchard, FBA (1902–73) known as E. E. Evans-Pritchard, was an English anthropologist who was instrumental in the development of social anthropology. He was Professor of Social Anthropology at the University of Oxford from 1946 to 1970. https://en.wikipedia.org/wiki/E._E._Evans-Pritchard

59. Lawrence Stone, see Appendix.

60. Richard Overton (Leveller) (fl. 1640–64) was an English pamphleteer and Leveller during the Civil War and Interregnum (England). https://en.wikipedia.org/wiki/Richard_Overton_(Leveller)

61. Ronald Godfrey Lienhardt (1921–93) was a British anthropologist. He took many photographs of the Dinka people he studied. He wrote about their religion in Divinity and Experience: the Religion of the Dinka. https://en.wikipedia.org/wiki/Godfrey_Lienhardt

62. Rodney Needham (1923–2006) was a British social anthropologist. His fieldwork was with the Penan of Borneo (1951–52) and the Siwang of Malaysia (1953–55) https://en.wikipedia.org/wiki/Rodney_Needham

63. Peter G. Rivière (b. 1934) is a British social anthropologist, Emeritus Professor of Oxford University and, with Audrey Butt Colson, a pioneer in the study and teaching of Amazonian peoples in England. In 1957–58 he took part in the Oxford and Cambridge Expedition to South America. https://en.wikipedia.org/wiki/Peter_Rivière

64. John Hugh Marshall Beattie (1915–90) was a social anthropologist of Africa, based for some years at Oxford. https://bit.ly/3t37c0x

65. William Lilly (1602–81) was a 17th century English astrologer. He is described as having been a genius at something 'that modern mainstream opinion has since decided cannot be done at all' having developed his stature as the most important astrologer in England through his social and political connections as well as going on to have an indelible impact on the future course of Western astrological tradition. https://en.wikipedia.org/wiki/William_Lilly

66. Frazerian, In the style of Sir J.G. Frazer, one of the founders of anthropology and the author of *The Golden Bough*. See endnote no. 67.

67. William Perkins (1558–1602) was an influential English cleric and Cambridge theologian, receiving both a B.A. and M.A. from the university in 1581 and 1584 respectively, and also one of the foremost leaders of the Puritan movement in the Church of England during the Elizabethan era. https://en.wikipedia.org/wiki/William_Perkins_(theologian)

68. Sir James George Frazer OM, FRS, FRSE, FBA (1854–1941) was a Scottish social anthropologist and folklorist influential in the early stages of the modern studies of mythology and comparative religion. His most famous work, *The Golden Bough* (1890), documents and details the similarities among magical and religious beliefs around the world. Frazer posited that human belief progressed through three stages: primitive magic, replaced by religion, in turn replaced by science. https://en.wikipedia.org/wiki/James_George_Frazer

69. John Emerich Edward Dalberg-Acton, 1st Baron Acton, 13th Marquess of Groppoli, KCVO, DL (1834–1902), better known as Lord Acton, was an English Catholic historian, politician, and writer. https://en.wikipedia.org/wiki/John_Dalberg-Acton,_1st_Baron_Acton

70. Sir Moses Israel Finley, FBA (1912–86) was an American-born British academic and classical scholar. His prosecution by the McCarran Security Committee led to his move to England, where he became an English classical scholar and eventually master of Darwin College, Cambridge. His most notable work is *The Ancient Economy* (1973) in which he argued that the economy in antiquity was governed by status and civic ideology, rather than rational economic motivations. https://en.wikipedia.org/wiki/Moses_Finley

71. The *Economic History Review* is the quarterly publication of The Economic History Society. Established in 1926, it was the first journal in the world dedicated to research in Economic History. It continues to be one of the leading academic journals in History and Economics. The *Review* publishes peer-reviewed advanced research on all aspects of economic and social history from around the world and from all periods, as well as reviews of new books and surveys of recent journal publications. https://bit.ly/39Sjwt2

72. The EHR was where medievalists would place articles which often contained numerous footnotes – as Trevor-Roper put it, 'Thin trickles of text through lush meadows of footnotes'.

73. Richard Cobb, see Appendix.

74. *The Annales*, Lucien Febvre, see Appendix.

75. Marc Bloch, see Appendix.
76. Le Roy Ladurie, *Montaillou*, see Appendix.
77. Quentin Skinner, see Appendix.
78. F.W. Maitland, see Appendix
79. Fernand Braudel, see Appendix.
80. G.M. Trevelyan, see Appendix.

PART two

Brian Harrison.

Photographs courtesy Alan Macfarlane.

Brian Harrison

Sir Brian Howard Harrison, FBA (b. 1937) is a British historian and academic. Harrison was Professor of Modern History at the University of Oxford from 1996 to 2004. He was additionally the editor of Oxford Dictionary of National Biography *from January 2000 to September 2004 (succeeded by Lawrence Goldman). Since 2004, he has been an Emeritus Fellow of Corpus Christi College, Oxford.*

Harrison has published extensively on British social and political history from the 1790s to the present. His first book was Drink and the Victorians. The Temperance Question England 1815–1872 (1971, 2ⁿᵈ ed. 1994), *based on his doctoral thesis entitled* 'The Temperance Question in England, 1829–1869'. *His most recent publications are two volumes in the* New Oxford History of England *series covering British history from 1951:* Seeking a Role: The United Kingdom 1951–1970 *(2009, paperback with revisions 2011) and* Finding a Role? The United Kingdom 1970–1990 *(2010, paperback with revisions 2011).*

National Life Stories conducted an oral history interview (C1149/24) with Harrison in 2012 for its Oral History of Oral History collection held by the British Library.

Harrison was appointed Knight Bachelor in the 2005 New Year Honours for 'services to scholarship'. He was elected a Fellow of the British Academy (FBA) on 30 July 2005. He is also an elected Fellow of the Royal Historical Society (FRHistS).[1]

I

Alan Macfarlane (AM): This is Brian Harrison who had a considerable influence on my life and career. It is a great pleasure and privilege to talk to you. I will start by asking when and where you were born.

Brian Harrison (BH): I was born in Hampstead, Belsize Park. My parents lived in Glenloch Court, a big block of flats in Belsize Park. My father was a buyer in the toy department in Peter Robinson, which was then an important London store. My mother had been in the hat department. She left there to work for McCracken and Bowen, who were women's hat makers in the Marylebone area. It is quite interesting the way they met because before my mother went to McCracken and Bowen. She worked as an assistant or something in Peter Robinson. When she left, there they organized a whip-round to give her a leaving present and my father contributed to that whip-round and with it they bought her a silver container, which I have still got upstairs, containing visiting cards, in fact, all types of small card. She went round to all the people who had subscribed because there was a list and thanked them. I am here now because she thanked my father, the buyer in the toy department. So, that's how and where they met.

My father was still a buyer at Peter Robinson when they lived in Belsize Park and my mother was a housewife, as was normal in those days. At that time as a married woman with a young baby you didn't have any career. She had a terrible time with me because I cried all the time apparently and she just ran away at one point. My father found her in the lift going down at Belsize Park because she loved going to the West End of London and loved the shops there. She just ran away from me! He was appalled.

This interview was conducted by Alan Macfarlane on 22 June 2012. The transcription for this interview has been provided by Radha Béteille, for this volume. These interviews are available for viewing on:
https://www.sms.cam.ac.uk/media/1402073
https://www.youtube.com/watch?v=aazqSnw2Q08
https://www.youtube.com/watch?v=N7N1bpffEIU

AM: How old were you?

BH: I was about two probably or one. I was probably one. I was born on 9 July 1937 and I just cried a lot. She couldn't stand it. She had no…you immediately go back because her mother died in the flu epidemic in World War I. And her father died, allegedly, of a broken heart, three years after that, when she was about four or five. She never had a mother, really, and she always felt the need for a mother because a mother would stand in, in that sort of situation, and would have said, well if the child is crying give it some equivalent of Godfrey's cordial or whatever to shut it up. My mother had no mother to guide her and she was absolutely at sea. Very fortunately there was a charming woman, a north country woman, very motherly, called Mrs Blackstock. Mrs Blackstock took my mother in hand, she had two children of her own, she said, 'If this happens, do that', and so on.

My father was a very interesting man in many ways. He had all sorts of theories and one of them was that you don't do any washing up on the weekend, so she found herself on Monday morning with these huge piles of washing up to be done and Mrs Blackstock helped her and said, 'You must get your husband in order!'

AM: These theories happily coincide with the fact that he wasn't around during the week?

BH: Yes. He didn't really like Mrs Blackstock because he was suspicious of her and her influence. Anyway, this may have had a very important effect for me because my mother told me that Mrs Blackstock's son Ewart, who was in the fire service, dropped me once when I was a baby on my head and my father was furious about it. He never let Ewart hold me again. But this may be responsible for all sorts of things.

The very first school report I had or very early on, I've got them all upstairs, the prep school headmistress said, 'He positively revels in work.' And that's what I have always done and I've been very happy in anything I have done. I enjoy working, I'm a workaholic. I have been very fortunate in being in a profession where work cumulates in some sense. It means that my life has some harmony about it which most peoples doesn't. No doubt yours is similar in this respect. There is no distinction and there never has been between weekends and weekdays or between holidays and non-holidays. It's all harmonious, it is all one. So, I work on a holiday and I enjoy my work and that goes way before school. It all started much earlier than that.

But, of course, I went to a good school, because my mother was socially ambitious. She viewed education as a way of moving up or at least avoiding moving down socially. My father was much in favour of education for the right reasons and felt that people should realize their full potential. Between them, they reached the same conclusion that I should be sent to Alcuin House School which was the little prep school with probably not more than a hundred pupils. Nothing like as grand as the Dragon School. I got a very good education there. Miss Dalgleish was very encouraging. I was a very nervous child and I had a term where I was completely off school altogether.

AM: How old were you?

BH: I was about six or seven. For some reason I was frightened of going to school. I don't remember being bullied or anything. My parents gave me a rest from school and I stayed at home. For a term, Miss Dalgleish wrote a letter saying, 'We're looking forward to seeing you come back next term', and I did go back next term. It was all alright after that. I was quite a nervous child, looking back. My parents were very good in trying to understand what the problems were and so on. But I got very good school reports. They had a really outrageous system by present-day standards. When you came top of the class, you were given what was called a list and the list was of all the pupils in that class in rank order of performance and I kept on getting all the lists! At the end of term, you used to walk up through the assembled company in a sort of ceremony to receive the list from the headmaster—T. D'Arcy Yeo was his name— so I walked off with all the lists. My parents knew I was bright and did everything they could to encourage it.

But for two quite different, but complementary reasons, it's that school that got me to Merchant Taylors' School, Northwood. And as I was saying, thinking yesterday, I was taught Latin there better.

My performance in Latin peaked at age 13. I was never taught at Merchant Taylors' better than I learnt it then. It was all prepared for what was called the Common Entrance —— no doubt, Alan took it. That was the way you got into a public school, you took it, then you didn't do eleven-plus or anything. You took it at 13 you either got it or you didn't and I got an exhibition, I did not get a scholarship, to Merchant Taylors' which was something like £40 a year, seems a piddling sum now. But it helped and my mother had a brother who was quite affluent. He helped out quite a bit, I think.

Going back a bit, because I was talking about my mother, my history does really go back. Broadly speaking, the situation was this, the Savill family, which is spelt without an 'e' they were always very keen on that. The Shaw Savill Shipping Line was quite a big operation in the Edwardian period, they were also in brewing. It was northeast London. They were also the estate agents, land agents. My grandfather Martin Savill was regarded as the 'poor' branch of the family. Obviously when my grandmother died, soon after my grandfather, died, I think of drink, not of a broken heart, but the two aren't distinguishable, the more affluent members of the Savill family took an interest and really wanted to help. There were seven siblings, I'm trying to remember, my aunt Margot, that's one, my mother, that's two, Gordon, who went to Australia, that's three, Jack who went to Canada, that's four, Merrry, shorter for Meredith, that's five, who was badly crippled and stayed in England and Geoffrey, and Tom, who served on the 'Worcester', training ship that makes seven. So, that's all of them. There were seven of them. Two of them had already gone off to Australia and Canada. They, subsequently, formed big clans in both colonies.

The other four stayed in England and Merry was very seriously crippled. He had rheumatoid arthritis. Like many crippled people in families, he became the centre of the family. He united the family. He was a charming person and very much loved by everybody. But they had him on their hands, so they had to look after him. Two girls, Margot and my mother, who couldn't earn very much. The only one who Tom was young and he couldn't earn at that stage though Geoffrey who was apprenticed to C.A. Vandervell, an engineering firm in Ealing. He was head of the family, at 20 0r 21. So, when both the mother and father are dead, there was quite a lot of pressure from solicitors for the rich members of the Savill family to take over, but my mother's sister and brothers wouldn't have any of it. They wanted to remain independent. They were terrified of being broken up, so they stayed together. The two went off to the colonies and the other five stayed together, including my mother. My mother always used to say she had an extremely happy childhood. But she was brought up by her brothers and by her elder sister, so she never had a mother to guide her through the business of being a woman.

I am always astonished that I ever appeared on the scene because my mother didn't know anything about sex, like a lot of women I suppose at that time and sex was not something one could easily talk about to her. Somehow, I was conceived, but she remained very innocent in all sorts of ways. I think, she was sort of in love with my father, I don't really know. In later life, she gave misleading signals to men, so they thought she was fond of them when really, she was just trying to be nice to them. It led to all sorts of misunderstandings, particularly when she separated from my father. She always said that difference in their age didn't matter. My father was about 20 years older than she was. But she always said that didn't matter because that was not the cause of the dispute. The cause of the dispute was that he was unreliable about money.

When I was a teenager, people used to knock at the door and say 'our bill hasn't been paid'. And my mother was quite terrified by that because her brothers had always paid their bills. Eventually my parents separated. But that was only when I came back from the Army after National Service and it didn't have any traumatic effects. I remember them arguing when I was a teenager, downstairs, they thought I was asleep, but I wasn't. They had quite fierce arguments. My mother used to burst into tears and my father used to get rather loud and my mother used to say, 'Don't shout!'

AM: Wicked boy!

BH: It's curious how children react, you can't predict. People will now say this is lethal. It wasn't at all, it was like a thunderstorm, I rather liked thunderstorms! It didn't worry me. It was just that something had happened, just like the pulling of the hair by the schoolmaster in the classroom. This just happened. This was where they came from really. But do ask any question.

AM: Just a little more about their characters. I've got something of your mother and your father apart from his theories about washing up, what else characterized him?

BH: Well, it was difficult because when my mother was turning against my father, which she did, took me as a teenager into consultation. Again, this is a fatal thing to do, nonetheless, I was always rather flattered because she talked to me about all sorts of confidential things. I remember she said....

AM: You were the only child?

BH: Yeah. I was the only child. She said, 'Well I'm thinking of moving into the front bedroom', which had been their big shared front bedroom. I usually agreed with her because I was very fond of her. But I said, 'Well, you can't do that, you can't push your husband into the back room'. Well, she did. But she took me into consultation about that, though she didn't take any notice of what I said! That happened quite a lot and it had the effect of putting me against my father, which was a pity because I can't answer your question about him very easily now, much as I'd like to be able to do so.

He was a clever man, very clever. He was an accountant by training and self-made, really. I don't know anything about my grandparents. My mother used to under duress entertain her mother-in-law at home at Christmas but very much under duress. Didn't like her at all. I never went up to Yorkshire where they lived. My father came from Hull, but his father allegedly ran off somewhere. I was told, to Canada. But I never found out, I don't go any further back on that, on that side. But I can go an awful along way back on my mother's side.

My father was a clever man, he thought for himself. In World War II, he resigned or left Peter Robinson. He set up on his own as a toy manufacturer on Percy Street just off Tottenham Court Road. I used to go there sometimes and they made a great fuss of me because his employees were refugees. Miss Rosenzweig was the woman who ran the workshop. You can imagine what her religious background was. She was a refugee, I think, from Czechoslovakia and very paradoxically—I really don't understand the mental process—my father was anti-Jewish even though he was making money out of them. He used to refer to Jews as 'shonks' which is some sort of insulting word for a Jew.

Frightful things had happened in World War II, but it didn't seem to affect that at all and it carried over to my mother. She would refer to Jews, and say about somebody, 'Oh well, that's because they are Jews'. You couldn't say that! By the 1950s or '60s, you couldn't say that. I would say to her, 'Look you can't say that about people. They are people, they're not special because they are Jews'. They are, but not in the way she was using it. My father was a very curious mixture. He tended to vote Liberal I think, but out of perverseness I suspect because nobody else did. He was disorganized. His study was a terrible mess, really frightful, heaps of stuff everywhere. My mother used to try and tidy it up but without any success. I was brought up (gesturing behind him) behind all these card indexes lies a mother who said, 'You must not be like your father'.

AM: I was wondering, there is a very close connection isn't there?

BH: I used to love going to my great aunt Bim who lived in Chelsfield. I used to go with my aunt Margot to Chelsfield at weekends to just visit her for the day and she would make gooseberry pie which I loved and still do love. So, I loved going there and after we'd had gooseberry pie, I'd clear out one of her cupboards and shelves. I'd say, 'You'll be glad when this'll be done Bim' and she'd say, 'I'm glad now Brian.' But I used to love clearing out cupboards. That's what historians do, they tidy up things, they make sense of chaos, they find buried treasure and so on. All that goes right the way back.

The War also had a profound effect because when I was three or thereabouts, we moved to Stanmore from Belsize Park. Stanmore was a suburban estate which was half finished. The War stopped the estate being built, now, of course, you can see it's all built up. There were lots of spaces between the houses where they had not had time to build the houses. They were full of railway trucks, all rusting, left over from the builders who had been interrupted by the War. We had the most wonderful time on these building plots. There were trees and fields round about. Bentley Priory near where the Bomber Command was. It was a lovely place to spend one's childhood and highly suburban. I've been suburban all my life.

AM: What does being 'suburban' in your life mean?
BH: It's a combination of privacy and companionship. It's an ideal mixture. I've never had any of these snobbish objections to being suburban. My mother used to occasionally use the word suburban pejoratively, but I never have. It's the ideal compromise, really. I had a little gang of friends of mine there and we roamed around totally uninterrupted as was common among children in those days. No doubt you did the same without any supervision. Nobody, no fear of any molestation or anything like that.

AM: You went off on your bicycles?
BH: We went off on bicycles or we were just roaming around.

AM: You had hobbies?
BH: Oh, lots, yes. Cigarette packet covers we picked up out of the gutter and stuck them in an album. Obviously, I was a great collector then and I still am. Those things there (gesturing behind him) are Temperance ware. So, I'm still collecting. I used to collect all sorts of things. I had a stamp collection. I never wanted for anything. And of course, if you've never seen a banana, you'd not worry about not having one. I remember my father drawing a banana round about 1947 — that's what they looked like. I remember having my first banana, which must have been a year or so after that and wishing that eating it would never end! I remember where I was sitting where I ate it on the steps outside the dining-room windows, looking into the back garden.

The War had the effect of maximizing the companionship side of the neighbourhood because the men were mostly away on war work or actually *at* war and the women got together. For instance, my mother and I had jaundice when I was nine. The neighbours weighed in and brought food. There was a great deal of fellow feeling that nourished the anti-Jewish feeling because the thing that really terrified everybody in the state was whether the place would be taken over by Jews. The Jews were moving out across Northwest London towards us because they were doing well. They had come out of the East End. They had got as far as Golders Green and Hendon and were likely to move further out. That was thought to be appalling because that would drag the estate down and you had to listen to them speaking to see they would drag the estate down. I remember my parents complaining about somebody shouting to her husband in the garden through an upstairs window. One just didn't do that sort of thing. It was a class thing partly. They were frightened of the estate going down as the expression was. It's not so much social aspiration that drives them but the fear of going down.

My mother's family, the seven siblings were at risk of going down. My mother's class consciousness and desire for education for me was to stop that happening in her case. They all clutched on to the one brother who had money, Geoffrey and he bailed them out. He never married. He was, to put it crudely, plundered, really. He was a very good-hearted man and they clutched on to him as he was their one refuge to prevent them from sinking. My father was dragging my mother down. She was always told that she had married beneath her. That was another source of friction. She used to refer to people as being provincial which meant that they came from the north of Watford. My father was decidedly provincial coming from Hull. He used to get awfully cross when she used that expression. But it was a class thing.

My father was a very kind man. He subsidized his brother Eddie, my uncle, in getting through university and he eventually became a university registrar. He did quite well. It was a great self-help tradition and kindness, but it's typical of my father. When I went to Malta on National Service, he used to send parcels of chocolate which I am extremely fond of. I'm a chocoholic. These parcels would contain a lot of chocolates and biscuits which I greatly welcomed. But they had gone white. He had not noticed that in the shop that he kept by that time, I will fill you in on that later, that they had passed their sell-by date! He was disorganized. He was very kind to send these parcels, but the parcels were largely uneatable even by me!

He had an accountancy business. The toy business eventually folded up and the accountancy business drained down to nothing. He was sinking and that is why the bills weren't paid.

My mother was determined he should not sink any further so she went out to work for a part-time job which was something middle-class women didn't do in those days. It was brave of her, and was in fact the making of her because she discovered that she was a very good manager. Eventually, her brother Geoffrey set them both up in a shop in North Kensington, a working-class area with black immigrants beginning to come in. They ran this sub-post office, corner shop, very well —— so much so, that they got a second shop in the Harrow Road. The way things were going, my mother continued to run the old shop in North Kensington and my father ran the Harrow Road shop.

When I came back from the Army when I was 21, I found that the marriage was breaking up, it was not a happy home-coming. My father was then running the Harrow Road shop on his own and I volunteered to open the Harrow Road shop on Sundays. He wasn't doing very well, so I said that I would open it on a Sunday for you and we will see if there are any customers there. Just to explain, I had worked behind the counter as a teenager for them in the other shop, and rather enjoyed doing so in the other shop. I am a natural entrepreneur partly as a result of that. I knew how to behave behind the counter. I went on my own on a Sunday, just one Sunday and thought that he really ought to know what his stock was like and why people were not buying it. I looked around and found some boxes of chocolates that had literally gone white and although there weren't many customers and I know why. A lot of the stock is not in good condition. 'It's alright. There's nothing wrong with it', he said. So, I said, 'I'm telling you but that is the situation'.

You couldn't tell my father anything really, he was never wrong, but I did my best. I did not persist with that experiment, nonetheless he was very good for me and to me. At that time, I needed to get some money together as I was coming up to Oxford. I went by bicycle to Kilburn because my mother was terrified that I would sponge off him, and said that I must get a job.

AM: That must have been a considerable pressure.

BH: Yes, quite. I was appalled. I didn't have the slightest idea how to get a job. I went to an employment agency. I filled in a form and was rather shocked to see how little I could offer because the only thing I could do was to type. I had had a good education in school and that was one of the reasons why I made myself a proficient touch-typist thereafter, because I thought that at the very least I would be able to do that. But, in fact, I didn't get a job as a typist. My father said he knew one of the buyers in Selfridges and would have a word with him and he did. I got a job in the gramophone record department through no merit of my own but just through my father putting in a word for me. I reluctantly say this, but I was extremely good at it. I developed two techniques. We were paid on commission, so it was important to do it well if you wanted money.

I had two techniques. One was to fix customers through eye contact as they were approaching the department at the counter, and the other assistants couldn't understand why they all came to me and not to them. Secondly, I had a little notebook in which I put useful record numbers so that when asked, I could find it quickly, and so I sold quickly. I suspect I earned more commission than anybody else there. They were very tolerant. They didn't take it out on me. They knew I was there for only six months before I went to Oxford. I was called aside by the head of the department, Mr Kemp, and he said that the personnel manager wanted to see me. And the personnel manager said, 'If you want to come back, and work for us you can. We will be pleased to see you'. I said, 'I didn't know what I wanted to do then but I will remember that and thank you very much'. I owe that to my father. My father put in a word and that worked out well enough.

I enjoyed selling records because I'm very fond of music. That is one thing I owed to my mother. My mother was very fond of music. She played Debussy a lot and she was trained during the World War II at the Wigmore Hall in piano playing. She used to play the piano. I still think of her when I hear certain Chopin nocturnes,[2] she used to play those and wonderful Schubert intermezzos.[3] As a teenager, that gradually developed, I got a gramophone player. I enjoyed selling records, it really interested me. And I was as I say really quite good at it.

AM: I would just like to ask you a little bit more about music. Firstly, taste, is it all classical music?

BH: Yes. I have a very vague memory of sitting with my back against a pillar in the upstairs classroom in Alcuin House School at the age of about seven, singing. I had a very good voice in the sense that I still have a good sense of tune. I can get into a tune without any revving up. I was obviously rather good at singing then, probably because my mother used to sing to me. My father used to as well. I can remember what they sang. I had that background. I never was taught the piano. I wish I had been, but my parents were very sensible, they didn't force it on me. So, I never learnt the piano, even though my mother played it. When I was about 14, I took an interest in learning the piano, my uncle Geoffrey paid for me to have a year's lessons at Merchant Taylors' School. I didn't make much progress on it. It's not really because I didn't enjoy it, but because I was terribly busy with O Levels at that time and then A Levels. I just didn't have the time to practice, so I gave it up after a year.

Nonetheless, I had gradually acquired a love of music. That was a time when long-playing records were coming out. I initially started out by buying 78s. I remember running between bus stops to accumulate enough money to buy 78s records at the end of the week because I was allowed to keep any travel money that I had saved.

The earliest things I liked were obvious things like Vaughan Williams's Fantasiaa on Greensleeves and Handel's 'Water Music' eventually we had some neighbours called Frank and Nellie Robinson who were extremely good to me in retrospect. My mother used to go up to chat to them in the evenings and eventually I was allowed to go with her. They had a long-playing gramophone record-player. They had Grieg's Piano Concerto on it. I fell in love with that. We had concerts at Merchant Taylors' School which were held at Watford Town Hall and you would get a free ticket. I used to go with friends to hear the recitals to Watford Town Hall. We used to get free tickets and I picked up most of what I knew about music then. Sibelius's[4] symphonies were very much the thing in those days and I still love them. Beethoven's symphonies, Tchaikovsky's symphonies and then I went to the proms and it all took off from there. In fact, I am going to six proms this year, but purely as a listener not as a performer.

AM: Can you see any connection between this and your work. Some people listen to music and are inspired, Maitland[5] for example. Do you work to music?

BH: No. Never. No. I find it too much of a distraction. There is no connection of that kind that I can think of. I am very interested in the history of music, but it's not well written about. Some really good books ought to be written about it. It doesn't tend to be written nor does the history of painting tend to be written about well and is not set into the context. So, I don't find books on the history of music at all interesting. I am interested in music and the technology of music and so on, but in a totally amateur way. The Robinsons were very influential on me. Mr Robinson was a self-made man and that was a term of abuse for my mother. He did not know what was what and how to speak properly. Nonetheless, he did very well. He worked in Kodak which had a huge factory in Wealdstone, nearby, at that time, and he made a lot of money. They were very well off. He epitomized prudence and success in my mother's eyes even though he was a self-made man. He was financially secure, and that is what she admired.

I think he was in love with her, in fact he made one or two propositions to her which she rejected. She was giving the wrong signals as usual. I think that Mrs Robinson, an extremely nice woman, once caught him with his hand on my mother's knee. My mother, during the daytime, went up to see Nellie Robinson and said, 'I am awfully sorry, there's nothing in this, but I'll stop seeing you if you prefer'. She said, 'No he likes you coming', basically she was quite secure in her hold on him. But she was also a very nice woman. My mother kept going, but that stopped any overt approach from him. He was fascinated by my mother and she admired him. I used to go with her to see them. They eventually fell out.

They were important in all sorts of ways because my father, when he was not being successful, I was about 14, had this pipedream of going to New Zealand, the new life. My mother had agreed to go to New Zealand. We were all set to go to New Zealand and Frank Robinson came to the house in the daytime and said to my mother, 'Don't go', and she put her foot down and didn't go. It was probably wisely because it would have been a disaster if they'd gone. That meant I stayed at Merchant Taylors' and the rest is history.

My mother, then later, again giving the wrong signals, this is fatal, when she was going out part-time to work, she needed to drive to work. She took lessons. She had learned to drive before World War II, but she nearly drove a hole in the back end of our garage, and my father said, 'You're not to do any more driving'. Anyway, she decided she must learn to drive. Going out to work was the making of her. She discovered all sorts of things she could do. She didn't realize one of them was learning to drive. She went out to drive with this driving instructor, Roy, who was about 10 years younger than her. The inevitable happened, she had an affair with him and separated from my father.

At that stage I stayed with my father, though a bit torn, and she went off with the man. Later on, her sister, who was a wonderful woman, Margot, I was very fond of her. She noticed that my mother had marks on her face. She asked her sister how she had got these marks on her face. My mother said it was the fat coming up from the frying pan, but in fact he was knocking her about. So, it was all hands on deck to get her away from him.

AM: So, what happened? How did you get your mother out of that scrape?

BH: I didn't get her out, she wanted to get out. The situation was, as I say she gave the wrong signals, she got tangled up in it, but had to be got out by somebody. She half wanted to get out and she came to live with her sister. She was very generous, my mother, she had lent her car, a Morris Minor, to Roy, the man she fell for or who fell for her. The strategy was to get this car back. He lived in North Harrow. My father loved this sort of thing. My father had a huge collection of detective novels. We devised a way of getting the car back. Roy had the car parked. We had done a reconnaissance outside his parents' house where Roy was living and we had a key to the car, a duplicate key. So, my father said, 'I'll drive you up there, you get into the car and I'll drive ahead of you and we'll go off'. It worked like clockwork! Just like something out of a film. He dropped me off, I got into my mother's car and it started first thing, thank goodness, and off we swept. I saw Roy in the front room astonished at what was happening, but he was too late, we had gone. So, we got the car back!

I should explain that Roy was a reasonable enough chap. I didn't particularly care for him, but I didn't dislike him. For a time, I used to go up to Selfridges with them. I was shuttling between the two parents. Eventually, Roy made it clear to my mother that he didn't want me in the car, so I then went with my father. Obviously, he didn't want me there. So, I knew him quite well. We got my mother away and she got a flat in Pembridge Villas in North Kensington which was near her shop. Uncle Geoffrey funded her in a little cottage, of which there's a picture in the hall of our house in Oxford. She lived there very happily. She was perfectly happy on her own. She used to go round to couples and suggest to the wife that it might be a good idea for them to part. She used to preach to them escaping from your spouse. She acted as a confidante to several members of her staff to get them away from their husbands!

AM: One psychological interpretation of this, you've mentioned the tidiness, sorting out and you've also mentioned your workaholic streak and I suppose someone might suggest that maybe some home unhappiness, moving from one family to the other, one short part of your life was your work.

BH: There's a lot in that in the sense that Oxford was a refuge from all this. I used to stay up in the vacations a lot rather than go to one or other home. It is certainly true in that sense. In another sense, I had the same fear that my mother had of slipping socially. I had seen them both slipping, rescued in my mother's case by her brother, and I was determined not to. The only way out of that was passing examinations. In that sense it's relevant.

I remember, for a time, I lived with my father who eventually married one of his assistants, Doris, a very nice woman. But it was a low-grade suburb of North London and I thought I am never going to sink any lower than this. You will obviously realize that I have absorbed all the class consciousness that my mother had, she put that into me. British society at that time was very class conscious then, it still is, particularly in the suburbs. You're right in that hypothesis. But you're not right about work being an escape, it was all there when I was five, in that school report. My parents were perfectly happy for the first 10 years of their marriage, it started to go wrong when I was a teenager.

AM: Coming back to when you were a teenager. At Merchant Taylors' were there any teachers who particularly inspired you? Do you remember them?
BH: Oh, yes.

I should start with Miss Dalgleish at prep school, who was a very good teacher. Very sympathetic teacher, encouraging. Then there was Miss Keast, who was a fascinating woman, who quivered, who had some sort of disability. I don't know what it was, but she quivered! Initially she terrified me, I think this was one reason why I had a term off from school because Miss Dalgleish was ill and I was very fond of Miss Dalgleish. And Miss Keast was taking over and I was terrified of her. She also had money spiders in her hair and it was all piled up. Children are very frightened by things like that, at least some children are. But they were both very good teachers, as a lot of unmarried women were in those days. D'Arcy Yeo, the Headmaster, was also very good though a bit of a sadist. He was a good teacher.

AM: Had he ever pulled your hair?
BH: He didn't pull mine for some reason but he had pulled some others. It was terrible. In retrospect. I somehow didn't see it as terrible at the time you just accept what happens. He gave me a very good education. I got into Merchant Taylors'. I was then on the science side, perhaps because I was quite good at maths. I stayed on the science side for the first three years at Merchant Taylors' and slipping down all the time in rank-order in the form. The subjects I was slipping in were science subjects, and I noticed this. I thought this won't do. I wasn't used to being at the bottom of the form, or getting near the bottom, which I was by the end of the third year.

So, when I was in Sixth A and I hated physics and I hated physics practicals. I have no practical aptitude at all. They were the absolute pits for me, I was no good at geometry either. There's something about geometry that really doesn't fit with me at all. I decided that this can't go on.

There was another boy, oddly enough, named Harrison. I remember the initials, he was G.E.B. Harrison. He had moved across from the science side to arts. I talked to him at one stage and asked him how he did it and what was it like. He said it was alright, it was very rarely done. I said that I'd like to switch. The school was against it. Harrison didn't discourage me, and my parents were against it because they thought it was a bad career move. I said I wanted to shift to the arts side and I did.

I was immediately in my element, I was good at Latin still, because I had inherited that from the prep school. I went into the History Sixth and the master who ran that was a chap called Alex Jeffries, an avuncular, very kind, very nice man, who was really a father figure for me. I had to some extent been put against my father by my mother and he was the father I didn't have. In fact, long before I came under his tutelage, I had got lost at Merchant Taylors'. When you go to a big school like that from a small prep school, you get lost and terrified. I couldn't find where I was supposed to be and at what time; I stood outside the masters' common room and looked for somebody who looked friendly, and it was Jeffries. I asked him where I should be. He said, 'Don't worry, I'll look at the timetable and tell you', and he told me where I should be and I went there. He was a friendly person even before I knew him.

He ran the 'History Sixth' Form. He was a very good teacher, not high-powered intellectually, but inspirational and encouraging. He encouraged us to give talks to the class, and I gave quite a lot of those. He was also extremely tolerant, which my father was not, and I admired that. He was a veteran of World War I. I remember two things about that quite vividly. He described what it was like to be an Army officer at that time, and he described the guns. He had a bevelled desk and he banged on the desk with his hands to show us what gunfire was like. He described how at one point he was trying to lead on his troop or platoon with a movement and nobody moved: they were all dead. It was very vivid and he was a brilliant teacher in that way.

Another good teacher I had in history Guy Wilson, who is still alive. He was very fresh from Cambridge, self-critical, and he started by giving us notes which we wrote down. At the end of the first term he realized that the method was not working and I think he changed to talks. It was he that made me into a Victorian. We read Monypenny and Buckle on Disraeli[6] and Morley's biography on Gladstone[7] and I got hooked. I was the only person in the class who liked Carlyle's *French Revolution*.[8] For that I was regarded as rather freakish. I still like it. I think it's a great book. He had that effect on me.

I had a very good English teacher, really brilliant man called John Steane.[9] He was an opera buff as well. He was a homosexual I now realize, though he never made any approaches to me. He was very empathetic.

AM: Is he still alive?

BH: No. He died about a year ago of cancer. He was totally inspirational, and a devotee of F.R. Leavis.[10] In A Level English, because I did A Level Latin and History, you had a piece unseen to criticize and on. I remember a piece of poetry from D.H. Lawrence[11] about a child sitting under a piano on a Sunday evening and hearing the tinkling of the keys. We would see this blind and be asked to comment on it. We didn't know it was D.H. Lawrence. I commented on it and I had some ideas of my own and I suddenly realized that I could actually have ideas of my own. I hadn't just read it, but also thought about it. Steane was very good in that way.

In another episode I still think that I was right, and he was wrong. We had a passage from Nashe[12] the Elizabethan author. He described the disembowelling of a man who had committed treason. The heart was taken out 'like a plum from a porringe pot'. I remember the phrase. I said in comment that this was a terrible image for us but probably would have been less terrible at the time because people were used in Elizabethan society to all sorts of brutal things happening. Steane said that mine was not a legitimate comment, it was a historical comment, it wasn't a critical comment. It was that sort of discussion that we had and was very inspirational.

I had another very good English teacher called R.B. Hunter who taught me for Wordsworth[13] which was one of the set books. We read *The Prelude*, and again I got quite hooked on it and I wrote what he thought was a good essay. He wrote at the bottom that I could actually go to Oxford or Cambridge, and that was the first time that anybody had said that to me. Very conscientious, very good teachers.

I got a scholarship to St John's, the Sir Thomas White Scholarship for History. I went up to the Merchant Taylors' Hall for the interview and it was a funny occasion. Keith Thomas was one of the tutors then, one of young tutors who I didn't know and he said, 'You said such and such in your essay'. and I said, 'Did I say that?', and they all laughed because I was incredulous that I could say such a silly thing. That went fine. We were invited as scholars for a dinner at the Merchant Taylors' Hall, the first time I had ever been to a grand dinner, I remember sitting opposite somebody and it was at the time when the British were having trouble in Cyprus and some government minister had said we would never leave Cyprus. I said it was a silly thing to say, and the minister said, 'Oh, that was my brother-in-law there!' I suppose I was pretty opinionated at that time, perhaps insufferable to some. Anyway, that got me to St John's, after doing my two year's National Service, and my friends were there. So, we sat together at what we call the scholars' table and I had a set of friends readymade. It was all dead easy.

AM: Two things about Merchant Taylors', did you have any particular activities there, in drama or in sports or anything that you…?

BH: I was hopeless at sport at school. I was absolutely hopeless in sports. I was short sighted. I had glasses from the age of eight. I remember coming back from the optician with the glasses fitted and my mother saying, 'You do look funny'. I was terribly upset, quite the wrong thing to say. I hated wearing glasses. It took me years and years to get used to them, and it meant I was hopeless on the sports field even if I had any aptitude, which I didn't. So, I went in for swimming, if you didn't like cricket you could go in for life-saving. I had no enthusiasm for saving lives but I had every enthusiasm for getting out of cricket. I have still got a friend (Nigel Williams) where the bond between us is a mutual hatred of rugby football on Saturday afternoons in the middle of the winter. It is a real bond there.

I remember when I went across from one side of school to the other, one rather patronizing young man called Willoughby, now deceased, said to me that everybody in the form (Classical Lower Sixth) did something distinctive. I thought, what am I going to do. I certainly couldn't shine on the sports field. What I did was, apart from doing well academically, was calligraphy. I must show you upstairs I've still got it on the wall, a huge piece of calligraphy which the art master said was a feat of character – an artistic product. I did that, but didn't do anything else. I worked very hard academically because I had to justify having moved across the school into the arts. My parents weren't well off, so I had to justify their expenditure.

AM: What about religion? Were you confirmed?
BH: Yes, I was. I'm rather ashamed of that fact now. The whole family was anti-intellectual and anti-religious. They didn't like anything involving pretentiousness or falseness. They didn't like people going to church, they thought they were hypocrites. Nonetheless, being confirmed was the rite of passage in your upward move or your intent to stay in the same position socially. So, I got confirmed and I went through a fairly religious phase as teenagers tend to do, at least, then did.

The Church of England was quite powerful as an influence in public schools then as you will probably remember. I struggled for some sort of faith at that time, but never found it. I greatly admired Cormac Rigby[14] who you may remember. He was a contemporary at St John's and I admired the way he used to go off to Mass regularly. He took David McLellan[15] with him. David, actually, became a Roman Catholic as a result of his influence, I think. At one stage I went to Cormac and said look I'd like to know more about Catholicism. He said, 'Well I can't tell you but there is a thing called the Catholic Truth Society, write to them and they'll help you'. I wrote to them and they sent me leaflets and I got a booklet which said, the title of it, 'The Pope is infallible' and that finished me off. I thought, no, I'm not having any of this. My parents were terrified if I'd become a Catholic, the only thing worse than becoming a Catholic was to become a ballet dancer! They were particularly worried that I might become that because I got very enthusiastic about ballet when I was about 14. The Robinsons used to take me and my mother off to the Royal Festival Hall to watch ballet. And I loved it and still do. That's the end of religion. I have always remained an agnostic and not an atheist but I'm not militant about it. I have never seen any evidence for religion, and if anything, being a historian has turned me the other way because one small episode in school which is relevant here is a sort of prank that we played in the Classical Lower Sixth where I was for a year, they made what is called a clepsydra. You probably know about this, it's a water clock.

In the Great Hall at school there were apertures in the ceiling which could be opened in the fencing loft above it and if you knew your way around the fencing loft you could open it. There was a plot at the end of the summer term in 1954 for putting a clepsydra above one of these holes, opening up one of the holes and putting the clepsydra on top of it and attaching to the arm that tilted when a certain amount of water had gone out, to a toilet roll, which then plunged down, much to everyone's excitement, into the Hall in assembly after prayers. We organized this conspiracy within the form and it worked like a dream! We meet every year to celebrate this event.

How did we get on to this?

AM: Religion?

BH: Ah school. I was appointed about 20 years ago historian of this group—they call themselves 'The Rollers'—so I wrote a history of the event. There were many contradictory accounts because I talked to all the people and they wrote to me about what had happened, some said the lavatory roll had fallen on the Headmaster's head, for example, which it didn't. Others said that one of the monitors tried to tear off a strip from it and failed to bring the whole thing down! It was really, quite a memorable event as they go, these events. Anyway, at the end, the history that I wrote of it I said that it's extraordinary that after only 20 years, when all of us are present, we don't remember exactly what happened, or even what day it was. A fortiori or words to that effect, what credence can be attached to many other documents prepared after the event? And, one of my contemporaries from Merchant Taylors' in the group, a nonconformist, objected to this, so I removed the direct reference to the Bible but that's what lay behind it. I have never felt any temptation towards religion, though when I listen to the radio now, radio broadcasts of some religious service I think how on earth can anyone believe in all that junk? Doesn't influence me in the slightest. I'm attracted, of course, to the buildings and the cultural significance of it.

AM: Dawkins[16] has a large collection of biographies of bishops.

BH: Oh, well, it's just religious history, because bishops were important in the 19th century and not because I am interested in religion as such. I'm interested in history.

AM: Okay, let's get to National Service.
BH: Yes.

AM: You were presumably 18 when you went to Malta and you spent the two years in Malta?
BH: Nearly two years in Malta. What you start off with is Catterick.[17] I was in the Royal Signals. I do wish my parents had kept my letters because I would love to read them now, I wrote back at least once a week to them, but my mother, true to form, threw away everything once she had read everything. She never kept anything, so they've all gone. I kept the letters I received from them. It was a most extraordinary experience. For the first six weeks we were simply treated as oiks, as they called ordinary soldiers, and were pushed around the drill square, rushing from pillar to post. It was like a nightmare, a most peculiar experience, but also at times extremely funny. It was like being a schoolboy again, laughing at masters behind their backs. We had a Corporal and a Lance-Corporal running our particular section in that six weeks, and I remember we were required to clean out the inside of the lavatories with our hands – a lot of reference to 'cleaning

out the bleeding shit', which was a combination of bad language that I had never heard before.

Keith Thomas says the same about language heard when doing National Service, really crude combinations of words. I remember thinking that it was a ghastly situation that I would have to get through somehow. There was a lot of talk at night after the lights were out, some of it extremely funny people among the people I was with. That was the first six weeks. Then we went on to OCTU (Officer Cadet Training Unit) for another six week or three months, I can't remember now, where we trained for the OCTU exam training to become an Army officer. That was quite a memorable experience because when we went from one side of Catterick to the other for this OCTU training place it was absolute hell. We were told we had to get the barracks, called 'spiders', that were left over from World War II and we were told that in that weekend of our arrival we had to get the whole thing in order and absolutely spic and span. We were driven from pillar to post. I remember seeing one chap cleaning a window with the cloth in one hand, and an Officer coming and saying, 'Both hands, both hands', we were told that if we felt we couldn't stand the pace we could sign ND (non-desirous) forms to opt out from it. I felt at times I would like to sign that form but I didn't. Eventually, on the Sunday night, at the end of the barrack room I suddenly heard a lot of laughter, and it was all a hoax. The next course above us had dressed up as officers having us on. It never left me the memory of what a uniform can do, it can completely change your relationship to people. And then we got trained. We did a lot of high-powered drill in our training as officers, but it was never as high-powered as at Merchant Taylors'.

We then went up for what was called WOSB – War Office Selection Board, and you had to do things like carrying a barrel across a stream, directing a group of people, and having projects for getting from A to B, also interviews. I passed that, I felt I should pass, public schoolboys didn't fail WOSB. I was very glad I did because I wasn't sure I would. Then you went on to Mons, which was another six-week course near Bisley. Again, a lot of drills, I remember. I learnt to lecture which was quite a good thing to do. A lot of skills I used, for instance, in those cards in there, (gesturing towards the back on his right) there are a lot of abbreviated words and they originated with the abbreviations we used in the Army. I've got my own personal shorthand, but it originated with that. You write 'accn' for accommodation, for example.

Eventually I got commissioned and I invited my parents to the commissioning parade in Catterick. Again, we went back to Catterick for the last part of the course, that had all sorts if unpleasant experiences. But nonetheless, survived that.

My parents were coming up and I said to my mother, 'Can you make sure my father dresses properly'. You know how terrified young people are about their parents and whether they look alright and so on. My father had embarrassed me terribly when he came to my public school because he just didn't bother with his appearance at all. My mother was dressed to the nines and she came along with her husband who was in shambles. He saw my letter to her I don't know how and took great offence. I then wrote to him and what my aunt said, it was passed around the family, had been a very tactful letter saying I'd be sorry if he didn't come, I didn't want to give any offence and so forth. He came and he was properly dressed! That passed off alright.

I was then free to go off to Malta. I went to Malta Signal Squadron and ran the military transport section there. There were about five or six Maltese drivers, grown men in their forties and fifties, and a few Maltese other ranks and a Corporal and some English, an Anglo-Maltese mixture. Again, I was struck by how easily one is influenced by one's environment. We despised the Maltese. They were incapable of running things. It was the time when people were saying that the Suez Canal couldn't be run by Egyptians. We called them 'The Malts', and I just inherited this from my surroundings. I didn't think this at first but, like a chameleon, adapted to my environment.

AM: This was 1955?

BH: I was in Malta from 1956–58. I learnt to drive there. I still don't have an English driving licence, I've driven ever since on an Army licence, because I had to learn to drive. It was ludicrous running a transport section without being able to drive. I used to take them out on test and I couldn't drive myself. That is the way the Army worked in those days. I learnt a lot of value there. I had a motorbike and I drove between there and the mess. Generally had an interesting life and it was a very interesting posting to have. I won't go into the details about that. But I also learned that I could run things. I knew I could operate behind the counter in my father's post office but I actually went into the post office with my father at the end, the post office department, a section of it. I picked that up quite quickly. The most complex business was issuing a money order payable abroad. You had to get through a number of hurdles to get a money order payable abroad. I learnt to do that. I taught myself Italian in Malta and did the Italian special subject later in the Modern History Honours School. I knew Malta like the back of my hand and in many respects enjoyed it though I wouldn't say everybody should do it but it was the first time I'd ever been out of the UK and it was an eye opener for me. So, is that what you want from National Service or do you want any more?

AM: Yes. That's probably fine because we'll move on to university.

BH: Another side was that I was terribly immature, like my mother, in sexual matters. I remember one of the officers who ran the military equipment section was fascinated by prostitutes. There were a lot of prostitutes in Malta and they occupied Strait Street, one of the well-known streets in Valletta. He took some of us to one of the places where you met these women, and I was appalled at the very thought of it. It never occurred to me to go to a prostitute! In all that department in life, I was totally ignorant, well I knew what happened but I naturally had no experience at all. In that sense I wasn't grown up at all. My parents, my mother thought that on returning home from the Army, I would be much more grown up than I was, a fully-fledged male. But I wasn't but of course that is a disadvantage of being an only child and going to a single-sex public school.

AM: Did you have girlfriends at all?

BH: I had friends who could be male or could be female, but there was no sexual component to it at all. That happened a lot later.

AM: So, your work on *Sex and the Victorians* came…?

BH: Partly self-discovery, yes. I don't want to exaggerate the degree of maturity you emerge from even from National Service.

AM: But you did come to Oxford a lot later than I did. You were about 21?

BH: Yes, I was 21. We thought we were terribly mature of course, but we weren't, at least I wasn't.

AM: Was that 1958?

BH: 1958. Yes. I went to Selfridges from January till October 1958 and started off with Keith Thomas, Howard Colvin and Michael Hurst as my three Tutors.

AM: Tell me about them as Tutors.

BH: Howard Colvin,[18] you probably know him, he was a very scholarly man, and it really was a case of absorbing scholarship by osmosis. He was a good Tutor and he was then just making the transition from being a mediaeval historian to an architectural historian and he had rolls of plans on the mantel shelf in his room. He was very interested in some photographs I took as I was quite a good photographer in those days. I took a lot of photographs in Malta and elsewhere when I was coming back across Europe to England through Italy and Austria. He was very interested in the photographs I took, particularly Wells Cathedral. I had a lovely photograph of the fan vaulting in Wells Cathedral. He wasn't a teacher in the sense that he wasn't really interested in teaching, as such. He knew how to write, but I didn't learn that from him. He was a good Tutor. He was a good influence and I was just bursting to learn. Coming to Oxford was just paradise to what had gone before, so I was keen to get the utmost out of it all.

We had Costin,[19] the President, who taught us Voltaire's[20] letters – *Lettres philosophiques* did you do that? It probably stopped before you came and Tocqueville followed on from that.[21]

We had the philosopher J.D. Mabbott[22] for political thought, I think. I did very well in Prelims and went in for the H.W.C. Davis Prize and came proxime to Prys Morgan,[23] who got it. We were both in St John's and St John's was getting a reputation for History by that time. I didn't encounter Keith until my second year for the 'Middle Period', and we didn't really get on. I thought he ought to know that I didn't need pushing and knew what I was doing, and he was very much the martinet. I worked out that you didn't have to do continuous British history but could select periods and get through that way. So, I refused to do anything on the 17th century, which was silly because he was a 17th century person. Anyway, I didn't do 17th century. He forced me to do a collection on that period, to write a few essays in that period, and it was the only time I borrowed my contemporary Richard Jackson's essay and copied it with some elegant variation. I wrote an essay on Cromwell about whom I knew nothing. But I got by. Keith was a martinet and for the best possible reason as he wanted his pupils to do well.

AM: He was very young, wasn't he? About 25?

BH: Yes, yes. That's right. We really didn't get on. We didn't have a row but he wasn't exactly....

AM: He didn't inspire you?

BH: No. Not really. I respected his intelligence and width of range. His lectures then were quite famous for the political thought paper, you may've been to some.

AM: Yes, I've been to some.

BH: And they really were inspirational. As a lecturer he was awfully good. The person who really inspired me was Jill Lewis at St Anne's. She taught me for the Italian Renaissance, and she took an awful lot of trouble. You sent her an essay and she would scribble on it and she had clearly had read it. I never felt that any of my St John's tutors really read my essays.

AM: Did you just give them your essays, or did you just read them out?

BH: I gave them the essays or I read them out, but I never got extensive comment on them.

AM: Because the system I had just a little later was that you never handed in your essay. You always sat, read for 45 minutes and then about ten or quarter of an hour they would make comments.

BH: I think it alternated with us. We went in pairs. I was either paired with Cormac Rigby or Prys Morgan as I remember it and one or other of us would read out his essay, which would last 20 minutes. But my essays were always rather long, especially for Howard Colvin. I said to him at one stage, 'Wouldn't it be sensible if I handed in my essay, and you read it and we talked?' 'Oh! That would mean that I would have to give up my day in London if I did that, my research day'. I thought to myself that I never to say that to a pupil of mine, if a pupil wants help from me. I'll never brush him off like that. Of course, I never was asked for that sort of service. In the end I did do what I felt I shouldn't in the ideal world and allowed the one that was read out not to be commented on. Initially, I tried to comment on them all, but I gave up. It's just impossible.

I thought, quite wrongly, that my Tutors were lazy. They were not lazy. They were just operating the Oxford system which only allowed a certain amount of time. They couldn't have done more than they did. Michael Hurst, who was a controversial character and eventually was pensioned off, in effect by St John's, who were rich enough to do it, because he had a row with a pupil. I think it came to blows. He treated me very well and was a good Tutor. He seemed to be interested, encouraging.

Paul Slack[24] told me about an episode in a tutorial with Michael who said, 'Now I think I am being particularly original here. Would you mind taking down what I am saying!' That was the sort of conceit Michael suffered from. And in the end, I had to break with Michael because he took you over if you weren't careful. He wanted me to be a disciple and I was not a disciple and did not want to be. In the end that meant you would have to break otherwise it wouldn't work.

AM: Was he a 19th century Tutor?
BH: Yes. And early 20th century, I think. As I say he was a good Tutor. It is a pity, it had to end that way, but it had to end that way. He asked me at one stage, 'Who do you think is the best historian?' So, I said Hobsbawm. He had expected me to say Michael Hurst. No go, I'm afraid!

AM: Were there any other lecturers, Isaiah Berlin?

BH: Oh yes.

Isaiah Berlin was a wonderful lecturer — on Marx and on Marxism. There were other lecture series and they were wonderful and they really were inspirational. I had a syndicate with Prys Morgan. Prys Morgan went to half a dozen that I wanted to go to and I went to the other half a dozen. We duplicated notes and gave them to each other. I learned a lot from Prys.

Prys was a highly cultivated chap, much more cultivated then and now than I am. I envied him because his father was a Professor of Welsh in Wales, and he had breathed it all in. Cormac didn't like him because he thought he was a fraud. Cormac was very, very demanding of people. Prys was a great actor.

AM: Is Cormac going to be happy to hear all this. We'll decide that later.

BH: Cormac knew where I stood on things. I think he rightly thought that I was a bit overwhelmed by Prys and that Prys was more of a fraud than I realized. I learned a lot from Prys and in general we had a good group of people there.

In the second year, I won the Gibbs Scholarship which was a godsend, because that gave me £300 a year for three years, which was a lot of money in those days. That started off my book collection. I wrote to Keith and said where did he get his books and he told me to give my name to a number of booksellers, that they would send their catalogues and then you order things from their catalogues. I did that for a long time. It involved a huge amount of work looking through catalogues, you must've done the same. And expeditions to Ilfracombe and seaside and cathedral towns and places like that.

AM: Hay-on-Wye?

BH: Hay-on-Wye I did go once. I was rather disappointed because they don't have many interesting books there, at least then. But in Ilfracombe, the Cinema Bookshop at that time was a gold mine. They are usually in cathedral cities, these bookshops. All my Victorian biographies of bishops came from there.

At that point, Keith came into his own in my life. When I won the Gibbs Prize, he realized that whatever he thought of me, there was something there. He was very encouraging to me as graduate student. To be written to by my own Tutor in his own hand, he had no responsibility for me at all. My supervisor was Peter Mathias,[25] but nonetheless Keith gave me every encouragement. I still have a great feeling of obligation, a model of what you might call 'aftercare'. He wasn't the man for me as an undergraduate, but as soon as I became a graduate student, he couldn't have been more helpful. He used to suggest books and things to read. He got me started on buying books and invited me to meals sometimes to his house. In every way, he was encouraging. He and Michael Hurst didn't get on. Michael Hurst was jealous of his influence and he was rising fast then. That was also incompatible with my liaison with Michael.

II

AM: What did you do next?

BH: I went to St Antony's first as a graduate student.

AM: You got a First?

BH: I had got a First, yes.

I remember picking up Cormac to go to our vivas. When I went into my viva, I expected to get a lot of questions and I didn't get any at all. I can't remember any details of it now, but the whole board of examiners was there. They simply said, 'What are you going to do in graduate work?' I learnt afterwards that I got the best First in my year, but I didn't realize that, I could hardly believe it. And Cormac said when I met him afterwards, he said, 'What happened?' So, I said, 'I'll tell you when we get to the other end', because in those days you could drive through Oxford and he was driving us back to St John's for some reason. Then I said, 'It's most extraordinary, I went in there and they didn't ask me any questions at all! They just talked about research'.

I had already been interviewed at St Antony's for a place as a graduate student there and I remember Theodore Zeldin[26] asking me if you didn't get in, what will you do? I said that I would swallow my pride and become a schoolteacher, which wasn't a particularly tactful thing to say, at least, it's not a very nice thing to say. But that is what I would have done. I would have modelled myself on Alex Jeffries and become a schoolteacher like him if I had got the chance.

But, in fact, I got in and again Prys came there as well, writing about Mediaeval Calais, Keith Robbins[27] from Magdalen who I then got to know was doing work on World War I, and I was doing 19th-century temperance. The idea of writing on temperance came from Harry Hanham in Manchester because I had the idea — of my few skills, one of them is writing a good letter. Somebody must have given me the idea of writing. If you want to research something, write to some key people whose work I admired and see if they got any ideas. So, I wrote to him and to Kitson Clark in Cambridge and somebody else, I don't remember who.

Harry Hanham said, and I have still got the letter, 'It may not be to your taste, but the thing that really needs writing about is the Temperance Movement'. I immediately saw the potential of that, you need to know something about Victorian society to see how surprising it was that nobody had yet written about it. So, that was my first book, *Drink and the Victorians* as it turned out. But it started as a D.Phil. thesis rewritten and drastically slimmed down. My disability has always been writing too much and it had to lose 100,000 words after its first draft. It was published by Faber, and the person who arranged that was the well-known London literary agent, Michael Sissons. I had written an article about temperance tracts in *History Today* in 1963 and he had seen it and said, 'Why not come to lunch?' I had lunch with him somewhere and he said, 'Let me know if you want to publish a book, I'll help you'. So, when I got to the stage of having a typescript, I sent him a typescript and he took it to Faber. And Faber said that it would have to lose 100,000 words but they would publish it if it did. They did publish it and they did a good job, actually.

AM: *Drink and the Victorians?*
BH: Yes, *Drink and the Victorians.* I had written a lot of articles before that, partly because I wanted to offload some of the vast amount of stuff, I had got somewhere else, so that I could refer to it in footnotes and I would not have to include it in the book. By 1971 when I published *Drink and the Victorians*, I had written a lot of articles on temperance history. I was launched by that stage and I broke with Michael Sissons, I'm afraid. I had written an essay on 'Moral Reform and State Intervention in the Victorian Period' for a book of essays edited by Patricia Hollis[28] called *Pressure from Without*, published in 1974. Edward Arnold offered me £50 for it and I asked Michael if I should accept it. He said, 'Oh! Nonsense, £100'. He said, 'I'll write to them'. So, he wrote to them. And Edward Arnold said, 'I'm awfully sorry, but it's only £50'. Then Michael had the cheek to take £5 off that as commission leaving me with £45. I was furious. I didn't say anything but from that moment I thought that I didn't need an agent.

AM: Can we go back to 1961? And one of the things that I really want to explore a little bit which is the method of breaking down historical information on to small cards. How did that first originate? Where did you get that idea from?

BH: I don't know where I got the idea from, but certainly by the end of my undergraduate days I had quite an elaborate card index. I had an index of quotations which I learnt off by heart, and an index of dates which I learnt off by heart. I knew an enormous amount in those days. That was its initial function, but I got used to shuffling around with cards. I didn't develop the present arrangement of facts on cards and bibliographical cards. That happened from the beginning of my time at St Antony's. I remember going to see James Joll, a historian of Germany, a homosexual. Anyway, I went to Joll as Senior Tutor, because I thought he was the person I ought to ask about how you did research. 'What do you do? Do you have a card index?' He said, 'Oh no, I don't have a card index, because all the cards fall out on the floor. I don't have a card index'. So, I really got nothing from him. This rather shocked me as I had thought I would get some guidance on research technique, so I invented the card index system for myself. It somehow grew out of the undergraduate cards that I also had, though it had a different function.

AM: You told me, I think, shortly after that that one of the influences was Beatrice Webb.[29]

BH: Yes, it was. But I don't think that I read that first. I certainly read it early on, but that validated what I was already doing or refined what I was doing.

AM: Was this at the end of *My Apprenticeship*?

BH: Yes. That's right. It was republished in their *Methods of Social Study*.

AM: I may have read an appendix on *Methods*, 'one fact one card'.

BH: That's right. It's wasn't as though I read that and had a sudden inspiration and did it from then onwards. I stumbled on for myself but then found it validated by her.

AM: And also validated by Keith Thomas.

BH: I did not know about the Keith Thomas envelopes in those days. He didn't talk about them. He's been extraordinarily frank subsequently, but I don't think we knew he had envelopes. I don't remember it anyway. I may have asked him, I don't know.

AM: The envelopes — to explain to the general public were lots of slips which he had cut up his notes into little sub-notes and put into envelopes under subject headings. That's what envelopes are.

BH: He was very well organized by comparison to me because while I was just looking through booklists wondering whether to buy books, he was looking through for references that would be useful and slipping some of them into his envelopes. I never thought of doing that, so in that sense he was far more efficient than I was. I think Peter Burke[30] was quite an influence at this point. Peter, as you know, was very intelligent, a highly intellectual person, and we used to talk after dinner quite a lot. Not just him, a group of us. He said that the important thing was to keep your horizons very wide when researching, don't just look out for one thing, and this is exactly what Keith does. He said he does this. I always try to do that, but it was Peter Burke who really influenced me on that.

The index started off as an index on temperance but eventually diversified and became a general index on everything in the world! Temperance is now only one drawer of 50, and there are all sorts of sections on political parties, Parliament, and so on.

AM: And in all there are over 1,000,000 cards?

BH: I think so, I never really counted them.

AM: Because you duplicated them. Different places, that is one of the problems with these card indexing systems that every fact as it were should be in two or three or four places.

BH: Initially we did not have Xerox machines then. The first Xerox machine I used at all frequently, was the one in Nuffield College where I went in 1964. At that point, I decided it was absurd typing out these cards several times, which I initially did, because there were so many sections, I would have to type the same card 15 times. And I got into the habit of Xeroxing cards into blocks, then I would cut them up and file them. It took ages and was frightfully boring. It all evolved organically from that. By that time it was launched and is still evolving.

AM: What proportion of your time was taking putting facts onto cards and cards into drawers and….

BH: It's impossible to answer that. I never ever measured it, but I worked extremely hard, all hours of the day. There were never Saturdays or Sundays, I always worked every day. I enjoyed it. It was partly ambition and ambition is important and you get that from school and from portraits in the Hall. When I was at St John's, I discovered that I was abler than I thought I was. Winning those prizes helped in that, and I then looked out of my window, I was on the top floor, the second floor facing straight into dessert room in the Senior Common Room. I saw a really rather nice panelled room with a big chandelier over the centre table and I used to see Dons going in there after dinner presumably to have dessert, or for their meals and I thought to myself that that was a nice life. I think of that quite often now. Now, I am an Honorary Fellow there, quite often having dessert in there, I think I've made it! But I never planned to be a Don, it wasn't something I planned to do, it seemed flying rather high. I just wanted to do as well as I could and if it led there, I was fine. It wasn't something I aimed at. And I have always remained surprised at having been a Don. I never thought I would. It would have been presumptuous to plan it and I certainly didn't think I was in the league at all.

AM: Can we come back to cards, the card indexing system before we move on? One problem I had when I adopted your method, was that after a certain size, in my case about 20,000 cards. As I progressed, I left it for a few months. The system seemed to get more and more difficult to operate. I didn't understand it at the time, but later I found it was a mathematical reason which is that the time it takes to file away things and to retrieve them goes up at a non-linear rate, it's exponential. The 20,001th card is much more difficult to file and to find than the 10,001th. The other thing I found was that I had to remember the categories that I had to set out, say 10 years earlier, both in putting things away and remembering and in finding them. Since my categories were constantly changing, over time it became a real mental effort to think where I would find my cards. Plus, the duplication problem you have mentioned. So, I in the end gave up for about 20 years and then I found the computer. I wondered if you had encountered either of those problems.

BH: Yes, I did encounter similar problems. The answer to it was constant subdivision, reshuffling and rearranging, so you had smaller categories in which you could find things. There is nothing like a computer for efficiency, so that problem has now gone away. Filing obviously took longer and longer, and looking back, it was becoming a real trial. That is why I am so glad I gave up filing. However, the material on computer is so fragile: that's the price you pay for its wonderful flexibility: combining and re-combining material, and continuously rewriting without all the labour of re-typing. The flexibility of computers involves risk in the sense that the stuff isn't secure, although in some ways it is more secure if you take copies of it elsewhere. I have now got it on the University backup system. You have got a duplicate which you never had before. In a way it's *more* secure. But there's an intermediate stage, where it's actually *less* secure with fragile information and that did worry me. So, I've always had backup arrangements of a modest kind—memory pens, and i keep two of them, one in the garage and the other in my study, and periodically swap them over—then run on to 'my main backup....'

My main backup system, though, is the university backup system which is totally secure as far as I am aware. I did predict to myself that computers would eventually be able to sort my stuff for me and before the access database was drawn to my attention, and in my love affair with the word-processor I was at first just printing cards from the computer. I got an arrangement whereby I could print out cards on the computer. the aim was simply to produce a card with that information on it. but I kept the information in its computerized form so that when I got an access database in 1997, I was able to transfer five or seven years of information into it. In 1992, when I started making cards on the computer I knew, I had a feeling, there was going to be some system where I would be able to use this stuff in a different way. In a way, the same happened with interviewing or laptops because roundabout 1986 I thought surely people would be carrying their computers around with them and that would be awfully useful if I am moving between libraries. In fact, I got one of the earliest portable computers round about 1986, and though I don't use it now, I've kept it in case it becomes a precious antique.

AM: What was it called?

BH: I have forgotten the name of it now. Learning is unlearning so you move on and you forget what the other stuff was. I have got it in the garage and I am keeping it might be of enormous second-hand value at some stage. I took it from archive to archive and when I was working on the history of the University, I used it a lot.

AM: ...a very tiny screen?

BH: I can't remember. Well, it has a screen. It must have had a screen. Yes, it had a screen.

AM: A very small screen.

BH: It had a small screen and no hard disc.

AM: You had floppy discs.

BH: Yes, that's right. I wrote an article in the College magazine about how computers came to Corpus. I wrote it because I just thought that we would forget what it was like in the early days. I re-read it the other day and thought that nobody could do this now because they have moved on and forgotten what it was like. I did interviews for that, I interviewed four or five Fellows of the College about how it started.

AM: What is the point of putting all these facts on to cards and how do you use it construct books and articles?

BH: The important thing is to enjoy writing. I enjoy the process of writing. And the agony of writing which I remember feeling very much when I was doing my drink book, is not being able to find stuff. It just adds such an additional layer of painful procedures. If you can make it instantly accessible, whatever, you want, it is not only ceases to be a chore, but it becomes a positive pleasure. Each time a thing comes up that you want, you think 'what a marvellous system I've got'. The initial impulse was to remove chores of writing, not the filing of it, but to make it easy to assemble the stuff in the order you want it when you come to write. Then the process of writing becomes pleasurable. If writing is enjoyable then you tend to write better, I think, on the whole.

The card index was not something you particularly look at one card and write that up and then look to the next one and write it. It is simply to make the information visible and available and then you can think so that you can write. The process of writing is a continuous process of discovery as I'm sure it is in your case, that is you don't know when you start on a chapter what you are going to say. But in the course of writing it, with luck you discover that ideas tend to take a form, in my case, unexpected juxtapositions. You think about one thing on one record and another thing on another, and you suddenly realize that they're related, there's some relation between them. That in a sense could be called an 'idea'. It may not be a brilliant one, but it's an idea.

The process of creation is also exhilarating and of course a highly personal matter too, whether it is good or bad it is yours. Nobody else could do it and that is why we are so different from the natural scientists because though all sorts of personal elements enter into the discovery there, as you must know better than most, because you have had a bad day with your eldest child that morning you are feeling really cross and aggressive so you invent something which you otherwise may not have invented. They all interact. The process of writing in the Arts, probably more than in the Sciences, but certainly in the Arts, is one of a continuous creation of a highly personal kind.

Anything that I write, whether it is good or bad, emerges out of my personality, experience, and my peculiar combination of reading, so you get all the satisfaction you would get out of sculpture or painting. It is highly creative. That is one of its attractions for me. But it is also attractive to me because it is cumulative, and on the whole within limits, I don't think I reach limits yet, you get better as time goes on. It requires an understanding of human nature and of human context, and of how things work. I think that, unlike some natural scientists, on the whole historians get better as they get older. Obviously, your brain goes off eventually, but one hopes it will be later rather than sooner. There's a certain cumulative aspect to it which relates to collection, collecting. I am collecting things all the time. They are facts, ideas, or insights, it is the same collecting instinct and the cards are substitutes for stamps. I am very competitive as well, so there is that incentive as well. I think that in research one starts off with rather low motives and these motives improve as life goes on. Initially, what I was fighting for was security and 'success' in some sense, but then the process in seeking those things becomes itself the object. You want to get it right and you just get interested. The ambition and lower motives get overlain by what I might describe as scholarly motive, so on the whole one is probably a nicer person later on in one's career than one was early on. But there are low motives initially I don't deny. I don't know if that answers your question.

AM: It is part of the answer to several questions. Another question is, how do you actually write? You get all these cards, you had your typewriter in the old days and your computer in front of you, you shuffle the cards around into patterns and then you start to write or do you do what Keith Thomas does which is to write a sentence or two, type a sentence or two and then get all the illustrative material to back up that proposition and clip it on with a paperclip and then write two or three more sentences and then paperclips and more slips or what.

BH: To begin with, I now write on the screen, I couldn't think of writing in manuscript, I wanted it to be instantly flexible. It is much easier if the cards are there in digitized form so that you could arrange them in the right order. Before I was able to do that, Access Database, I would arrange the cards in what I thought was the right sort of order and that would give me my initial text, but then very frequently one would rearrange them once they were on the screen. The big virtue of computers is that you can reshuffle the stuff so easily. You can try it there and if it doesn't work, you can move it down there. And that flexibility you don't have when writing a manuscript. I can never understand people who can use a computer saying they always put their first draft in manuscript because that's the time that you move the stuff around most.

AM: I'll put the case afterwards....

BH: Maybe some people are much clearer-headed than I am so they know exactly what they are going to say when they start writing. I don't. I just throw stuff down. The Warden of Nuffield used to say to us, 'Get something down, it doesn't matter what it is like, get started'. And then on you go. I do that. I haven't said anything about Nuffield, by the way, do you want me to say anything about that?

AM: Let's finish on writing. Do you write in the mornings, afternoons, evenings?

BH: Oh, any time. I am a morning person. I can't usually do serious work after about nine o' clock at night and no doubt when I get older it'll be eight o' clock, and then seven o'clock, and so on....

AM: Do you write many drafts of things or...?

BH: In the old days when one had to retype each draft, I used to go through seven drafts in anything I published. Now, I have no idea how many drafts I do, because I don't print it out as I go along, I just do it all on screen.

AM: Further on this creative, talking to many people, Max Weber said, 'We will never have our ideas at the desk, you need to go away from it and go for a walk'...Do you find this?

BH: Yes. I mean. I wouldn't say I always had my best ideas away from the desk, but certainly quite frequently I will wake in the morning to find something has become clear that wasn't so before, just through sleeping on it. Or in the bath. I always used to carry cards with me in my pocket wherever I went, I don't so much now because I don't wear a jacket, I always had some cards in my top pockets so that I could write ideas down whenever they came to me. You could have ideas anywhere. The great attraction for me of writing contemporary history, for at least a decade, any casual conversation could turn out to be academically fruitful. When I went to the dentist, for instance, I might ask, 'When did you learn dentistry and why did you go in for it'. You could ask lots of questions and they would be quite fruitful. My mother always used to ask me when I would stop asking questions. All children do that, but I have sought to perpetuate that childish trait into extreme old age. I am inquisitive by nature, and being a historian gives you every excuse for asking people questions and questions about raw material. Someone criticized me for being naive, I thought maybe I am, but all historians should be naive, and should approach reality with surprise. Why are they like that, and why are people like that, and couldn't it be done some other way, or whatever. To that extent I am a disciple of Wordsworth. I do think that young people have a freshness of outlook which one really needs to try to retain. To appear worldly-wise and all-knowing is wrong in my view. One should be learning all the time. There's that dimension of it as well. I have never minded asking people questions and in a sense, you have a license to do. That is one reason why I have done a lot of interviewing because the whole business is asking questions and I find that interesting. When we studied Wordsworth's *Prelude* for A Level I did well enough at it, but I never really got the point: I realized many years later that it was a good text to set for teenagers, because then is the time that they're losing the 'visionary gleam', or in danger of losing it.

AM: Tell us about the interviewing.

BH: The first serious interview I did was with Douglas Veale, who was the Personal Private Secretary of Neville Chamberlain when he was Minister of Health. He was a retired Fellow of my College. He came round to the first house we had. I did two interviews with him about Neville Chamberlain. He was very incisive, very clear, as civil servants can be. This convinced me that it was a technique worth having.

AM: What date was this?

BH: This was in 1967–68 and at that time Paul Thompson[31] was getting going, and I used to go to History Workshop meetings and Paul Thompson was preaching his gospel then. I was a follower but not a disciple, because I felt, you may not agree with this, he was too bitten by social anthropology and not sufficiently critical of the stuff he received or sufficiently analytical of it. Nonetheless, he got it going. I went on a BBC course that was organized by him about interviewing people; it was good for me in a number of ways. I'm not an extroverted person but interviewing made me much better in company than I would otherwise have been. I got used to putting people at their ease and getting them to talk. I think it was good for me in a general way.

It really originated with my father giving me his Grundig tape recorder (very expensive at that time) in about 1959. It was a huge thing like a suitcase, and I remember wondering if I would be able to lug it around when I was 64. They weren't small in those days. I used it for recording music off the radio. I set it off, highly improperly, at the first tutorial I ever gave, because it starts with Keith Robbins looking round the door to tell me, in urgent tones 'they're coming, they're coming'. And there emerged a dreadful tutorial with two pupils I had from St Edmund Hall. I talked all the time. I was terribly nervous, as a young tutor is, whereas the essence of being a good tutor is to let *them* talk. It was just ghastly. That was one of the earliest tutorials I took.

AM: Did you learn from listening to it?
BH: Yes, I did. And I thought this is really terrible. Then on one of the BBC courses we were sent out to interviews with rather patient people, and I interviewed a cockney woman in Camden Town in her kitchen. We played the interviews afterwards to the group and it was a dreadful interview…something like, 'tell me how your mother ran the kitchen' and so on. We just weren't connecting at all. I didn't know how to do it even then, eventually I got better at it. I did a big project interviewing suffragettes and feminists. That collection is now in the London Metropolitan University in the Women's Library, though the Library is in danger at the moment. It is called the 'Harrison Collection', and contains about 200 interviews, and some of them some were awfully good. We made a radio programme for Radio 4 about three months ago where Peter Snow presided, where extracts were played. There was a wonderful one of Maud Kate Smith, who was on her deathbed in some old people's home, talking about being forcibly fed. She had a bright, chirpy voice, and talked in such a cheerful way about this ghastly procedure. It came over brilliantly on the radio and there was a close following

on Twitter as a result. She died soon afterwards, but at that stage she was still not saying who was involved in her sabotage attempts —— she was trying to destroy the canal system by blowing up an aqueduct in the Birmingham area. But there were many other episodes in that project which were quite memorable. People would burst into tears during interviews and I didn't know how to cope at first, but people are prepared to talk more freely to a stranger on very personal matters.

I did a lot of interviewing for the history of the University as well. Oral history emerged somewhat more centrally for that, as I organized 48 seminars on the history of the University—Keith Thomas gave one of them—and I did word-for-word transcripts of them. We not only had the paper but also the conversation afterwards with names attached. They are now quite an important record of what the University's elite were saying in the late 1980s about the University's recent history as they themselves had observed it. They were quoted in footnotes in volume eight of the History. The seminars became 'an event' that people came to because their friends were there. They also knew that it was being taken seriously so anything they said they said carefully but I don't think they distorted what they said. You must have experienced this. Seminars get a momentum of their own and you don't think about what would be said of them 20 years hence, they just say what they are thinking of at the time. Roy Jenkins says that somewhere about the cabinet. He says that he doesn't mind being frank in cabinet because the concerns of the cabinet are immediate, 30 years hence, he doesn't care what people will be saying. He said there was no harm having diaries kept by other colleagues, though he didn't keep one himself and I agree with that. The seminars were very, very useful. They also became very useful because they were targets to contributors to aim at. It is a great problem, as you know, of getting stuff out of people. So if you say, 'Well you'll all be addressing this seminar, such and such, on your chapter', that would get them started and they would write something for that and then let's comment on that.... So, it was really very useful from that point of view.

I also interviewed people like Isaiah Berlin, Max Beloff,[32] and so on, just to try and understand how their subjects worked. But it is so time-consuming that I didn't use it much for the *New Oxford History* volumes, I would never have written them if I had continued on that line. I interviewed a dentist called Downer about the history of dentistry, which interests me because there was no book on it. I also interviewed Cicely Saunders, the founder of the Hospice movement. She was a marvellous woman. I would like to have done more interviews but I just decided it was just too time consuming. You can't use it unless its transcribed and that takes seven times as long as the interview. If the interviews are two hours, you've got another 14 hours to add to that. I just never had the time

AM: You didn't think of filming the interviews?

BH: It never occurred to me. I wouldn't be capable of it.

AM: Of course, you would, it's terribly simple. It is a different form of interview. You did College servants, was that part of the University?

BH: No that was 1969. It was a teaching device. What happened was that some very good students of mine, my second year as a Tutor there, said they wanted to write some history of their own. Trevor Aston was there then with all the accoutrements of *Past and Present*, he encouraged it when we made a tape recorder available so the students went around. They didn't all use a tape recorder, I did because I used my father's tape recorder. They wrote in manuscript. It was really very laborious for them. I've got the notes all written out in manuscript. That was an oral history project of a slightly different kind. There, there was a teaching device. There were these College employees in our midst who didn't respond to inequalities of wealth with jealousy but with admiration. They weren't envious, they wanted to be seen with these people, so that they could tell their friends that they had met so and so. This was very odd because this was the period of Marxism, Marxism was fashionable, class-consciousness was the thing, the Labour Party was going places, so these people were oddities. In fact, they were a lot more sensible than we were but we did not know it at the time. It worked very well, but I am surprised how much time the students were prepared to give to it as it didn't pay off at all in their degree result.

AM: Can we come back to Nuffield? That was the next stage after St Antony's. What would you like to say about it?

BH: Quite honestly. I was frightened of Nuffield as a Junior Research Fellow (1964–47). I applied to go because it was the place to go if you were a modern historian. It was then, and still is, a highly professional place, very competitive and very serious. That was why it was disliked in the rest of Oxford. There was no pretence of amateurism at all. We were all seriously in business as social scientists of one sort or another. It was very good for me as it exposed me to not only economics, but political science and sociology, and to a certain extent to social anthropology, though not much. It was interdisciplinary. There were some very interesting people there including Rod Floud, Patricia Hollis, Gareth Stedman Jones, Robert Currie. Raphael Samuel came into discussion groups we had there. Max Hartwell was extremely encouraging to us all —— it was what they now describe as an intellectual hub.

I wrote an article with Patricia Hollis and later we edited Robert Lowery's autobiography together. I found it published in instalments in a little-known Temperance periodical. I then took it along to her and said, 'Is this important?' She was working on the Unstamped Press movement in the 1830s and she said it was important. I suggested we write an article in the *English Historical Review* about it, and then we edited the autobiography which was published in 1979. That was the atmosphere because there was a lot of inter-fertilization.

Another person I ought to mention is John Walsh. He was a wonderful man, very encouraging, a historian of Evangelicalism and Methodism. The first time I ever met him, he simply looked round the door of my room in St Antony's and said, 'I'm running a seminar, would you like to come to it?' I said, 'Of course, I would'. I was very flattered that someone like him should come to my room and ask me whether I would go. So, I went. He used to fill in yellow slips when you went to the Bodleian Library to take a book out. He would send me these slips with references to temperance that he had found. He was awfully generous, a very nice man.

I was not the only graduate student deeply indebted to him. He was a friend of Keith Thomas, a semi-contemporary of Keith Thomas so they knew each other. And all this time, Keith was very encouraging. You need encouragement as a graduate student. The first year, Peter Mathias, my supervisor (in Cambridge), left me alone and I just did what I wanted to do. He then said, 'It's time you started writing now'. It wasn't before time either. I thought, in retrospect, he should have got me writing earlier. He was a very good supervisor, very encouraging, and conscientious in reading my stuff. I used to go over to Cambridge on the railway that then existed between the two cities. My first bit of writing turned out to be the second chapter of *Drink and the Victorians*. He wrote at several points on the text that I had been 'uncritical' of the evidence. In general, it frightened me to the extent that I wondered if I had got on the wrong track, if I would be any good as a historian. I remember sitting in the bedroom I had in Queen's College in Cambridge, wondering if this had been a big mistake. But he was encouraging and very supportive, and I needed to be told that. He was critical and a very good supervisor. What with him in Cambridge and Keith in Oxford I was very well looked after. In the end, Peter used to call me a Stakhanovite,[33] I just flooded him with chapters on drink, and finally took off from him in a way. I was always a social and political historian, not (like Peter) an economic historian. I was never very interested in economic history and sociology was the subject that interested me. There I got a lot of encouragement from sociologists in Nuffield, particularly Chelly Halsey[34] who was extremely encouraging, a very nice man, and eventually we collaborated in writing things for the history of the University. There were a lot of encouraging senior members there.

AM: Did you know Clyde Mitchell?[35]

BH: No. but I know the name. Norman Birnbaum[36] was there for a time, an American sociologist. And Jean Floud[37] was there. She was my model of an intelligent woman, well turned-out, very incisive, and tough as old boots. 'Don't be bloody silly', I remember her telling Chelly Halsey when we were doing a selection. I thought my goodness she's a woman and a half!

AM: You then went on from Nuffield to your first teaching job?

BH: Yes. Three jobs came up in the same year, in 1966. The job at Queen's, which Ken Morgan got, came up first in 1965 and I wondered whether to apply. I didn't think I would get it and it would also get me tangled up with the Prestwiches, which I didn't want to do and Keith was not keen on the Prestwiches either. This is where Keith is so good, he advises you on your career, what to do when, that sort of thing. I think it was with his encouragement that I did not to go in for that. Then in 1966 three jobs came up at the same time, one in Oriel, one in Christ Church and one in Corpus. I was in for all three. I got a postcard from Michael Brock[38] at Corpus, who asked me to call on him to talk about my future. Naturally, I went in my best suit at once. To cut a long story short, they did what now would be quite impossible. The Fellows invited me to dinner at Corpus and I talked to several of them. They had little tables that you could swap around.

I remember being grilled by Christopher Taylor, the philosopher, about Gladstone's drinking habits. They just offered me the job though I gathered afterwards that there had been a competition of some sort. Presumably, they had invited applications, one of which was mine, and they either didn't interview anyone else or if they did, they vanished off the scene. Anyway, I got it and Keith said, 'It is a very nice College, take it', and so I did.

Michael Brock was very good at initiating me into the teaching process. I was a bit of a firebrand then. I was very much a Nuffield person. In some ways I always remained a Nuffield person. I didn't go for the amateurism of Oxford and the pretence of not taking work seriously. I remember getting into trouble with the College secretary because I was Xeroxing so much on the machine. She was obviously thinking of the expense to the College. The College was perfectly rich and well able to afford it. It was very good expenditure of its money. At Nuffield you just took things like that for granted and that was where I started Xeroxing cards. You just took it to the College office and you Xeroxed and nobody asked any questions.

I thought that attitude would apply in Corpus, but it didn't and I was rather disapproved of.

AM: Did you enjoy the teaching?

BH: Yes. But there were three nagging things. President Hardie, the first I served under, was enlightened enough to say when I was invited to go for a semester in Ann Arbor in 1970, that I should go even though I'd not stacked up much sabbatical entitlement, so, I went, and was very much taken with the American teaching system —— that is the lecture based, course-paper based system. I gave something like 40 lectures on British history and liked found it a useful experience, and also had a memorably interesting graduate class on 'reforming movements' it. I thought the American system much more compatible with writing. There was no fixed syllabus and you could teach what you liked. Thereafter I was always an outsider as far as the Oxford teaching system was concerned as I didn't believe in it.

Secondly, I hated examining and I didn't believe in the then four-class system. I do not believe that human nature is divided into four categories. I was invited, a fortnight ago, to talk to a gay-lesbian society and said I did not believe in this bifurcated view that the world is divided into homosexuals and heterosexuals, nor did I think the category of bisexual is much good either. The world is divided into a spectrum from one extreme to the other, and it is no more divided into two or three categories in that sphere than it is divided into four categories in intellectual calibre. I felt alienated from the examination system, I hated examining.

I felt that the pupils I taught were good didn't necessarily get the right marks, and people whom I thought incapable of getting Firsts, got them. That worried me. I had to pretend that I believed in the system, which I didn't think was delivering the right results, and that really lasted until the end of my career. It involved a certain degree of hypocrisy but you can't say to students that you don't believe in the system you are being examined in, you just have to pretend that that is the system and that's what you do. I was unhappy in that dimension. I liked the one-to-one teaching and I think I probably became a better teacher the older I was because pupils initially seem a bit of a threat, they are near one's own age and how are you going to get an essay out of them. That all vanishes when you are older.

Keith is a very sophisticated tutor in many ways, though I did not see that as an undergraduate. He knew that the tutorial was not an occasion in which one delivered information which was then absorbed, it was an opportunity for discovering your own thoughts and being able to convey them clearly to other people. The best tutor was not necessarily the person who knew most about what he was talking about, he could be somebody quite different. In fact, there was an exhilaration about learning something in a tutorial from a pupil who didn't know about what you were teaching. I think I was a bit overwhelming as a Tutor at first, but I think I got better. I like young people, and like the opportunity of talking with them on an equal basis. I never made them wear a gown, and if they wanted to smoke in a tutorial I pretended not to mind, because it ought to be an equal thing.

AM: What about lecturing?

BH: I hated lecturing, mainly because it is peripheral to the Oxford system which is tutorial based. Partly, it may sound a bit silly, I never really thought I knew the truth, so that lecturing was didactic, and I preferred the tutorial system in that sense as it is question and answer. You don't necessarily know the answer, whereas in a lecture people think you do. Quite apart from that I am not a particularly good lecturer and not a spontaneous performer, and I think you have to have a histrionic flair to be a really good lecturer, maybe even a certain conceit. I could never be an A.J.P. Taylor,[39] for example. I admire him immensely for what he was able to do and Berlin, still more so, he was a wonderful lecturer. I think Michael Howard[40] said that an important thing with a lecture is for it to go through the brain, so that what you say is what you are thinking at the time, not to read out some screed. I'm sure that is very good advice and I haven't got a good enough memory to do that convincingly. I didn't enjoy lecturing. I didn't enjoy examining. I was quite good at administration and could have had an administrative career, but I didn't want to because I had various relatives who said, 'Brian's doing a lot of research, but is he able to find anything?' And I was quite determined to write things to prove them wrong. In the end, I got the bug for writing, I liked writing and now I suppose I always did like writing because I liked writing letters. I got better at writing and enjoyed writing, so that's the way it went.

AM: Two more questions, one is about the role of your wife in your life and the other is to choose one of the many projects which we haven't had time to deal with like the Oxford history or the Oxford Dictionary of National Biography and single out what is your most interesting contribution…?
BH: To me or to other people?

AM: To you. And you can do them in either order.
BH: I got started as a graduate student before I met Vicky. We first met in 1964. We didn't get married until, I am ashamed to say, I can't remember, 1966 or 1967, anyway it was one of those two years! We married on the first day that the Registry Office was open in January that year, it must've been January 1967, I think. I was strongly against a church wedding because I didn't believe in the religion, and greatly disappointed her parents because they would have liked a normal wedding. We were complementary, both in personal terms and academically. She was doing a D.Phil. in the natural sciences and I was doing mine in history or had got it by then, I did my D.Phil. in 1966. She was working quite hard in the labs when we first got married. We didn't know how things were going to turn out, whether she would join me in some joint operation or was she going to have a career of her own.

It was really Robert Maxwell who got her alerted to the fact that she is good at communicating. She is a very good writer. She is a meritocrat, unlike me. She went to a grammar school in Workington and made it to Oxford through her own inherent ability, she didn't have a privileged background at all, she had parents who encouraged her a lot. We were both sort of meritocrats in a way, but she more than me. She then went and wrote to Maxwell and found that she was good at this, she then went into the popularization of science, a very wide approach rather than professional science.

Through osmosis again, I gained a certain self-confidence about writing in that area more than I would otherwise have had. I could ask her things when I was getting things wrong in that area and she also gave me a certain scepticism about science. She is very sceptical about doctors, for example. I had never thought about and just believed everything they said like my mother did. My mother went into her final operation that killed her, totally confident that it would cure her completely. I remember her waving as she went into Intensive Care at St. Mary's Hospital, Paddington. The person we were with was a friend of hers who said, 'Courage, courage, courage'. She had great courage and she believed in doctors too.

In the natural science we were complementary, in character we were very complementary. She is like her mother, very diplomatic, whereas her mother says of me that Brian is so open, and that is not praise! I think I have probably become a bit more discreet as a result of her influence. She comments on things, I ask what a layman would make of this, she'd say, 'I can't understand what you are saying'. She's very helpful in that way. But we are both busy. We've both had separate careers, so we are a marriage of opposites in some ways. We couldn't have had that situation if we had had children, we had no children. Two careers would have been quite impossible in that case. Not having children was not by design, it just didn't happen. The pattern of our life was in some sense determined by that. I have always been interested in children and I am rather fond of children. I like trying to think myself into their ways of thinking. David McLellan's awfully good on this. He talks to his grandchildren and they are very logical. It particularly interests David, because he comes to breakfast quite regularly, I see him quite often, and their way of thinking is attractive to a philosopher. They interest me, partly because we haven't had children and partly because I would like to be a child myself, and think it rather important to remain a child, feeling that the world is strange.

What do I like best?

A lot of people say that I am best known for *Drink and the Victorians*. It was my first book and one is always proud. One is always pleased to see one's name in print, it's a vanity factor there.

I really enjoyed it, and soaked myself in temperance, as it was not my world at all, I was coming at it from outside. I later learnt that father's father had actually preached temperance standing on top of a public lavatory in Hull. I didn't know that at the time I took it on. My father was always very interested in what I was doing. My mother could not understand it and thought it bizarre. But my father was interested. I wish he'd lived to see it. I dedicated my first book to him. It is a classic case of only retrospectively discovering one's parents when it is too late. I never really knew him whereas I knew my mother all too well, but they were both very good parents in their way and I owe a great deal to them.

Women's history was always messed up by militant feminists who were extremely tiresome. I am a feminist but not militant. Militancy is incompatible with the historical outlook which should be balanced, getting things in proportion, measured, and I felt uncomfortable in this world and eventually got out of it. I was intending originally to write a big history of British feminism but I gave up because I didn't feel the climate was right. I did write a lot of articles and two books, but I didn't write the book I originally intended.

I enjoyed doing the history of the University a lot. I think that if anything 'made' me it was that, because I got known in the University for the seminars, and then handled this big volume, which wasn't easy but very exhilarating and very enjoyable to do. Although I only wrote three chapters in it of about 20, I did have a grasp of the whole thing. That was my volume.

Probably the thing I have enjoyed doing most has been the *New Oxford History of England* because I started writing my first of two volumes when I was working on the Dictionary and wrote the first four chapters in draft. It was the first thing I did in retirement and got it done in retirement. It was a real building operation. It took ages and I don't think I could've done it now. It built on everything that I had done. I drew on the card index, right, left and centre and all the newspaper reading I had been doing. I haven't said that PPE [Philosophy, Politics, Economics] was very important. In a peculiar situation at Corpus I taught PPE and history. And PPE is very much modern, pushing you towards the modern, so I went more and more modern and I learnt a lot from political scientists. That comes out of PPE much more and not out of my history course.

I really enjoyed writing my two volumes in *The New Oxford History of England* a lot. I did a huge amount of reading for it in the 90s and then started writing in about 2003, and published the first volume in 2009. That was more personal as a volume. My name, of course, doesn't appear in its subject matter anywhere, and I think it would have been wrong if it did, though Paul Addison in his history of the period, he himself features. I think it's a mistake, it spoils his volume to some extent. I also enjoyed it also because I had been brought up on the old *Oxford History* volumes, Woodward especially. And the thought of actually writing them myself was beyond my wildest dreams. I met E.L. Woodward,[41] the *Age of Reform* man in the Senior Common Room in Corpus in 1966 when I got the fellowship and I had not yet taken the job, but they had invited me to dinner now and again. There was Woodward, legendary figure and I said, 'Goodness me! I was brought up on you', he was pleasant to talk to but he had crumb or something on his chin. I pondered whether to tell him that he really ought to remove the crumb but everyone there regarded him with such reverence that I didn't dare say anything to him in the end.

AM: How would you assess your character?

BH: There is one element of it which is timidity which is actually an important characteristic of a historian. Timidity in the sense of not being confident that your views are correct and not actually being very confident about one's career and doubts about where one's going. I was certainly surprised when I got a scholarship to Oxford, certainly surprised when I became an academic, very surprised to become a professor, and when it came to the envelope arriving from Number 10, I burst out laughing!

AM: I was going to ask you with all the social climbing that you've been ascribing to yourself, when you became Sir Brian, was it a moment of ultimate triumph?

BH: Well, no. In the sense, it was something I never ever dreamt of. My mother would have been so pleased for all the wrong reasons but she had died by then, so there's that element. I am also timid in a physical sense. I remember being frightened of bigger boys as a child, and though I had a girlfriend though not in a sex sense, a friend who was a girl, she said, 'Don't be frightened, he can't eat you', or something to that effect. 'Just go through the field, he won't do anything.' And he didn't. That carried on into the sports field though the main problem there was poor eyesight.

By the time I got into the Army, they wanted to train you in being tough. So, we were put in the boxing ring. A famous friend of mine, Nigel Williams, the course before mine, one of his contemporaries put in the ring, hit the target and said, 'Sorry'. The officers didn't like that at all. I was quite determined when I got into the ring to go down fighting! I really made quite a good impression because whenever I was knocked down, I got up quickly! There was a physical element to it. But there is also an intellectual element of it as well. I always used to wonder how on earth anyone could give a lecture and answer any question that came at them and be freely able to answer them. I could never do that. But I later found that you can always turn a question round so that you can answer it, and anyway after a few years as a historian there is a huge armoury that you can draw upon.

Likewise, early on in committees in the College, knowing the right moment to intervene is quite important. I didn't know how to do that. I remember at one stage, David Maclellan saying rather endearingly that when he did intervene in meetings, they would just carry on as though he hadn't spoken. but you eventually pick it up, though few people are as good at it as Keith.

My blooding on that was when we had the vote on whether to admit women to Corpus because in 1971–72 the opportunity of admitting women to Corpus came up to consider the matter, and I supported it on the naive grounds that it would be just to women to admit them. That was quite the wrong tack to take. What I should have done was to say that it would be in the interest of the Corpus to admit women, and that never occurred to me until after the event. Of course, we were defeated, but we put up a good fight. I think we got 13 votes to 12, but it needed to be a two-thirds majority.

Anyway, we went mixed in 1979, seven or eight years later. I did then in 1971 nerve myself to intervene and I put up a paper to the Governing Body with the encouragement of another Fellow. I did take quite a prominent part in that, but it was a real effort to do it. On another occasion, Val Cunningham, the English Tutor, had far more self-confidence than I did, tended to quote poetry in Governing Body meetings. I remember him quoting Shakespeare – once being in it you've got to go on or something like that, a quotation in, not *Hamlet*, but *Macbeth* about how you ploughed in so much blood and you've got to go on. He quoted that at one point, so in the next I made a speciality of quoting that famous and wonderful poem by G.K. Chesterton[42] *The Donkey*. I had made a report on something in the College and the Bursar got it, but before it got to the Governing Body dealt with a number of issues that I had raised, I had said that the report should come straight to the Governing Body, there should be no interference regarding the Fellow's report on the Governing Body, I quoted *The Donkey* because I said, 'We might be pretty lowly creatures, we Fellows for most of the year round, but we had our day'. And I quoted *The Donkey*!

AM: I've got one last question, you have studied many great historians, history has been your life, what would you think have been the four or five essential qualities you talked about, you talked about timidity, for a good historian?

BH: One thing I thought you were going to ask me about, but I'll say it anyway because it is important in a way. When I went in for a fellowship at Jesus College, Oxford, with John Walsh's encouragement, because he was a Fellow there, I talked to Christie who was the Headmaster of Westminster and then became the Principal of Jesus. John Walsh reported to me afterwards that I had been asked about my other interests and said I spent all my time doing history, it's a very broad subject and that was reported as a black mark with Christie. I can see why, but I don't agree. It may be that a mathematician needs to become a good flautist, but it seems to me that history is such a wide subject, it includes flute playing and natural science, that I find it totally satisfying not having any other predominant interest. I love music, I listen to music. I remember a wonderful woman, Elizabeth Rawson,[43] an Ancient Historian, at Corpus. She was the aesthete in the College and decided the colour of curtains. She was a very cultivated woman. She once said in friendly fashion that she didn't think that art ultimately was my first priority and she was right in the sense that it could not divert me from my historical occupations. I was interested in the history of art, but in my case, I didn't think art was a more important than history.

I don't think that about music, given the overwhelming pleasure that music gives, it goes on and on through generations. If I had another life, I would like to have been a great composer. To be able to give so much pleasure to so many people is really something. But in general, she had a point. And I have never felt any obligation to pretend to be an enthusiast in any other area, history is quite sufficient for me. Getting back to your question, was what?! Sorry!

AM: My question was what are the four or five qualities....

BH: Oh, yes! One quality I don't think is necessary to have necessarily is to have hobbies or other interests or to be an amateur. I am a Nuffield person and I believe in being a professional.

AM: What is being professional?

BH: Being professional is, being dedicated, getting things as right as you can, checking references and getting your footnotes right, polishing your prose as thoroughly as you can. I always had this image in my mind of a bricklayer while doing the *New Oxford History of England* of tapping a sentence to see whether you have expressed it as concisely and clearly as possible. Another analogy when I was doing the history of the University was exploring, making your way through a forest, finding things out. I think you have got to be inquisitive, very determined to stick at it, balanced, sense of proportion and perspective, you have got to understand of human nature, be precise, meticulous, methodical and have the desire to express yourself clearly for the reader. That is the recipe for the perfect person, which I am not, but those are aspirations. All those qualities and skills are important. I don't like narrative. I don't like chronology. I want explanation, however inadequate. I want analysis. I don't like schematic sociological obsessions, but I like the sort of questions sociologists ask. I also like the receptiveness and assimilative quality that social anthropologists have, listening to people. Interviewing is important for me, I like asking questions, I like listening to people, you always try and quote them in their own language if possible. There are a whole range of qualities. History is a very civilizing discipline, very broad. You don't need any interests other than history in my view.

NOTES

1. Wikipedia. 2020. https://en.wikipedia.org/wiki/Brian_Harrison_ (historian)

2. Nocturne, in music, is a composition inspired by, or evocative of, the night, and cultivated in the 19th century primarily as a character piece for piano. Polish composer Frédéric Chopin wrote 21 nocturnes for solo piano between 1827 and 1846. They are generally considered among the finest short solo works for the instrument and hold an important place in contemporary concert repertoire. Although Chopin did not invent the nocturne, he popularized and expanded on it, building on the form developed by Irish composer John Field. https://en.wikipedia.org/wiki/ Nocturnes_(Chopin)

3. Intermezzo in music and theatre is an entertainment performed between the acts of a play; also a light instrumental composition. https:// www.britannica.com/art/intermezzo-music-and-theatre

4. Jean Sibelius (1865–1957) was a Finnish composer, the most noted symphonic composer of Scandinavia. https://www.britannica.com/ biography/Jean-Sibelius

5. Maitland, see Appendix.

6. *The Life of Benjamin Disraeli: Earl of Beaconsfield, Volume 5* by William Flavelle Monypenny and George Earle Buckle was originally published in 1910.

7. *The Life of William Ewart Gladstone* by John Morley.

8. *The French Revolution: A History* was written by the Scottish essayist, philosopher, and historian Thomas Carlyle. The three-volume work, first published in 1837.

9. John Steane, see Appendix.

10. Frank Raymond 'F.R.' Leavis (1895–1978) was a British literary critic of the early-to-mid-twentieth century. He taught for much of his career at

Downing College, Cambridge, and later at the University of York. https://en.wikipedia.org/wiki/F._R._Leavis

11. David Herbert Lawrence (1885–1930) was an English author of novels, short stories, poems, plays, essays, travel books, and letters. His novels *Sons and Lovers* (1913), *The Rainbow* (1915) and *Women in Love* (1920) made him one of the most influential English writers of the 20th century. https://www.britannica.com/biography/D-H-Lawrence

12. Thomas Nashe (1567–1601) [also Nash] was an Elizabethan playwright, poet, satirist and a significant pamphleteer. He is known for his novel *The Unfortunate Traveller*, his pamphlets including *Pierce Penniless*, and his numerous defences of the Church of England. https://en.wikipedia.org/wiki/Thomas_Nashe

13. William Wordsworth, see Appendix.

14. Cormac John Rigby (1939–2007) was a broadcaster and priest. https://www.theguardian.com/media/2007/mar/29/religion.broadcasting

15. David McLellan, see Appendix.

16. Richard Dawkins, FRS, FRSL (b. 1941) is a British ethologist, evolutionary biologist, and author. https://en.wikipedia.org/wiki/Richard_Dawkins

17. Catterick Garrison is a major garrison and military town 3 miles (5 km) south of Richmond, North Yorkshire, England. It is the largest British Army garrison in the world. https://en.wikipedia.org/wiki/Catterick_Garrison

18. Howard Colvin, see Appendix.

19. William Costin, see Appendix.

20. Voltaire, see Appendix.

21. Alexis de Tocqueville, see Appendix.

22. John Mabbott, see Appendix.

23. Prys Morgan, see Appendix.

24. Paul Slack, see Appendix.

25. Peter Mathias, see Appendix.

26. Theodore Zeldin, see Appendix.

27. Keith Robbins, see Appendix.

28. Patricia Hollis, see Appendix.

29. Beatrice Webb, see Appendix.

30. Peter Burke, see Part III, p. 125.

31. Paul Thompson, see Appendix.

32. Max Beloff, see Appendix.

33. An exceptionally hard-working or zealous person.

34. Albert Henry 'Chelly' Halsey (1923–2014) was a British sociologist. He was Emeritus Professor of Social and Administrative Studies at the Department of Social Policy and Intervention, University of Oxford, and a Fellow of Nuffield College, Oxford. https://en.wikipedia.org/wiki/A._H._Halsey

35. James Clyde Mitchell, FBA (1918–95) was a British sociologist and anthropologist. https://en.wikipedia.org/wiki/J._Clyde_Mitchell

36. Norman Birnbaum (1926–2019) was an American sociologist. He was an emeritus professor at the Georgetown University Law Center, and a member of the editorial board of *The Nation*. https://en.wikipedia.org/wiki/Norman_Birnbaum

37. Jean Esther Floud, CBE née McDonald (1915–2013) was a prominent educational sociologist and later an academic. She was Principal of Newnham College, Cambridge, from 1972 to 1983. https://en.wikipedia.org/wiki/Jean_Floud

38. Michael Brock, see Appendix.

39. A.P.J. Taylor, see Appendix.

40. Michael Howard, see Appendix.

41. E.L. Woodward, see Appendix.

42. Gilbert Keith Chesterton, KC*SG (1874–1936) was an English writer, philosopher, lay theologian, and literary and art critic. He has been referred to as the 'prince of paradox'. https://en.wikipedia.org/wiki/G._K._Chesterton

43. Elizabeth Donata Rawson (1934–88) was a classical scholar known primarily for her work in the intellectual history of the Roman Republic and her biography of Cicero. https://en.wikipedia.org/wiki/Elizabeth_Rawson

PART three

Peter Burke.

A characteristically helpful note about diary writing across Europe.

Photographs courtesy Alan Macfarlane.

Peter Burke

Ulick Peter Burke (b. 1937) is a British historian and professor. He was born to a Roman Catholic father and Jewish mother (who later converted to Roman Catholicism).

He was educated by the Jesuits and at St John's College, Oxford and was a doctoral candidate at St Antony's College, Oxford.

From 1962 to 1979, he was a member of the School of European Studies at the University of Sussex, before moving to the University of Cambridge, where he holds the title of Professor Emeritus of Cultural History and Fellow of Emmanuel College, Cambridge. Burke is celebrated as a historian not only of the early modern era, but one who emphasizes the relevance of social and cultural history to modern issues. He is married to the Brazilian historian Maria Lúcia Garcia Pallares–Burke who is the author of several books (in two of which she collaborated with her husband).

Burke is not only known for his work on the Modern Age but also for his research on cultural history across its entire spectrum. As a polyglot, he has managed on the one hand to incorporate information from a good part of Europe and has also achieved a wider readership for his books. They have been translated into more than thirty languages. In 1998, he was awarded the Erasmus Medal of the European Academy, and he holds honorary doctorates from the Universities of Lund, Copenhagen, Bucharest, Zurich, Brussels and Oviedo.

Some of his notable publications include, The Italian Renaissance *(1972),* Popular Culture in Early Modern Europe *(1978),* The European Renaissance: Centres and Peripheries *(1998)* A Social History of Knowledge *(2 vols, 2000–2012), and* The Polymath *(2020).*[1]

|

Alan Macfarlane (AM): It's a great pleasure to have the chance to talk to Peter Burke, a very distinguished colleague and my first historian–anthropologist rather than anthropologist–historian in this series. Peter, what I usually start with is to ask people to talk about their families and family background. I know you have a very interesting mixed parentage so you can go back as far as you like, as long as you don't do eight generations. Just back to grandparents and downwards, what they did, what they were like, what effects they had on you.

Peter Burke (PB): I jump in and say that I'm the kind of Englishman, none of whose grandparents were born on this island. But two from the extreme west of Europe and two getting on for the extreme east of Europe. Two from Galway, arriving in England, at a typical time for Irish immigrants to come, I suppose, 1904. My father was born in Birkenhead a week after they arrived, to his eternal sorrow, because he would have liked — would have loved really — to have been born in Ireland. And the whole of his life he talked about the English as 'the English', which I'm sure has some funny consequences for my sense of identity. Even though he didn't really go back to Ireland very often.

And then my mother's family, her father came from Vilnius. He called himself a Russian but that's because Vilnius was firmly part of Tsarist Russia. He would have left, let me think, he left in 1883. And my grandmother, who came from Łódź, the Manchester of Poland, she left in 1887. And the earliest family document, I just found it again last week when clearing out, is her French grammar. She has a grammar, French–Polish but the Polish is written in Cyrillic, and so it's an interesting document of one particular moment in the history

This interview was conducted by Alan Macfarlane on 26 March 2008. The transcription for this interview has been provided by Rittika Dhar, for this volume. These interviews are available for viewing on:
https://www.sms.cam.ac.uk/media/1120921
https://www.youtube.com/watch?v=GVR3YdyQQBA
https://www.youtube.com/watch?v=JvB5yozQsmM

of eastern Europe. And clearly, the Russian–Lithuanian and Polish parts of the family wisely chose to come out in the 1880s because that was the time of the pogroms.

AM: They were Jewish?

PB: That's right. Completely, as far as I know. I'm mixed, sort of. By Jewish tradition, I'm Jewish because my mother's Jewish. And by Catholic tradition, I am Catholic because my father's Catholic. And in any case, my mother was converted, I never knew how deeply but in order to get married to my father, she was perfectly happy to do this. And then, she was in the funny situation of having to bring me up as a Catholic during the War when he was away because he spent the War in Italy and Egypt. And maybe she didn't do it with great fervour, I mean she did it absolutely as she was supposed to but I found giving up Catholicism was absolutely no problem. I never had that sort of deep emotional attachment to it. I'm fond of Catholic culture and the bizarre thing is, when I went to Poland for the first time, I felt at home in it and its Catholicism, despite of course the Communist state and the tradition of anti–Semitism that was still alive. I went in '64 and in '69, you could read in the newspapers that General Moczar[2] and his fascists were still persecuting Jewish academics and others.

AM: What languages did your parents speak? Because you're a very good linguist, did you get anything from your parents?

PB: To me, they only spoke English but they met at a German club, the Deutsche Verein, and so it was an interest in learning German that led to them meeting one another in London. And my mother must have had very good German once because she spent a year in Berlin, (1930–31, so late in the Weimar Republic), and was always very enthusiastic about that. But she went back only once after 1933, couldn't bear the atmosphere and never went again.

My father was a real linguist. Never formally, not more than Latin and Greek and French at school, same as me. But he became a professional translator, mainly French and German, in the British–American Tobacco Company. But he learned languages as a hobby and his proudest moment was, he said, that he was once introduced at a party as the man who'd forgotten twenty languages. That was the sort of compliment he really was pleased to be given. And he tried everything. In the war he was in Cairo, so he started learning Arabic. And then they sent him to Caserta, he started Italian. And when he was a bookseller, which is what he became later on, I remember him learning to read Chinese and above all, Japanese, so that he could sell Japanese prints, things like that. So yes, I have in that sense carried on the family tradition.

But no Irish. I don't think even my grandparents would have known more than twenty or thirty words of Irish because they grew up before the real age of linguistic nationalism. I'm sure they believed in home rule but I don't think they thought that you needed to learn this language, even in the west. You know, you still can't get a job in University College, Galway, without Irish. I once saw a job advert, at a time when I was interested in jobs in history, and it said, 'Please send 40 copies of the application and bear in mind the interview will be in Irish'. So, I didn't apply.

AM: It must be one of the few languages you don't speak. Which languages do you speak fairly reasonably?

PB: Romance languages. Even then, not quite all of them. I started Romanian as well but…French, Spanish, Italian, Portuguese and a bit of Catalan. And all of them like that character in Umberto Eco's *Name of the Rose*, remember Salvatore? Because he speaks a total mix of the Romance languages. If I don't speak a total mix, I don't think I can utter more than two or three sentences in any one of them without contamination from one of the others. I go to an Italian lecture now and instead of saying 'come' I say 'como'. Afterwards people say why did you do that? It's too similar, it interferes.

AM: What about reading? You can read all these languages?

PB: I read the Germanic languages as well, just about all of them. And I can decipher certain Slav languages. I really made the effort with Polish, partly, I suppose, because of my grandmother and partly because of wanting to work on 17th century history, where Polish is much more relevant than Russian. Muscovy really was on the edge of Europe but Poland was a great power, making a big impact on the rest of Europe. And I said to myself, when I finish Polish, I'll start Russian but then I never finished Polish. I got stuck in it somehow but it has been great fun and it's still useful. I can pick up a book, I know exactly what it's about. I can't be always sure what the author's saying but then, of course, it's not a problem in Cambridge to find somebody who can give you the translation of just the paragraph you know you really want.

AM: To return to your parents, can you say something about their characters and the way you think they may have influenced you?
PB: That's not so easy. My mother, definitely more extrovert and more outgoing, would have liked to have much more social life, but she was a different person in the nuclear family from when she was telephoning her sisters. It struck me already as a small child, when she got on the telephone to one of her four sisters, she became a different person. Much more continental. She started to gesture, spoke much more loudly and all sorts of Yiddish words appeared which she never used otherwise except in front of my grandparents. I was aware that there was this language and I suppose I still know twenty words of it but she never spoke it in front of my father.

And my father was much more of a solitary person. He made a few friends but he said there were very few people he'd cross the road for if he saw them on the other side. He didn't really want people to come home to dinner and so on. He liked just to be with us and his hobby was reading by himself. I think I've inherited a bit of that. I like to alternate, periods of sociability and periods of being by myself, I can't manage without both. I don't think I can think without being by myself but in order to think the right thoughts by myself I need to be in intense conversation with other people, maybe an hour before. So, I suppose, I hadn't really thought about this from the character side but yes, I'm sure I owe quite a lot to both of them.

AM: Turning to your schooling, you went to a Jesuit school. Which one?
PB: St. Ignatius, Stamford Hill, which is a grammar school so I started at eleven. And I had been at the prep school from nine. But of course, the Jesuits used to say, famously, 'Give me a boy at the age of seven and I'll make him into what the Order wants, what God wants' and so they missed out on me by two years. And

indeed, when we were 16 there was one of these Jesuit retreats, compulsory for all of us, which was just like the part of *Portrait of the Artist as a Young Man*,[3] complete with the hellfire sermon. When I read Joyce a year or two later, I just had that sense it was a rerun of my own life, because his Jesuit school, Clongowes Wood, was more fashionable than mine but absolutely the same tradition. I can remember they told us all, 'Pray to have a vocation to the priesthood' but they couldn't hear us so I prayed not to have a vocation to the priesthood.

AM: Would you say that, at any time, you really were deeply believing in the presence of a God or were you always sceptical? You've done a lot of work on scepticism and so on.

PB: I found the sceptical position to be attractive for a very long time, definitely from the sixth form onwards. I really enjoyed finding objections to the arguments that the Jesuits, like other intellectual Catholics, employed to demonstrate the existence of God. So, we learned Aquinas[4] as the truth, not as the history of philosophy. I still probably know the *Five Ways to Prove the Existence of God*[5] by heart. But of course, I couldn't resist making objections. And my teachers enjoyed this. Maybe if had been the Benedictines[6] or the Dominicans,[7] they would have disapproved of this but the Jesuits think that this is playing the game and they would find answers to my objections and we would enjoy ourselves. I think they always thought they'd win me over in the end but I don't know.

It was quite fun doing this and it went on in Oxford where I tried, formally, to leave the Church and was instantly visited by Jesuits and the Catholic chaplain himself. Not very intellectual, but a very charming upper–class Englishman Monsignor Valentine Elwes, like a figure straight out of Evelyn Waugh,[8] absolutely perfect specimen. Father Val also told one Jesuit and one secular priest to come and see me and convince me not to leave. The first was a very smooth Jesuit called Joe Christie, I never saw him again. The second a very serious, very small, very intense secular priest and the first thing he said as we went for a walk along the river to talk about religion, 'I could be in your position next year'. And he was called Anthony Kenny,[9] now better known as a Master of Balliol and a President of the British Academy, having left the priesthood not so many years after we had these conversations.

AM: Was there anyone, in your school, any teacher who particularly influenced you and sometimes there are one or more people who....
PB: I don't think so, but I ought to say I had a history Master who really did have ambitions for me. I suppose I don't think he had a big influence because I woke up one morning when I was seven and said to my mother, 'I'm going to be a Professor of History'. I'm not sure what I thought being a Professor of History meant. I'd heard of lectures, but had absolutely no idea, of course, of what a University was like. So, in that sense, I was sure I wanted to be a historian but Father O'Higgins, he put a lot of effort into making sure I did well at A Level and S Level. And there were only three of us in the class and finally, for S Level, I was the only person left. Later his superiors took him out of teaching and sent him to Campion Hall in Oxford, and for years he was a sort of research fellow there. Good but not all that good. He did a very decent monograph about the English Enlightenment. But he was serious about history and maybe, seeing for the first time, somebody who was serious in that way might have influenced me more than I ever thought at the time.

AM: You took History as your entrance for Oxford.
PB: That's right. My A Levels were English, History and Latin. I wanted French but it was on at the same time as Latin on the timetable. So that concession had to be made. But I never regretted having read a lot of English literature and criticism and written essays about John Donne[10] in the Sixth Form. I did the open scholarship at St John's, it seems, I can't quite believe it, 60 years ago this year. And of course, in that old–fashioned way, the candidates went and lived in the college for three days, taking exams and being interviewed.

AM: It can't be 1960?
PB: Well, 1954. But it would have been December.

AM: It's 50 years. 1954.
PB: You're right. Sorry, that's right. I'm going to sleep.

AM: You would have been a child prodigy....

PB: No, 17 and three months. The interviewers demanded to know how many months. They were quite interested by that sort of thing.

AM: Fifty years ago. And you got an open scholarship?

PB: Yes. I didn't expect to, because nobody from my school had done this and you know how it is, the hundred or two hundred students living in the college like undergraduates for three days. I remember sitting at dinner next to this incredibly confident public school boy and he was telling me all about how the system worked. I had no idea about it so I thought he would get in and I wouldn't. In fact, I got the scholarship and he was never seen again. And afterwards, I thought, why did he know so much about it? He'd probably done this thing three times because he'd failed twice.

AM: Were you at that time interviewed by Keith Thomas?[11]

PB: No. In '54, the interview was run by Costin[12] who had given up History to be the Senior Tutor and was going to go on to be the President of St John's, just as I got there. And a terribly shy, young–looking man, not quite as young as he looked, Howard Colvin,[13] who taught me medieval history, while really wanting not to teach that but the history of architecture which finally the university let him do. And of course, he had a second distinguished career writing about the history of 17th–18th century English architecture.

AM: You got the open scholarship but before you could take it up, you were enlisted into the great British Army.

PB: That's right. Because they actually said to me at the interview, 'What would you say if we offered you a scholarship on condition that you did National Service first?' And I said instantly, 'Apply to Cambridge'. And then afterwards, the Senior Tutor wrote me this letter which my father saw, 'We won't make this the legal requirement but I must insist that the wisest thing for you at this stage is to join the Army' and so I did.

And it was the wrong moment in the year, because I had a clear idea, if I'm going to be in the Army, I want to do the Russian course, I want to be sent to Germany and then I'd go to Oxford with two languages that I'd like to know and didn't know a word of. But I was going in in September, so that means the people who'd read modern languages all over the country were doing their deferred national service and had better qualifications than me. So, I missed out on all that and they decided to make a clerk of me.

I did basic training in Catterick[14] which was horrible but illuminating. It took me about twenty years to realize what the point was of some of the things that they made us do. I thought of it again after seeing the videos of what was happening in Iraq a few weeks ago because actually…yes, I think this is very interesting.… in the barracks, they were very keen on polishing boots and we were told that we had to appear on parade the next day with very brightly polished boots. We were issued with boots which were totally unpolished. We were then told, informally, that there's only one way to get the high polish. You burn it on with a spoon. You heat a spoon in the candle, you apply it to the black polish and it burns in. It destroys the waterproofing and it's forbidden. We were simultaneously told, get this result but the only means is forbidden. And so obviously, we all did it and we all said we didn't do it. And I thought this is totally absurd, I'm living in a kind of Dadaist world and years later I thought that maybe when an officer tells his men, 'Be gentle with the prisoners but just get them to talk', somehow, they would have learned the lesson.

And then I had clerks training and then I got posted, but this was my good fortune, to Singapore to be the Pay Clerk in a regiment of what the army called, in its bureaucratese, 'locally enlisted personnel'. Which meant Malays, meant Chinese, meant Indians, mainly Tamils, meant Anglo–Indians in the sense of mestizos, one Filipino that I can remember, anyway it was a wonderful ethnic mix. And the British, characteristically, only trusted the British with money so they needed not only the pay captain but the pay corporal to be English although we were assisted by Chinese clerks in the office. But I was the one that had to go to the bank with the pay captain to draw the regiment's weekly wages. This was great fun because it meant going into the Hong Kong and Shanghai Bank carrying a loaded sten gun. Actually, I didn't enjoy it as much as I should have done because I spent my time worrying about whether the magazine would fall out because

I was not terribly good at putting these things together, worrying whether I'd disgrace myself. But I did notice that when you got in with a loaded sten gun you got to the front of the queue very fast.

AM: You might have become a bank robber after that!

PB: That's right but I'd still be worrying about what was going to happen to the magazine! And that's when I really, effectively, was doing something like fieldwork without knowing. I think until I was 21, I had not come across the word 'anthropology'. Then I picked up a book by Evans–Pritchard,[15] not one of the famous ones, but a little introduction to the subject. And as I began to read his description of field work it suddenly clicked with me it's what I had really been doing for more than 18 months in Singapore District Signal Regiment because there wasn't much else for me to do. A boring job that didn't take very long to do and this fascinating mixture of people who looked different, who spoke differently, who had very different customs and I wanted to observe it and write it down in a notebook. It was a real culture shock. The really shocking bit of the shock was, I think, in the first week when I realized how corrupt the regiment was. I'd come straight from school. I wasn't used to things not working according to the rules and the officers didn't see anything. In the hours that they were in the regiment everything worked in the way that it was supposed to work but they went home to the officer's mess, at 4 or 5 in the afternoon and they didn't come back till 8 o'clock the next morning and the regiment was dramatically transformed while they were away. And there were so few British of the 'other ranks' as the army called us, that nobody put on any theatre in front of us.

So, take the stores. The quartermaster sergeant somehow faked the books so that large quantities of equipment ended up in the market in town which was known unofficially as the Thieves' Market, and if you lost a piece of equipment, you always replaced it there for a third of the price, rather than the official price. The drivers used to siphon the petrol out of the tank of the lorries and sell it and they managed to fake the routes. Several friends of mine were engaged in a protection racket so that the local Chinese restaurant was paying them a weekly sum not to have the windows smashed in.

But the best of all of these things was the racket of a tremendously dignified and elderly Indian, whose day job was delivering tea to the officers, which he did very well, with his staff. And for his night job, he simply rented out space in the regiment for civilians to sleep. And they had to be gone by 6 in the morning so that they were invisible to the authorities. I can't imagine how much rent he was getting in this way or how many years it went on. So, I suddenly realized, I was in a totally different world in these ways, it was not just the fact that the soldiers were all these different colours. The first day of arrival, all the British new arrivals, six of us, we were called in front of the Commanding Officer. And the CO made a little speech, a sermon really, which he must have done a lot of times. And he said, 'These are not black bastards, they are your brown brothers'. And in fact, there'd just been a scandalous incident, I think two weeks before we arrived. A kind of very small race riot because one of the Malays was playing the piano too loudly in the Malay bar, the NAAFI,[16] for the liking of one of the English. So, he went to the kitchen, helped himself to a slice of bacon, went and smeared it on the piano keys, thus effectively stopping piano playing for the evening. Well, of course there was a complaint and the CO had to sort it all out and so he added 'brown brothers' to his speech.

He even told us, this was a real preparation for anthropology, almost the only thing that he told us about life in the regiment was, 'Don't offer anybody anything with your left hand, don't accept anything with your left hand because the Malays think it's unclean'. And it was a regiment with four cookhouses and I was terribly tempted by the Malay one, obviously walking past and smelling the food. And then, I realized, of course, that there would be no knife and fork in there. And there were all the Malays, elegantly eating their rice and curry with one hand. And I think to myself, 'How many months would it take me to learn to do that? Will I ever learn to do that?' And the only time I saw that again was in Berlin because I was there the same year as André Béteille.[17] And his daughters came, and his wife, just once to see him. And because we'd become friends, he invited me and Maria Lúcia to dinner. And the daughters ate, again with great elegance, with their hands while the parents ate with us with a knife and fork. So that was my one big regret that I wasn't physically adaptable enough. I would have loved to have done it. The Malays would have found it great fun. They enjoyed having an Englishman asking about their customs all the time, they kept asking me if I was going to turn Muslim. Especially the day that I came with a souvenir I bought, one of these green velvet *songkoks*[18] and came back with it in a box which I revealed to everybody as I passed the guardroom and so they started making jokes about was I going to turn up at the mosque next Friday?

AM: Do you think all this experience, in a sense you've answered it, led into the fact that you are one of the few historians who really, seriously read anthropology and applied anthropology to your work and been interested in popular culture and so on? Was it this experience, do you think?

PB: It's what I now think. I didn't think about this at the time. I picked up an anthropology book, was instantly fascinated, started to read more without stopping to ask myself why am I so interested. But then thinking back, the books were describing situations which were recognizably like what I'd just been doing in Singapore. Well, not just, I had been in Singapore five years earlier. So, I started not with any kind of high theory but I started reading and applying ethnography and found it quite fascinating. And the thought even crossed my mind, would it be fun to read anthropology in Oxford afterwards and if so, I was sure I would do fieldwork either in Kelantan[19] or Terengganu[20] because I found the Malays such charming people. I'd visited these villages, I'd realized they were very hospitable, it would have been great fun to do fieldwork in such a place. I had a very easy rapport with all the Malays that I had met, there were about 400 of them in the regiment. One night when I was 'duty clerk' and had to stay in the office after hours, I went through all their files. Almost everybody had had one of two jobs. Rubber tappers, paddy planters joined the army when things were going badly. And when I complained to them about the food, I remember somebody saying to me, 'We've never had three meals a day before. Why are you complaining?' They thought the food in the army was absolutely wonderful.

AM: Well, perhaps we now ought to get back to Oxford. After this liberating experience you then went to Oxford to read history.

PB: The first week, I have to say, I went to see the Senior Tutor and said I want to study Chinese. And he said, 'If so, you'll lose your scholarship'. So, I though no more of it. But it would have been a temptation. I might have had a career, in fact, like Jonathan Spence.[21] A year older than me, he went to Cambridge and read history. Or Mark Elvin,[22] who was at Oxford not long after me and became, like Spence, a distinguished historian of China. But anyway, the next thing was my tutor asked, 'Do you want to do medieval history?' At school, the Middle Ages had been my enthusiasm (knights in armour, Gothic architecture, romances of chivalry, Froissart's chronicle…) but for some reason at that point I decided no, early modern.

AM: At that time, you had to do all history.

PB: You had to do English 1, 2 and 3. But for what they delightfully called foreign history, you could choose one of eight periods. And I think Howard Colvin expected me to choose the late middle ages and in fact I chose the 16th–17th centuries. And that meant, because this new young tutor had come to the college, I think he arrived a week before me from All Souls, Keith Thomas, it meant that he tutored me for European history as well as for English 2.

AM: Well, Keith is going to loom large at some point so perhaps…

PB: That's right. This is the cue.

AM: This is the cue. He was my DPhil supervisor too and I only met him at the end of my academic career. What was he like as an undergraduate teacher and later on?

PB: So, starting with 1958, he was quite shy, he was extremely earnest. There was no sign of the later famous irony and I remember first him telling everybody, 'History's become terribly professional'. He wanted everybody to work really hard, he encountered some resistance because half my year had been in the army for two years and they'd got used to not engaging in a lot of intellectual activity. And the other thing, I think, he had a very interesting way of giving every essay a social twist in the tutorials. He would set a perfectly conventional political history question and so we might then, from the book list, be inspired to give a very conventional political history answer, which up to a point was what he wanted but in the last ten or fifteen minutes he would open the thing up by saying 'But you could look at it this other way too' and it wasn't in the books or articles. And I later started to think, he was probably imitating his own tutor, the Balliol Marxist Christopher Hill.[23]

When I began giving tutorials (because Sussex began with the tutorial system with two students at a time), of course, I'd never done it before. How do you do it? You do it by imitating your own tutors. So, the first year I spoke like Keith and now I'm guessing that in his first year, he spoke like Christopher. Though Maria Lúcia's interviews contradicts this because Keith now claims, I don't know with what plausibility, that Christopher never said a word in tutorials.

AM: Several of the interviews say the same thing. About three or four of them say the same thing.

PB: Very intriguing that he got away with saying absolutely nothing.

AM: That's right. Nor suggesting anything.

PB: And then, there's the later Keith. So, when I was a graduate student and a kind of a restive critical graduate student, of the kind that was making a noise about what was wrong with both the undergraduate system and the graduate system, and Keith had just become the editor of the Oxford Magazine and asked me to write about it and so on. He also organized a few talks about history and something and Asa Briggs came and spoke on 'History and Sociology' and of course, Keith did 'History and Anthropology'. And that was an oral presentation of what would about two years later be the *Past and Present* 'History and Anthropology' article. So that meant I did know while I was still a graduate student at St. Antony's that Keith's interests had gone that way.

But what had impressed us as undergraduates was his article in the *Journal of the History of Ideas*, 'The Double Standard'. So, suddenly a whispering campaign went through the three years of undergraduate historians that our tutor, whom we thought was much more conventional than that, had published an article about men's attitude to women, all these kinds of things. And in this funny journal, the *Journal of the History of Ideas*, we didn't know that was a kind of history, with nothing to do with our weekly book lists. And this was true of Keith many years later, he would go on setting conventional history questions and giving people conventional history book lists while cultivating a kind of history that was very different, if not at odds with it. I've never compartmentalized in this way but interestingly, for whatever reason, and I still am not sure I know, Keith preferred for a long time to teach in one way and research in another.

AM: You are one of the great historiographers of history and if you had to place him, obviously there's still many things he may produce, but if you had to place him in the ranks of historians, thinking of the great historians you've written about, Febvre[24] and Bloch[25] and Braudel[26] and others, where would you place him?

PB: His style is much closer to Bloch than the others because the other two were both flamboyant. They even exaggerated what made them different from conventional historians. Bloch preferred understatement, he innovated without making so much of a fuss about it. Keith briefly made a fuss about it. I think he was invited to write that article for *Past and Present* and then he was asked to write the still more notorious article for the *Times Literary Supplement* about the new models and methods which I know annoyed Geoffrey Elton[27] so much. And after that, maybe as a result of the flak that he got on those occasions, he decided he was quietly going to renew history but not make a song–and–dance about doing it. So that's very much the Bloch style, *Le Rois Thuamaturges*, it's one of the most innovative books of history published anywhere in the 20th century. But it does not begin with any kind of manifesto whereas Lucien Febvre was always writing and rewriting manifestos. He also delivered the goods with the great *Rabelais* book and others so I'm not saying that he wasn't a real innovator.

And then, Trevor–Roper[28] was flamboyant in another way, not in the sense of saying that he wanted to write a new kind of history, though he was always sympathetic to *Annales* and he always had a European vision. But he liked to be flamboyant in his denunciations of his colleagues. Keith prefers the question, 'What do you think of X?' and then very quietly, 'you know I do think some of his or her work is a bit overrated'. No more than that. Trevor–Roper was my research supervisor and therefore, someone whom I heard a lot from. I think that's the best way to put it because we didn't have real conversations but he talked at me a lot. And it was just like his public performances. It was always denouncing people.

Actually, it is such a funny story how I came to have Trevor–Roper as a research supervisor, I think that ought to go on record as well. At that point, the Regius professor used to interview anybody that wanted to do historical research which meant almost entirely research in the History Faculty. In Oxford in 1960 you signed on immediately for D.Phil. Some people chose the B. Litt (including Bob Darnton) but there was relatively little interest in anything in between the BA and the doctorate. And so, I turned up and Trevor–Roper said, what did you want to do and I said I had a couple of early modern European topics in mind, one of which was the Jesuits. And then he said, got any supervisor in mind? And I said yes, Anne Whiteman,[29] and he said something to her disadvantage.

And then I said, well maybe John Stoye[30] and he said something to his disadvantage. At that point, two simultaneous thoughts occurred. One was that I could go through the whole history faculty and this man would then say something bad about everybody and simultaneously, I thought that for some reason he wants me to ask him to do it. Then I just said, well if you're interested...and the next moment, I found he was my supervisor. And that meant I saw him every term and he walked up and down the room delivering a lecture. It may or may not have been a real lecture for the day after. Queen Victoria complained about Mr Gladstone, 'he addresses me like a public meeting'. That was Trevor–Roper exactly. The whole rhetorical works and he never even looked at me. I think he always had a problem interacting with most people, maybe there were a few people who escaped from this, but he couldn't easily relate to people face to face. He had relatively few friends, he had a few disciples but I never wanted to be a disciple. So, at some point after he had treated me in a very friendly way as a patron to a client, I was getting a bit restive with that role and wanted to convert it to something a bit more egalitarian. But there was no space for that and we just drifted apart.

AM: Was that after you finished your D.Phil.?

PB: Well, I never finished the D.Phil. We stayed quite close until after I published an essay about Tacitism.[31] In what was basically commissioned as an article on the history of the enthusiasm for Tacitus in the 16th and 17th centuries and its influence on historical writing, I couldn't resist saying that I thought *The Last Days of Hitler* was written in the Tacitust tradition and of course Trevor–Roper was an ex–classicist. And he loved that and at that point, he was still regarding me as a good disciple but a year or two later, I suspected he discovered that I'd got involved with History Workshop and that was the end. Meeting Raphael Samuel[32] was one of the great formative experiences for me, after meeting Keith, after meeting Trevor–Roper, after meeting Arnaldo Momigliano[33] (to whom Trevor–Roper gave me an introduction but to whom I became much closer than to Trevor–Roper).

AM: Let's finish on those two then. If you had to put people into football divisions and the first division consisted of, well for me the first division of great historians would be Maitland,[34] some great universal thinkers, Tocqueville,[35] Montesquieu,[36] Montaigne,[37] these sort of people. Top of the next division are R.H. Tawney,[38] Namier,[39] these sort of people. Then there's a division below that. Where would you place Keith? Would you say he was kind of in the Namier–Tawney division?

PB: I put Namier well above Tawney though I feel that Tawney must have been a very much more sympathique person than Namier. I would put Keith above Tawney but well below Namier. I think Tawney wrote like an angel but was not any kind of real innovator historically. I think Namier made a major breakthrough, Keith certainly made a breakthrough. But for sheer intellectual power, that's a different criterion, where I think Trevor–Roper may be a tiny bit ahead of Keith, not a lot. But then the most intelligent people I have spoken to in my life, isn't it funny that two out of three are more philosophers than historians, Isaiah Berlin[40] with whom unfortunately I never got on all that well although I would have liked to have done. He didn't seem to approve of me. But he understood what you were saying before you got three words out and he would answer, so you never finished sentences because there was no need, so you could cover a lot of ground very fast. And Momigliano could do that though he only talked about what was on his mind at the time so you had to bluff him or pant to keep up because suddenly he bowled you a question about Thucydides[41] and you didn't want to seem stupid because you wanted to go on talking to him. And desperately you had to say something about Thucydides to keep the thing going. And the third one was Leszek Kołakowski,[42] whom I met very rarely but again there was that sense that you didn't really need many words to communicate.

AM: Momigliano, you said he influenced you and you were fond of him. Can you say anything more about his work and his influence on you?

PB: Maybe one sentence as a prologue to that is that I had meant to do research on the Jesuits in the Jesuit Archives in Rome and I thought I had set this up rather well because I realized a doctoral student doesn't simply write to the archivist of the Jesuits, not in those days, 1960, anyway, without an intermediary. I went to Campion Hall and Campion Hall produced a Spanish Jesuit whom I later met, a very gifted historian, a Catalan called Miguel Battlori and he wrote a letter to the archivist. And then I wrote. But even so, it wasn't good enough. I got a letter back in slightly wooden English saying, 'Father archivist is not happy with someone going to the archive for making thesis of doctorate'.

He was an Italian. I didn't know Italy. I'd been to Italy twice at this point but I didn't know Italian culture. And I misread the letter because, so I believe now, it was really an invitation to negotiate. It was saying no but saying no gently which means, if you turn up on my doorstep, we'll have a cup of coffee and I'll end up letting you in. But of course, I didn't want to be paying my airfare to Rome only to be turned away from the door of the archive and I was too literal–minded. I was reading the letter as if it was from an archivist in Britain where the rules are the rules and letters mean what they say, but I was going to work in a culture where the rules are not quite the rules and letters don't quite mean what they say.

I hadn't done the anthropology of Italy thoroughly enough so I needed a new subject and I went for the history of historical writing, which I was already extremely interested in. And I chose an anti–Jesuit as it happened, not to punish them, but just because I thought this was a wonderful historian, a Venetian called Paolo Sarpi[43] whom I continue to believe was one of the great historians of the 17th century on a level with Lord Clarendon. Trevor–Roper was certainly the only person in Oxford and maybe the only person in England at that time who would have known who Sarpi was and shared my particular enthusiasm. He had read the *History of the Council of Trent*. In that sense he was the right supervisor even if he wouldn't talk to me about what I was working on.

And that meant historiography because I realized (Trevor–Roper didn't think of it, I thought of it), that if you didn't study the reception of the ancient historians in the 16th and 17th centuries then you wouldn't understand what the great historians of the time were doing. I thought, who were the most read historians in the 16th–17th century Europe? Livy,[44] Tacitus, Sallust,[45] maybe Polybius.[46] Thucydides unfortunately a bit lower down on the list. So, I've got to study the translations and that's part of the background. And Sarpi is a Tacitust. When Trevor–Roper saw I was starting to go in that way, he said there's somebody in London you absolutely have to meet and that is Momigliano. So, I went to see Momigliano and we chatted and we stayed in touch. I took a liking to him. He took a liking to me. He was doing a lot of work at that time on the reception of the ancient historians, especially Tacitus. And we stayed in touch till the end of his life. Whenever I bumped into him, it was like continuing the same conversation for twenty years. And he always assumed you knew everything about whatever was in his head at a particular moment, which wasn't always true but we communicated enough. I think that maybe he's the greatest scholar that I've ever encountered, which is not quite the same thing as the most intelligent intellectual or maybe even the most innovative historian. I think all these categories are a little bit different. But anyway, I did find him immensely impressive.

Of course, I met Mom, as everyone called him, at the height of his powers. The problem with Keith is I met him when he was young and shy and unknown. It took me time to adjust to his becoming a great man. I think maybe I was even a little bit late to recognize this, though when *Religion and the Decline of Magic* came out in '71 and I reviewed it on the radio, I realized it was in the class of Lawrence Stone's[47] *Crisis of the Aristocracy* and Edward Thompson's[48] *The Making of the English Working Class*, the three big fat books which British historians have produced since 1960. I still hold by that judgement.

AM: You mentioned two people there, Edward Thompson and Lawrence Stone. Did you know either of them well or anything beyond reading their books?

PB: Lawrence, definitely. He was lecturing at Oxford and Christopher Hill and Lawrence Stone were *the* lecturers at Oxford for early modernists. And I never missed one. Stone was very histrionic and very self–dramatizing. Edward Thompson was somebody whose books I read and whom I never met, I think this is right, until that conference you organized and the famous occasion where he said 'I'm a Marxist empiricist' and Ernest Gellner, sitting next to him, replied, 'No you're not!' viewing the statement as a contradiction in terms'.

I did meet Thompson a few more times and would have loved to have known him better. Though he was a difficult character, he was a fascinating one. Could clearly be very charming, indeed I saw him being very charming but I heard about him being very difficult. Lawrence, I kept up with, and it was thanks to him that I got to Princeton because he went to that chair in Princeton, which Trevor–Roper characteristically commented to me, was 'the appropriately named Dodge Chair of History'. Lawrence obviously talked to people in the Institute of Advanced Study.

One of them was Felix Gilbert,[49] this very gifted German émigré historian who lived two intellectual lives. He wrote about the Italian Renaissance very well but he wrote about 20th century

Europe, especially Germany. And he had a chair at the Institute and I think he must have said to Lawrence he was looking for younger scholars to go to the Institute as visiting fellows. It was full of old men basically. And Lawrence mentioned my name but then I had to get references and of course, I had to get a reference from Trevor–Roper. I got such a funny letter back, 'I suppose you know Lawrence Stone is in Princeton. I do not know whether that would be an incentive to you or not'. So, I wrote back, saying I'm applying to the Institute, the person at the Institute whom I need to meet is Erwin Panofsky,[50] because I'm writing a book on the Renaissance and Panofsky is the most important person in the world for me to meet. I got the reference but I also got a sense of a certain cooling suspicion because Trevor–Roper guessed, absolutely rightly, that Lawrence had something to do with the invitation.

When I went to Princeton, I used to shuttle between the Institute and the Firestone library, where I was doing the research, and the history department where there were tremendous graduate seminars. I think the first week I was in Princeton Tom Kuhn[51] came to talk to the graduate students in history and there was something like that every week. The best tradition of the American–style graduate seminar, so that was an education in itself.

Edward Thompson, was an intellectual influence because like so many people in the early 60s, especially Oxford historians who were interested in any kind of history that wasn't political, I was very interested in Marx and very sympathetic to Marx though no kind of 'ist'. I spent a lot of time in St. Antony's reading Marx and Weber.[52]

That was another education. It's not only people who influence you, it's environments. St John's, Oxford was a great environment for relatively conventional history and also the Oxford history faculty at that point. But it wasn't such a good idea, I think, to do research in your own old undergraduate college because middle common rooms at this point, 1960, were only just starting up. I thought I'd have the sensation, if I stayed with St John's, of outstaying my time, my friends had gone down and that sort of thing.

Anyway, it was good to be funded and Keith said why don't you try St. Antony's because they've got those senior scholarships they give out, £450 a year compared to my open scholarship of £350, a hundred pounds that in those days really made a difference. And so, I found myself in this college where most people were studying the 20th century and very few people came from Britain. In fact, there was even a division in the college fellowship, what should St Antony's do and James Joll[53] at that point had the idea, first of all, however strong the emphasis on the 20th century it should always be complemented by having a few people in the college with other interests. Let's be a bit like those more rounded older colleges. And secondly, although it's absolutely right to have all these people from outside, let's take in three or four Oxford graduates every year if only so that they can explain British culture and Oxford culture to people who have just appeared from Budapest, Tel Aviv, Dar es Salaam and Tokyo. And that environment was very important to me. My best friend was Ecuadorian, Juan Maiguashca, I'm still in touch with him so many years later, and he had come straight from Paris where he'd been a pupil of Pierre Chaunu.[54] I had an intellectual interest in Annales and I was meeting somebody who was a foreigner on the fringe of that famous group, it was very exciting.

The whole atmosphere was very continental, people were not afraid to talk about philosophy over dinner, not like St. John's, maybe any Oxford college. Maybe Worcester was like this. You didn't talk about that sort of thing at dinner, maybe you went and had coffee in somebody's room and you had a serious conversation but at dinner you ought to be just talking politely to your neighbour and not intensely about whatever the latest idea was. So, St. Antony's was a revelation that there's another culture of conversation around and I gravitated to Mediterranean or Latin people. You might count South Americans because of the Spanish tradition. So that environment was very important.

On Marxism, everybody at St Antony's seemed to be into social theory and I was reading Marx and Weber and then I opened the lecture list and there was a word in it I didn't understand. 'Alienation'. It looked interesting and this was a seminar which also looked interesting because it was a joint sociology and philosophy seminar organized by Iris Murdoch[55] and Norman Birnbaum.[56]

I turned up and of course, Oxford seminars are different from Cambridge seminars because at Oxford seminars, there is a very great risk that if you turn up the first week, you'll be giving a paper later in the term. The two teachers announced the topic and gave the introduction and then they grabbed people in the audience and made them give papers. And I'm not very good at saying no to things. By the fourth or fifth week, I was giving a paper on the concept of alienation in the context of recent American sociological studies of factory workers and Norman Birnbaum provided the bibliography. That was the deal, he gave you the reading. This was a fascinating moment, I read a book, the author of which I forget because it doesn't really matter, it was called *The Man on the Assembly Line.*[57] The book was really interesting to me, it wasn't what the sociologist said so much as the long quotations from interviews.

The worker says to the interviewer, 'I don't like it here because they treat the men here like the machines'. I quoted this. And then, at the end Norman says, 'Why did you choose that book? I gave you a choice of six books and then you did a report entirely on one'. And I said because it was the only one where you heard the voices of the people that were being studied, rather than just the voice of the person studying. And I still remember a couple of people laughing and Norman saying, 'You shouldn't laugh because this is absolutely crucial in sociology. You really have to listen to people talking'. He had an ethnographic approach to sociology at a time when some sociologists were working from questionnaires and statistics and so on.

II

AM: In the ancestral lineage, Keith Thomas was your teacher and Keith's teacher was Christopher Hill. Did you come across Christopher much?

PB: Quite a bit. I asked him to talk to the college history society. This was a typical way in which you get to know a leading historian in another college and he was absolutely charming. I continued to see quite a bit of him on and off. He was invited to Sussex when I was in Sussex in the early days. When he became Master of Balliol, I wrote a letter to congratulate him. He had a marvellous postcard that he sent me, he said he hoped that Brighton in the Broad would live up to the tradition of Balliol by the Sea. But I don't think I continued to get so much from him intellectually. As a Marxist, he was never as interesting as Eric Hobsbawm[58] or Edward Thompson because they were more creative with the concepts. He was a man deeply learned in 17th century England. He was also a Marxist but he didn't develop his Marxism at all. He just stuck with it and so his work came to seem less interesting. My admiration for him is above all, as a person. I think he was a wonderful choice as Master of Balliol.

AM: Both Christopher and Keith were in the tradition of what Trevor–Roper described as 'thin trickles of text through lush meadows of footnotes'. Not so much, but basically, they were great quoters of thousands of pamphlets and so on. Did either of those people influence you in the way you actually wrote and studied history, by using quotations or not?

PB: I don't think so, that is, I think there were so many historians before them who had used quotations effectively and I never had a moment of sudden discovery that a few quotations together would tell a story very well, so you'd hardly need to intervene. It's still a great challenge and a great pleasure to manage the quotations. I like quotations which bounce off one another and each of them modifies your perception of the other one, the placing and so on. And I certainly have never gone in for footnotes on a Thomasian scale, maybe that was the fault of my apprenticeship with Trevor–Roper who took these things much more lightly and used to make jokes about ponderous people and long footnotes, despite his admiration for Gibbon.[59]

AM: This is possibly a point to ask you about your writing methods. I've seen samples of your writing. Do you write with a typewriter, a computer? What's your traditional method and how much do you change things and redraft?

PB: Ever since 1985, I've written on the computer, as soon as I got one. I found that it was easier to write on the disk than it was to write on paper and now I constantly revise. I like to pick up a subject, work on it, drop it for a week or two, do something else, come back to it. I also like to drop a subject for years and then come back to it. I'm working on a couple of articles now, one of them was a paper at Oxford in 1970, I never felt I'd got it quite right. On various occasions I have taken it up again. Now, in memory of Roy Porter, another good friend and colleague, a lovely man,[60] I think I can actually send the thing off. Definitely returning to things, elaborating things, occasionally dropping things but usually just another layer of encrustation. And before the computer, I was literally a scissors and paste person. I typed, I didn't write, I typed it and then I didn't like it but I thought I could use some of it again so I would cut it up, and really, I did have a big glue pot. But the problem with scissors and paste, you may remember, is that you get the glue on the desk and then you have the bits of paper sticking to the desk, sticking to one another. The move to metaphorical 'cut and paste' has been a real liberation for me.

AM: And do you like writing?

PB: Yes, especially any draft after the first. And also, this goes back to school, sentences come in my head as I'm walking and I always have to have a little notepad. It's very peculiar, completely formed sentences emerge in the way that poems do for poets. Of course, I've got to write all the other sentences. The great thing is, read a book or be writing notes, do something intensely, then stop, go for a walk and then the unconscious just throws up something. I don't know how long it would have taken me to find it but I'm just given it. It's just great luck.

AM: Do you regularly go for walks while you're working?

PB: The best system of all that I've found is, this is another curious thing, that writing is a good start for research rather than simply the end product. Only when I start to write about something do I discover what I really need to know. I write in the morning, throwing up a whole list of queries. Cambridge is wonderful for this, I walk to the University Library, on walking to the University Library I stop two or three times because a sentence has come. In the library I try to solve all the questions that came up in the morning. Next morning, insert these passages, rewrite, go on a bit, new questions, go back to the library the next afternoon. For me, it's an absolutely ideal system with the most intense activity being the writing when I'm freshest in the morning while I've got a bit more patience in the afternoon to go through the books and let people tell me things in their own time, as authors will. I don't work very much in the evening. It's funny, different people have very different rhythms.

AM: The other person, or school, which you are very much associated with is the Annales School in France. How did you come in touch with them and particularly with the work of Braudel?

PB: Definitely while I was an undergraduate, I'd found Braudel's *Méditerranée* and read it and was already enthusiastic about it before I took schools. I think Braudel was the first person where Keith used this famous technique and I remember him saying, I think Braudel's rather overrated, don't you? And to this day, I cannot work out whether that was because he thought that or whether he was just trying me out or what. But anyway, that incident fixes in my mind exactly when I was reading it.

Then I went to other people from Braudel's footnotes and I went back to Febvre to whom the book was dedicated and found that despite the over–flamboyant style (at least for me, for most English people), he was saying really exciting things. I did think as a graduate student that it might be interesting to go and work with Braudel but I never did. The Jesuits would have been okay because there is a piece in the *Méditerranée* where he talks about their role in Philip II's takeover of Portugal and I'd come across a book written by a Portuguese Jesuit which managed to demonstrate the contrary. I thought of sending Braudel a note, did he know that a particular statement in a particular paragraph of the great book had been undermined by this piece of research. I think that such a note would have intrigued him, coming from a graduate student and that I would at least have been invited to go and call on him if I was in Paris.

But maybe it was a good thing not to go. He's a powerful intellectual presence at a distance. When I did meet him, I once interviewed him for the BBC and afterwards I met him a few times, he's such a powerful personality that the danger would be of being taken over, becoming a Braudelian in a groupie sort of way. Just as I didn't want to be a Marxist but wanted to learn from Marx, I wanted to learn from Braudel but not be any kind of Braudelian. Trevor–Roper was helpful there because of all British historians in 1960, he was probably the most openly sympathetic to Annales without ever belonging to the school or anything like that.

For many years now, I have at least tried to approach things by asking the big Braudelian questions, things about connections. In other words, 'total history', not in the sense of absolutely every detail but total history in the sense that you look at every domain of human behaviour and you always ask if each of them has made an impact on all the others. And also, Braudel's stress on the *longue durée*. Even if you are studying 10 or 50 years, always place them in the larger context. However big your topic, it can always be put in a still bigger context, in space or time, that's what I've learned from him.

I've had fun teaching in the Cambridge supervision system. For one week, you give people an essay on the Ottoman Empire and they write about the times the Turks invaded central Europe but of course, there are other times the Turks didn't. Then you ask them, have they any explanation of why there were moments when a particular Sultan is trying to capture Vienna or Belgrade and other times not? Is it just aggressive and unaggressive Sultans? Wouldn't it be a good idea to look at the Ottoman Empire's eastern frontier? Of course, we don't know so much about the history of Persia but enough to know that sometimes the Turks were on the defensive. Sometimes, as a parting shot, I'd say, 'Well, maybe one ought to know what's happening on the eastern frontier of the Persian Empire as well'. And I never would have said that if it hadn't been for reading Braudel.

AM: Let's move on from Oxford now to Sussex. When did you go to Sussex and what was it like?

PB: I'm very proud to be able to say that I went in 1962, that is, I arrived while they were laying the dining hall floor. We were in these prefabricated huts on the edge of the campus because the Arts Building wasn't ready on time. There was the real sense that we were starting something which was terribly exciting, and also the sense there is no tradition in this place, we are going to have to make a tradition now, that's also a good experience for a historian. The second meeting of the School of European Studies, somebody already quoted the first meeting as a precedent. I should have written it in a diary but I remember thinking, this is how historical traditions get created. It was a great liberation.

I applied for the job because I'd heard Asa Briggs[61] talk about history and sociology at this series of Oxford lectures and he'd happened to remark casually that all this kind of interdisciplinary thing, that was just what was going to be institutionalized at the University that was going to start in the following October. I actually wrote to him and said, 'Are there going to be any jobs' and he sent me a postcard saying advertisements will be in three months' time. I duly applied and got the job.

There was this challenge to invent new courses because all the people senior to me were trying to invent new courses themselves and they had no time to tell the assistant lecturers what to do. There were so many of us aged 25, fresh from being graduate students and research fellows and all were allowed to do our own thing. And then the chances for collaboration, on one side with sociology and on the other side with literature, also with philosophy if I wanted, were enormous and I benefitted to a very great degree. I would have been very happy to collaborate a bit with anthropology but the first professor was Freddie Bailey[62] and he caught me one day with Malinowski[63] under my arm, I'd just got it out of the university library. He grinned and said, 'You know, we anthropologists don't believe in that stuff anymore' which was a little bit of telling somebody' no trespassing', I think, though he did it in a very nice way. 'You people won't understand that we've got our own development' and so on.

Sociology, I think, sociology is more like a city maybe and anthropology more like a village or a tribe, sociologists thought I could just as well teach sociology as anybody else if I wanted. And of course, Asa in particular, being a historian, thought that I could do it. And right from the first year I was teaching a course in sociological theory. That's how I learned it actually, week by week reading the textbooks. Helped by the fact that Norman Birnbaum, in whose seminar I had given the Oxford paper, he'd volunteered to write me an extra reference for the Sussex job just to tell Asa that I had given a paper about sociology. It must have been quite competitive, that job, I don't know who else was in for it, and maybe being given a fourth unsolicited reference was just the thing that made the difference. Anyway, the sense then that it was permissible to invade other people's disciplines, that there were people who would welcome you into learning about theirs, that they would teach a joint seminar with you, it was wonderful to have that support when I was branching out in these ways.

I'm equally grateful for the fact that Cambridge was the opposite when I arrived in 1979. And it was like standing in the cold shower. You had to justify every borrowing from another discipline in the history faculty because by that time, I had got the confidence but maybe I was a little uncritical of the interdisciplinary approach. So, to be forced to justify to these people why I'd spent all this time reading books written by people in other disciplines, that was quite good as well.

AM: Were there any people in Cambridge, obviously Geoffrey Elton springs to mind, were there others who were forcing you to explain?
PB: Oh yes, especially when I and Bob Scribner, who was a very close colleague for a few years while he was in Cambridge, we set up this course called Historical Anthropology and of course it had to go through the faculty board. And the faculty board kept sending it back, they would find some very trivial reason for sending it

back but it was happening too often, so of course, we smelt a rat. Derek Beales[64] was opposed to it on principle so one year, when he wasn't in the chair, the chairperson asked me to come to a meeting to explain what I wanted to do with this new paper. Derek didn't say anything on that occasion, it was too embarrassing for him to have a confrontation like that. And then the faculty board sent me such a funny note that it was fine to teach this course, I quote, 'as long as there was no theory in it.' So, of course, we said yes and of course, we took no notice and it was a course that the students really loved and it ran for six years and I'm very happy to have had the chance to teach it. At that point in the 80s, although there was the opposition in the faculty, there were other lecturers who said, 'Well, why don't you let them have a go? These are two trained historians, they're not going to be unhistorical, maybe the students will find it fun'. And those colleagues won.

AM: The other cold shower which affected you when you came to Cambridge was Emmanuel College. Can you say something about that?

PB: That's right and to be fair, it wasn't a colder shower than most colleges would have been because it was and remains a very friendly place but it was still a culture shock coming from Sussex, where everything was informal and we had a rather informal kind of lifestyle. So much so that I'm not sure that I even owned a tie in 1979. I know I got married in one but I'm not sure whether I'd kept it. I either wore open neck shirts in the summer or polo necks in the winter. I arrive in Emmanuel and I start dining and I notice out of the corner of my eye that other people are wearing ties but I don't object to other people wearing ties so I thought no more about it. And to the credit of the college, nobody complained the whole term and then there's this annual meeting of the 'parlour' which is a slightly larger group than the SCR , and they pass a resolution reaffirming the good old custom that gentlemen dining in the evening, clergy excepted, should wear ties. But we were all sent a copy of this, they didn't send anything especially to me so I thought that was such a very gentle reminder that I was prepared to conform whereas if I'd been told you have to wear a tie, I might have reacted like Wittgenstein[65] and given up dining, because he had that problem, I remember, with Trinity College in the 1930s. There were so many little customs, sometimes exasperating but sometimes just fascinating, that I started to take notes. And it was a way of coping with the culture shock to pretend that I was the anthropologist and write everything in my notebook. Some younger colleagues knew I was doing it and if someone in the governing body said something very stupid, somebody else might whisper in my ear, 'Put it in your notebook!'

I didn't really think more of this until in 1982 there was a conference on art history in Italy and there was Bourdieu[66] who was working on art at the time but also on higher education. When he heard that I was from Cambridge, he had all these questions. He wanted to know, how does the university work? In the course of all this, I somehow found myself telling him, 'Well, I've got field notes on the college'. He roared with laughter and he said, 'Choose any name you like. I'll publish this in the *Actes de la Recherche en Science Sociale*'.

I took him very literally and in about a week I just wrote an article and signed it 'William Dell'[67] and called it 'St. Dominic's: Notes towards the Ethnography of a Cambridge College'. This was so that real Cambridge insiders would know which place I was writing about because Emmanuel, as you know, is on the site of the Dominican Friars in Cambridge. And William Dell was once a Fellow of Emmanuel who was asked to give the university sermon. He was a hero of Christopher Hill's actually who wrote an article about him because Dell gave the university sermon in front of the Vice Chancellor in full regalia but spoke against 'gowns, hoods, tippets and such like anti–Christian forms and follies' and also against the use of Latin in the university. Dell was a real radical Puritan of the kind that Oliver Cromwell[68] and Christopher Hill loved.

Actually, Cromwell took him out of Emmanuel and made him Master of Caius but he was ejected at the Restoration of Charles II in 1660 and went to a country living in Bedfordshire. The first thing he did was ask John Bunyan[69], who was of course not a member of the Church of England, to preach from his pulpit. So right down to the end of his life Dell liked doing unconventional things, so I thought that was a nice nom–de–plume. So, there it is, it's had a great life as a form of samizdat among graduate students. But Cambridge, being, like England in a sense, so much a culture of the implicit, I could not tell whether some of my conservative colleagues knew about this article or not. I suppose I shall never know.

AM: Returning to another person I know has influenced you a lot, how was it that you came across Raphael Samuel and what influence has he had on your work?

PB: Yes, Raph I met in Oxford in 1964, when I had a term's leave and was thinking of getting back to my doctoral dissertation. At that point, he was very interested in the history of religion and popular religion and he was starting a series of graduate seminars. There was Gill Thomas, not yet Gill Sutherland and there was Gareth Stedman Jones[70] and there was a very quiet young man who, as I remember, didn't say anything in the seminars but he still came every week, Roderick Floud.[71] There might have been another couple of people, I've forgotten. We had a very informal series of seminars where I talked about Jansenism and John Walsh[72] came and talked about Methodism. And Raph about the 19th century and so on. He was one of the most charismatic people I've ever met and after Edward Thompson, the one who did most, I think, to give working class history a kind of epic quality. When he spoke about it, it just sounded like the most important subject in the world.

We kept up ever since because in Sussex, which was oriented towards the history of the 19th and 20th centuries, I couldn't do research. I used to go twice a week to the British Museum which was where the British Library still was and kept bumping into Raph in the round reading room. And we would go out to lunch and talk and so on. That lasted years and years, he was kind of an elder brother figure because he was always encouraging me to do things. He wanted me to be more committed to the Left and he was always greeting me with fist clenched though I never really got around to doing this in return. He used to organize these incredible Ruskin conferences which by the early 70s I remember somebody in *The Guardian* said had the atmosphere of the small pop festival. And there was this conference on 'Childhood and history and children's liberation'. And because I was interested in the ideas of Philippe Ariès,[73] who was after all part of the Annales, and Raph knew this, he asked me to give the talk about whether childhood has a history. Was it invented in France in the 17th century, as Aries claimed, and what can it mean to say this?

I remember a couple of small children crawling on to the platform and of course, in such an atmosphere nobody was ever going to pick them up. So, I went on lecturing while surrounded by small children. There was another conference about socialist history which was very interesting and at some point, I remember saying (we had to kind of confession where we were speaking from), so I said I was a socialist and a historian but I wasn't a socialist historian because I didn't think that history could be written from just one point of view. And an elderly trade unionist got up and said, 'You mean we ought to write history from the boss's point of view?' Those seminars at Oxford and the big workshops made an impact but above all in this case it was Raphael's personality and seeing history from below that impressed me. Maybe I wouldn't have written that book on popular culture in the 70s if I hadn't become a great friend of Raph's in the 60s.

AM: The other person who was very dynamic and who was a great writer in the same league as yourself is Roy Porter. Did you ever meet Roy?

PB: Well, I didn't meet him till the late 70s. I was asked to speak to a student history society, actually, the Emmanuel History Society, not knowing that I was later going to have a connection with that college. They wanted me to give a talk on some general subject and I said history of mentalities. Should there be a history of mentalities? And so, I gave the talk and there was this youngish man, shirt wide open and his hair all over the place and he asked the first question about what do I think about the relation to mentalities and ideology and this turns into a kind of conversation rather than just me answering the question and he seems very sympathique and I got to talk to him afterwards and that was Roy. A very few years later we started to collaborate and I forget how many books we both contributed to, even the ones we edited together add up to three or four let alone the ones we wrote chapters for. He was nearly 10 years younger than me, but very much pursuing within British history the kind of approach I was trying to pursue for European history.

AM: Which perhaps takes us to the last question. If you had to summarize what you think the question behind your work, the major questions behind your work have been, what are you really seeking for? It's a very difficult summarization but in two or three minutes could you outline that?

PB: The two very big historical problems I have been wrestling with almost all my life, one is about how far there is a European history, that is, how much there's a common culture for all those countries. I never wanted to think of Europe as just Western Europe, I wanted to study it from Galway to the Urals. I suppose it's really for a psychoanalyst to answer this rather than oneself, but I've come to think of this as trying to bring my two pairs of grandparents together since they came from the western and eastern edges of Europe and so in some sense so do I, and so to be a whole person, I have to try to look at Europe as a whole.

The other question that emerged relatively early for me was the history and theory one. Surely if sociologists, anthropologists and, later, so I started to think, geographers and political scientists as well, have insights into human behaviour, then they must be relevant to history. If they're true we've got to use them and maybe the best way of testing them is to try to use them in history because almost all the social science concepts are coined in the context of the present, somewhere or other. So, if you take them back a couple of centuries, you're always asking, Is this theory a key that only fits one particular lock or is this some kind of master key that might open more locks. I do think that historians have got quite a useful function in this debate, even though we steal so many concepts from our colleagues in the social sciences, but give them so very few concepts in return. The one thing we can do is always this testing in a new set of circumstances, which is quite a harsh but quite a valuable test for any concept to go through. I suppose those are the two big things that I've been trying to do through doing smaller things all my working life.

AM: The last question really, recently you've married a Brazilian. I wondered if you wanted to say something about Maria and about Brazil, which you're going off to after a time.

PB: It's hard to make it a short question. I suppose again, trying to stand outside and look at myself from outside, I've always been drawn to Latin cultures. I was very excited to start working on Italy by doing the Italian Renaissance special subject when I was an undergraduate. And I took to the country instantly and then to Spain as well. And then when somebody arrived in my college to invite me to lecture in Brazil, I both found that individual captivating and was deeply attracted by the idea of getting to know Brazil. And that was Maria Lúcia whom I happened to meet on Emmanuel soil because she came with this suggestion that I give a course of lectures in São Paulo. Discovering her and discovering São Paulo and discovering Brazil have become mixed up together, an unending thing, this discovery. And I remember trying to see Brazil as a kind of Italy, an enormous and even more chaotic sort of Italy, and also seeing that in some ways this analogy didn't work because of the huge spaces of a country in the Americas. And then of course, discovering that Maria Lúcia's family is about as culturally mixed as mine because she's Spanish on one side, Italian on the other, yet speaks Portuguese, a combination that is a very typical Brazilian sort of thing.

So, between us, we are quite a mixture. Her father was an immigrant. My grandparents were immigrants and in Brazil they take it for granted that everyone is an immigrant. The first question they ask you is 'Where you're from?' Then you say Britain and they ask, 'Where's your family from?' The assumption that it's going to be somewhere else, I find this very refreshing. And thanks to Singapore and thanks to Italy, I was already adjusted to the idea that the apparent rules may not be the real rules or as the Brazilians love to put it, the distance between the legal country, *país legal,* and the real place, *país real,* can be quite a big distance.

AM: Well, I think on that nice Brazilian note, we sadly ought to end. But I want to thank you very much indeed, Peter. Interviewing you, I almost felt at times I was interviewing myself. Our experience and interests and ways of looking at things are so very similar. It was a particular pleasure. So, thank you very much indeed.

PB: Well, thank you for giving me the chance.

NOTES

1. Wikipedia. 2020. https://en.wikipedia.org/wiki/Peter_Burke_(historian)
2. Mieczysław Moczar (1913–86) was Polish Communist leader and organizer. As a leader of the underground resistance during World War II, he was noted for his skill in fighting the German secret police. https://www.britannica.com/biography/Mieczyslaw–Moczar
3. *A Portrait of the Artist as a Young Man* is the first novel of Irish writer James Joyce. A Künstlerroman written in a modernist style, it traces the religious and intellectual awakening of young Stephen Dedalus, Joyce's fictional alter ego, whose surname alludes to Daedalus, Greek mythology's consummate craftsman. Stephen questions and rebels against the Catholic and Irish conventions under which he has grown, culminating in his self–exile from Ireland to Europe. The work uses techniques that Joyce developed more fully in *Ulysses* (1922) and *Finnegans Wake* (1939). https://en.wikipedia.org/wiki/A_Portrait_of_the_Artist_as_a_Young_Man
4. Thomas Aquinas (1225–74) was an Italian Dominican friar, philosopher, Catholic priest, and Doctor of the Church. An immensely influential philosopher, theologian, and jurist in the tradition of scholasticism, he is also known within the latter as the *Doctor Angelicus* and the *Doctor Communis*. https://en.wikipedia.org/wiki/Thomas_Aquinas
5. The Quinque viæ (Latin for 'Five Ways') (sometimes called 'five proofs') are five logical arguments for the existence of God summarized by the 13th–century Catholic philosopher and theologian St. Thomas Aquinas in his book *Summa Theologica*. https://en.wikipedia.org/wiki/Five_Ways_(Aquinas)
6. The Benedictines, officially the Order of Saint Benedict, are a monastic order of the Catholic Church following the Rule of Saint Benedict. They are also sometimes called the Black Monks, in reference to the colour of their religious habits. They were founded by Saint Benedict of Nursia, a 6th–century monk who laid the foundations of Benedictine monasticism through the formulation of his Rule of Saint Benedict. https://en.wikipedia.org/wiki/Benedictines
7. The Dominican Order, formally known as the Order of Preachers is a mendicant order of the Catholic Church founded in France by the Spanish

priest Saint Dominic. It was approved by Pope Honorius II via the Papal bull Religiosam vitam on 22 December 1216. Members of the order, who are referred to as Dominicans, generally carry the letters OP after their names, standing for Ordinis Praedicatorum, meaning of the Order of Preachers. https://en.wikipedia.org/wiki/Dominican_Order

8. Arthur Evelyn St. John Waugh (1903–66) was an English writer of novels, biographies, and travel books; he was also a prolific journalist and book reviewer. His most famous works include the early satires *Decline and Fall* (1928) and *A Handful of Dust* (1934), the novel *Brideshead Revisited* (1945), and the Second World War trilogy, *Sword of Honour* (1952–61). He is recognized as one of the great prose stylists of the English language in the 20th century. https://en.wikipedia.org/wiki/Evelyn_Waugh

9. Sir Anthony John Patrick Kenny, FBA (b. 1931) is an English philosopher whose interests lie in the philosophy of mind, ancient and scholastic philosophy, the philosophy of Wittgenstein and the philosophy of religion. With Peter Geach, he has made a significant contribution to analytical Thomism, a movement whose aim is to present the thought of St. Thomas Aquinas in the style of analytic philosophy. He is one of the executors of Wittgenstein's literary estate. He is a former President of the British Academy and the Royal Institute of Philosophy. https://en.wikipedia.org/wiki/Anthony_Kenny

10. John Donne (1572–1631) was an English poet, scholar, soldier and secretary born into a Catholic family, a remnant of the Catholic Revival, who reluctantly became a cleric in the Church of England. He was Dean of St Paul's Cathedral in London (1621–31). He is considered the preeminent representative of the metaphysical poets. His poetical works are noted for their metaphorical and sensual style and include sonnets, love poems, religious poems, Latin translations, epigrams, elegies, songs, and satires. He is also known for his sermons.

11. Keith Thomas, see Part I, p. 3.

12. William Conrad Costin, MC (1893–1970) was President of St John's College, Oxford from 1957 to 1963. Costin was educated at Reading School and St John's College, Oxford. He served in the Great War with the Gloucestershire Regiment. He was Proctor of Oxford University in 1935. He wrote: *Great Britain and China, 1833–1860* (1937); *The Law and Working of the Constitution: Documents, 1660–1914*, (1952); and *History of St John's College, 1598–1860*, (1958). https://en.wikipedia.org/wiki/William_Costin_(academic)

13. Howard Colvin, see Appendix.

14. Catterick Garrison is a major garrison and military town 3 miles (5 km) south of Richmond, North Yorkshire, England. It is the largest British Army garrison in the world. https://en.wikipedia.org/wiki/Catterick_Garrison

15. Sir Edward Evan Evans–Pritchard, FBA (1902–73) known as E.E. Evans–Pritchard, was a British anthropologist who was instrumental in the development of social anthropology. He was Professor of Social Anthropology at the University of Oxford from 1946 to 1970. https://en.wikipedia.org/wiki/E._E._Evans–Pritchard

16. The NAAFI is a place where people eat and buy small items.

17. André Béteille (b. 1934) is an Indian sociologist and writer. He is well known for his studies of the caste system in South India. https://en.wikipedia.org/wiki/Andre_Beteille

18. The songkok or peci or kopiah is a cap widely worn in Brunei, Indonesia, Malaysia, Singapore, the southern Philippines and southern Thailand, most commonly among Muslim males. https://en.wikipedia.org/wiki/Songkok

19. Kelantan is a state of Malaysia. It is located in the north–eastern corner of the peninsula. https://en.wikipedia.org/wiki/Kelantan

20. Terengganu is a sultanate and constitutive state of federal Malaysia. The state is also known by its Arabic honorific, D ru l– m n ('Abode of Faith'). https://en.wikipedia.org/wiki/Terengganu

21. Johnathan Spence, see Appendix.

22. Mark Elvin, see Appendix.

23. Christopher Hill, see Appendix.

24. Lucien Febvre, see Appendix.

25. Marc Bloch, see Appendix.

26. Fernand Braudel, see Appendix.

27. Geoffrey Elton, see Appendix.

28. Hugh Trevor–Roper, see Appendix.

29. Anne Whiteman was History Tutor of Lady Margaret Hall (LMH) from 1946 to 1985. https://www.history.ox.ac.uk/anne-whiteman

30. John Stoye (1917–2016) was a British scholar and historian who specialized in Renaissance Europe. His seminal work, *The Siege of Vienna: The Last Great Trial between Cross and Crescent*, was originally published in 1965 as *The Siege of Vienna*, garnered new critical attention in 2000 with an updated and revised edition, and another in 2006. https://www.encyclopedia.com/arts/educational–magazines/stoye–john–1917

31. Tacitism, Tacitus, see Appendix.

32. Raphael Samuel, see Appendix.

33. Arnaldo Momigliano, see Appendix.

34. Frederic Maitland, see Appendix.

35. Alexis de Tocqueville, see Appendix.

36. Montesquieu, see Appendix.

37. Montaigne, see Appendix.

38. R.H. Tawney, see Appendix.

39. Lewis Namier, see Appendix.

40. Isaiah Berlin, see Appendix.

41. Thucydides, see Appendix.

42. Leszek Kołakowski (1927–2009) a Polish philosopher, a critic of the Communist regime who was invited to leave the country in 1966 and moved to the USA and then to Britain.

43. Paolo Sarpi, see Appendix.

44. Titus Livius, Livy (59/64–17 AD) with Sallust and Tacitus, one of the three great Roman historians. His history of Rome became a classic in his own lifetime and exercised a profound influence on the style and philosophy of historical writing down to the 18th century. https://www.britannica.com/biography/Livy

45. Gaius Sallustius Crispus, Sallust (86 BC–35/34 BC) was a Roman historian and one of the great Latin literary stylists, noted for his narrative writings dealing with political personalities, corruption, and party rivalry. https://www.britannica.com/biography/Sallust

46. Polybius (200 BCE–c. 118) was a Greek statesman and historian who wrote of the rise of Rome to world prominence. https://www.britannica.com/biography/Polybius

47. Lawrence Stone, see Appendix.

48. Edward Thompson, see Appendix.

49. Felix Gilbert, see Appendix.

50. Erwin Panofsky, see Appendix.

51. Tom Kuhn, see Appendix.

52. Max Weber, see Appendix.

53. James Joll, see Appendix.

54. Pierre Chaunu, see Appendix.

55. Dame Jean Iris Murdoch, DBE (1919–99) was an Irish and British novelist and philosopher. Murdoch is best known for her novels about good and evil, sexual relationships, morality, and the power of the unconscious. Her first published novel, *Under the Net*, was selected in 1998 as one of

Modern Library's 100 best English–language novels of the 20th century. https://en.wikipedia.org/wiki/Iris_Murdoch

56. Norman Birnbaum (1926–2019) was an American sociologist. He was an emeritus professor at the Georgetown University Law Center, and a member of the editorial board of *The Nation*. https://en.wikipedia.org/wiki/Norman_Birnbaum

57. *The Man on the Assembly Line* by Charles R. Walker and Robert H. Guest was published in 1952 by Harvard University Press.

58. Eric Hobsbawm, see Appendix.

59. Edward Gibbon, see Appendix.

60. Roy Sydney Porter, FBA (1946–2002) was a British historian known for his important work on the history of medicine. He retired in 2001 as the director of the Wellcome Institute for the History of Medicine at University College London (UCL). https://en.wikipedia.org/wiki/Roy_Porter

61. Asa Briggs, see Appendix.

62. Freddie Bailey, see Appendix.

63. Bronisław Malinowski, see Appendix.

64. Derek Beales, see Appendix.

65. Ludwig Wittgenstein, see Appendix.

66. Pierre Bourdieu, see Appendix.

67. William Dell (c. 1607–69) was an English clergyman, Master of Gonville and Caius College, Cambridge from 1649 to 1660, and prominent radical Parliamentarian. https://en.wikipedia.org/wiki/William_Dell

68. Oliver Cromwell (1599–1658) was an English general and statesman who led the Parliament of England's armies against King Charles I during the English Civil War and ruled the British Isles as Lord Protector from 1653 until his death in 1658. He acted simultaneously as head of state and head of government of the new republican commonwealth. https://en.wikipedia.org/wiki/Oliver_Cromwell

69. John Bunyan (1628–88) was an English writer and Puritan preacher best remembered as the author of the Christian allegory *The Pilgrim's Progress*. In addition to *The Pilgrim's Progress*, Bunyan wrote nearly sixty titles, many of them expanded sermons. https://en.wikipedia.org/wiki/John_Bunyan

70. Gareth Stedman Jones, see Appendix.

71. Roderick Floud, see Appendix.

72. John Walsh, see Appendix.

73. Philippe Ariès, see Appendix.

Appendix
Biographical Information
(in alphabetical order)
Compiled by Radha Béteille

PHILIPPE ARIÈS (1914–84)

Ariès was a French medievalist and historian of the family and childhood, in the style of Georges Duby. He wrote many books on the common daily life. His most prominent works regarded the change in the western attitudes towards death.

Ariès regarded himself as an 'anarchist of the right'. He was initially close to the Action française but later distanced himself from it, as he viewed it as too authoritarian, hence his self-description as an 'anarchist'. Ariès also contributed to *La Nation française*, a royalist review. However, he also co-operated with many Left-wing French historians, especially with Michel Foucault, who wrote his obituary.

Ariès is likewise remembered for his invention of another field of study: the history of attitudes to death and dying. Ariès saw death, like childhood, as a social construction. His seminal work in this ambit is *L'Homme devant la mort* (1977), his last major book, published in the same year when his status as a historian was finally recognised by his induction into the École des hautes études en sciences sociales (EHESS), as a directeur d'études. https://en.wikipedia.org/wiki/Philippe_Ariès

ARISTOTLE (384–322 BC)

Aristotle was a Greek philosopher and polymath during the Classical period in Ancient Greece. Taught by Plato, he was the founder of the

Lyceum, the Peripatetic school of philosophy, and the Aristotelian tradition. His writings cover many subjects including physics, biology, zoology, metaphysics, logic, ethics, aesthetics, poetry, theatre, music, rhetoric, psychology, linguistics, economics, politics, and government. Aristotle provided a complex synthesis of the various philosophies existing prior to him. It was above all from his teachings that the West inherited its intellectual lexicon, as well as problems and methods of inquiry. As a result, his philosophy has exerted a unique influence on almost every form of knowledge in the West and it continues to be a subject of contemporary philosophical discussion. https://en.wikipedia.org/wiki/Aristotle

ASSER (DIED C. 909)

Asser was a Welsh monk from St David's, Dyfed, who became Bishop of Sherborne in the 890s. About 885 he was asked by Alfred the Great to leave St David's and join the circle of learned men whom Alfred was recruiting for his court. After spending a year at Caerwent because of illness, Asser accepted.

In 893, Asser wrote a biography of Alfred, called the *Life of King Alfred*. The manuscript survived to modern times in only one copy, which was part of the Cotton library. That copy was destroyed in a fire in 1731, but transcriptions that had been made earlier, together with material from Asser's work which was included by other early writers, have enabled the work to be reconstructed. https://en.wikipedia.org/wiki/Asser

GERALD EDWARD AYLMER, FBA (1926-2000)

Aylmer was an English historian of 17th century England. Gerald Aylmer was the only child of Edward Arthur Aylmer, from an Anglo-Irish naval family, and Phoebe Evans. A great-uncle was Lord Desborough. Educated at Beaudesert Park School and Winchester College, he went up to Balliol College, Oxford for a term before volunteering for the Navy, where he was a shipmate of George

Melly. Returning to Balliol, he was tutored by Christopher Hill. He graduated in 1950, spent a year at Princeton University as a Jane Eliza Procter Visiting Fellow, and completed his thesis, 'Studies on the Institutions and Personnel of English Central Administration, 1625–42' (1954) as a Junior Research Fellow at Balliol. The thesis, in two volumes, was 1208 pages long: The Modern History Board subsequently introduced a word-limit.) https://en.wikipedia.org/wiki/Gerald_Aylmer

FREDERICK GEORGE BAILEY (1924–2020)

Bailey who published professionally as 'F.G. Bailey' and was known to friends and students as 'Freddie', was a British social anthropologist who spent the second half of his career in the United States at the University of California, San Diego (UCSD). He received his PhD in social anthropology from Manchester University, working under Max Gluckman, and is closely associated with the Manchester School of social anthropology. A prolific writer of some sixteen books in anthropology, he is probably best known for his studies of local and organizational politics. https://en.wikipedia.org/wiki/F._G._Bailey

DEREK EDWARD DAWSON BEALES, FBA (B. 1931)

Beales is a British historian. He has written the definitive work on the Holy Roman Emperor Joseph II.

He was educated at the University of Cambridge, where he gained a BA in 1953, an MA and a PhD in 1957. He was appointed a Fellow of Sidney Sussex College, Cambridge in 1955 and a University Lecturer in History in 1965, which he held until 1980. He was then Professor of Modern History at Cambridge until 1997.

He was editor of *The Historical Journal* from 1971 until 1975. From 1984 until 1987 he was a member of the council of the Royal Historical Society. In 1989 he was elected a fellow of the British Academy. https://en.wikipedia.org/wiki/Derek_Beales

SIMONE LUCIE ERNESTINE MARIE BERTRAND DE BEAUVOIR (1908–86)

Beauvoir was a French writer, intellectual, existentialist philosopher, political activist, feminist and social theorist. Though she did not consider herself a philosopher, she had a significant influence on both feminist existentialism and feminist theory.

Beauvoir wrote novels, essays, biographies, autobiographies and monographs on philosophy, politics, and social issues. She was known for her 1949 treatise *The Second Sex*, a detailed analysis of women's oppression and a foundational tract of contemporary feminism; and for her novels, including *She Came to Stay* and *The Mandarins*. Her most enduring contribution to literature are her memoirs, notably the first volume, 'Mémoires d'une jeune fille rangée' (1958), which have a warmth and descriptive power. She was also known for her open, lifelong relationship with French philosopher Jean-Paul Sartre. https://en.wikipedia.org/wiki/Simone_de_Beauvoir

MAX BELOFF, BARON BELOFF, FBA, FRHISTS, FRSA (1913–99)

Beloff was a British historian and Conservative peer. From 1974 to 1979 he was principal of the University College of Buckingham, now the University of Buckingham.

In 1990 Lord Beloff was one of the leading historians behind the setting up of the History Curriculum Association. The Association advocated a more knowledge-based history curriculum in schools. It expressed 'profound disquiet' at the way history was being taught in the classroom and observed that the integrity of history was threatened. https://en.wikipedia.org/wiki/Max_Beloff,_Baron_Beloff

ISAIAH BERLIN (1909–97)

Berlin was a naturalised British philosopher, historian of ideas, political theorist, educator, public intellectual and moralist, and essayist. He was renowned for his conversational brilliance, his defence of liberalism and pluralism, his opposition to political extremism and intellectual fanaticism, and his accessible, coruscating writings on people and ideas.

His essay *Two Concepts of Liberty* (1958) contributed to a revival of interest in political theory in the English-speaking world, and remains one of the most influential and widely discussed texts in that field: admirers and critics agree that Berlin's distinction between positive and negative liberty remains, for better or worse, a basic starting point for discussions of the meaning and value of political freedom.

Later in his life, the greater availability of his numerous essays began to provoke increasing interest in his work, particularly in the idea of value pluralism; that Berlin's articulation of value pluralism contains many ambiguities and even obscurities has only encouraged further work on this rich and important topic by other philosophers. https://plato.stanford.edu/entries/berlin/

MARC LÉOPOLD BENJAMIN BLOCH (1886–1944)

Bloch was a French medieval historian, editor, and Resistance leader known for his innovative work in social and economic history.

In 1929 Bloch and his senior colleague, Lucien Febvre, founded the *Annales d'histoire économique et sociale*, a journal dedicated to overcoming disciplinary and national boundaries and promoting a more human, accessible history. After a modest start in the tumultuous 1930s, the *Annales* achieved prominence after World War II and gave its name to an influential international school of historical research. During the Great Depression, when bolshevism, fascism, and Nazism threatened Europe, Bloch summoned historians to transcend racial and ideological formulas, engage in comparative, collaborative, and transnational projects, and use the tools of the social sciences to sharpen and expand their critical skills.

Published in 1949, *The Historian's Craft* is Bloch's best-known and most accessible work. It is both a valuable guide to historical methodology and a stirring statement of a scholar's civic responsibility. After the Nazis occupied all of France, he joined the French Resistance in 1943 and became a leader. Captured by the

Vichy police in March 1944, Bloch was tortured by Gestapo chief Klaus Barbie and killed by a German firing squad. https://www. britannica.com/biography/Marc-Bloch

PIERRE BOURDIEU (1930–2002)

Bourdieu was a French sociologist, anthropologist, philosopher and public intellectual. Bourdieu's major contributions to the sociology of education, the theory of sociology, and sociology of aesthetics have achieved wide influence in several related academic fields (e.g. anthropology, media and cultural studies, education), popular culture, and the arts. During his academic career he was primarily associated with the School for Advanced Studies in the Social Sciences in Paris and the Collège de France. https://en.wikipedia. org/wiki/Pierre_Bourdieu

FERNAND BRAUDEL (1902–85)

Braudel was a French historian and a leader of the Annales School. His scholarship focused on three main projects: *The Mediterranean* (1923–49, then 1949–66), *Civilization and Capitalism* (1955–79), and the unfinished *Identity of France* (1970–85). His reputation stems in part from his writings, but even more from his success in making the Annales School the most important engine of historical research in France and much of the world after 1950. As the dominant leader of the Annales School of historiography in the 1950s and 1960s, he exerted enormous influence on historical writing in France and other countries. He was a student of Henri Hauser (1866–1946).

Braudel has been considered one of the greatest of the modern historians who have emphasized the role of large-scale socioeconomic factors in the making and writing of history. He can also be considered as one of the precursors of world-systems theory. In his works Braudel shows a revolutionary change of focus in the craft and analysis of history from individuals or events to world systems. https://en.wikipedia.org/wiki/Fernand_Braudel

ASA BRIGGS, BARON BRIGGS (1921–2016)

Briggs was an English historian. He was a leading specialist on the Victorian era, and the foremost historian of broadcasting in Britain. Briggs achieved international recognition during his long and prolific career for examining various aspects of modern British history. He was made a life peer in 1976. https://en.wikipedia.org/wiki/Asa_Briggs

MICHAEL GEORGE BROCK, CBE, FRHISTS, FRSL (1920–2014)

Brock was a British historian who was associated with several Oxford colleges during his academic career. He was Warden of Nuffield College, Oxford from 1978 to 1988.

Brock continued after 1948 at Corpus Christi College until 1966, serving as a junior research fellow, senior tutor, proctor, librarian, and dean. He then became Deputy President to Sir Isaiah Berlin at Wolfson College, a new graduate college at Oxford. He held a visiting professor position at the Hebrew University in Jerusalem, Israel. https://en.wikipedia.org/wiki/Michael_Brock

JAMES CAMPBELL, FBA (1935–2016)

Campbell was a British historian with a particular interest in the Medieval period and Anglo-Saxon studies. He studied at Lowestoft Grammar School, where he found an interest in history. He took early entry to Magdelen College, Oxford, at the age of 17 and graduated with a first in 1955. The following year he took up a Junior Research Fellowship at Merton College. By 1957, at the age of 22, he became a Fellow at Worcester College, University of Oxford, where he served as the University's Senior Proctor for 1973–74. He remained at Worcester College until his retirement in 2002. Campbell's particular interest in the Medieval period and Anglo-Saxon studies. Although he never published a book himself, Campbell was the editor of *The Anglo-Saxons* (1982), a collection of essays on Anglo-Saxon England, for which he wrote the section on the period from AD 350 to 660. He was elected as a Fellow of the British Academy in 1984. https://en.wikipedia.org/wiki/James_Campbell_(historian)

PIERRE CHAUNU (1923-2009)

Chaunu was a French historian. His specialty was Latin American history; he also studied French social and religious history of the 16th, 17th, and 18th centuries. A leading figure in French quantitative history as the founder of 'serial history', he was professor emeritus at Paris IV-Sorbonne, a member of the Institut de France, and a commander of the Légion d'Honneur. A convert to Protestantism from Roman Catholicism, he defended his Gaullist views most notably in a longtime column in Le Figaro and on Radio Courtoisie.

Chaunu had an important impact on historiography, whether with regard to quantitative history, his studies of Latin America, or the social and religious history of France during the Ancien Régime. https://en.wikipedia.org/wiki/Pierre_Chaunu

RICHARD CHARLES COBB, CBE (1917-96)

Cobb was a British historian and essayist, and professor at the University of Oxford. He was the author of numerous influential works about the history of France, particularly the French Revolution. Cobb meticulously researched the Revolutionary era from a ground-level view sometimes described as 'history from below'.

Cobb is best known for his multi-volume work *The People's Armies* (1961), a massive study of the composition and mentality of the Revolution's civilian armed forces. He was a prolific writer of essays from which he fashioned numerous book-length collections about France and its people. Cobb also found much inspiration from his own life, and he composed a multitude of autobiographical writings and personal reflections. Much of his writing went unpublished in his lifetime, and several anthologies were assembled from it by other scholars after his death. https://en.wikipedia.org/wiki/Richard_Cobb

SIR HOWARD MONTAGU COLVIN, CVO, CBE, FBA, FRHISTS, FSA (1919–2007)

Colvin was a British architectural historian who produced two of the most outstanding works of scholarship in his field: *A Biographical Dictionary of British Architects, 1600–1840* and *The History of the King's Works*.

Born in Sidcup, Colvin was educated at Trent College and University College London. In 1948, he became a Fellow of St John's College, Oxford where he remained until his death in 2007. He was a member of the Royal Commission on the Historical Monuments of England 1963–76, the Historic Buildings Council for England 1970–84, the Royal Fine Art Commission 1962–72, and other official bodies.

Yale University Press produced a third edition of *A Biographical Dictionary of British Architects, 1600–1840* in 1995, and he had just completed his work on the fourth edition at the time of his death. On first publication this reference work of heroic scale immediately became the standard in its field: it 'changed the face of English architectural history', according to David Watkin. In the revised edition, Colvin expanded the range to include Scottish and Welsh architects as well. The work includes every building within its time range with which the name of an architect can be associated, based on documentary evidence from extensive archival research, both by him and a growing network of correspondents. He was particularly an enemy of attributions based on style alone. This resulted in an index that is an architectural gazetteer, and which also gives a comprehensive listing of architectural books published in Britain, listed by author.

Colvin was knighted in 1995. He served as president of the Society of Architectural Historians of Great Britain 1979–81; and a special issue of their journal *Architectural History* was produced in his honour in 1984. https://en.wikipedia.org/wiki/Howard_Colvin

WILLIAM CONRAD COSTIN, MC (1893–1970)

Costin was President of St John's College, Oxford from 1957 to 1963. He was educated at Reading School and St John's College,

Oxford. He served in the Great War with the Gloucestershire Regiment. He was Proctor of Oxford University in 1935. He wrote: *Great Britain and China, 1833–1860* (1937); *The Law and Working of the Constitution: Documents, 1660–1914* (1952); and *History of St John's College, 1598–1860* (1958). https://en.wikipedia.org/wiki/William_Costin_(academic)

MARTIN JAMES DAUNTON, FRHISTS, FBA (B. 1949)

Daunton is a British academic and historian. He was Master of Trinity Hall, Cambridge, between 2004 and 2014.

Daunton is the son of Ronald James Daunton and Dorothy née Bellett. He was educated at Barry Grammar School before going to the University of Nottingham where he graduated with a Bachelor of Arts degree in 1970. He studied further at the University of Kent PhD 1974 and received the degree of LittD from the University of Cambridge in 2005. https://en.wikipedia.org/wiki/Martin_Daunton

SIR GEOFFREY RUDOLPH ELTON, FBA (1921-94)

Elton was a German-born British political and constitutional historian, specialising in the Tudor period. He taught at Clare College, Cambridge, and was the Regius Professor of Modern History there from 1983 to 1988.

Elton elaborated on his ideas in his 1955 work, the bestselling *England under the Tudors*, which went through three editions, and his Wiles Lectures, which he published in 1973 as *Reform and Renewal: Thomas Cromwell and the Common Weal*.

His thesis has been widely challenged by younger Tudor historians and can no longer be regarded as an orthodoxy, but his contribution to the debate has profoundly influenced subsequent discussion of Tudor government, particularly on the role of Cromwell.

Elton was a staunch admirer of Margaret Thatcher and Winston Churchill. He was also a fierce critic of Marxist historians, who he argued were presenting seriously flawed interpretations of the past.

In particular, Elton was opposed to the idea that the English Civil War was caused by socioeconomic changes in the 16th and 17th centuries, arguing instead that it was largely due to the incompetence of the Stuart kings. Elton was also famous for his role in the Carr–Elton debate when he defended the 19th century interpretation of empirical, 'scientific' history most famously associated with Leopold von Ranke against E.H. Carr's views. Elton was also a strong defender of the traditional methods of history and was appalled by postmodernism. https://en.wikipedia.org/wiki/Geoffrey_Elton

JOHN MARK DUTTON ELVIN (B. 1938)

Elvin is a professor emeritus of Chinese history at Australian National University, specializing in the late imperial period. He is also emeritus fellow of St Antony's College, Oxford. He is noted for his high-level equilibrium trap theory to explain why an Industrial Revolution happened in Europe but not in China, despite the fact that the state of scientific knowledge was far more advanced in China much earlier than in Europe. Essentially, Elvin proposed that pre-industrial production methods were extremely efficient in China, which obviated much of the economic pressure for scientific progress. At the same time, a philosophical shift occurred, where Taoism was gradually replaced by Confucianism as the dominant intellectual paradigm, and moral philosophy and the development of rigid social organization became more important than scientific inquiry among intellectuals. https://en.wikipedia.org/wiki/Mark_Elvin

LUCIEN PAUL VICTOR FEBVRE (1878–1956)

Febvre was a French historian best known for the role he played in establishing the Annales School of history. He was the initial editor of the Encyclopédie française together with Anatole de Monzie.

Febvre's first thesis on Philip the Second and the Franche-Comté, published in 1911, showed the strength of this approach. In this work, Febvre reconstructed the life of villagers and town dwellers in a small traditional province in France by contextualizing historical events in terms of the geography and environment of the times.

Another influential work of Febvre dealt with Protestantism. Published in the *Revue Historique* in 1929, 'Une question mal posée' attempted to study popular religion by trying to observe and quantify human behavior.

As time went by, Febvre grew increasingly suspicious of theology. He refused to see people as bound by forces beyond their control. He came to the view that religion and old ways of thinking were impractical, maybe even dangerous, in modern times.

In 1929, Lucien Febvre, along with his colleague and close friend Marc Bloch, established a scholarly journal, *Annales d'histoire économique et sociale* (commonly known as the Annales), from which the name of their distinctive style of history was taken. The journal followed Febvre's approach to describing history. Its approach was to educate the world about the dangers of old-world thinking to avoid possible future economic and political disasters. Its purpose was to influence academic circles to 'study ... the present so as to reach a profounder understanding of the past'. This journal was like no other scholarly publication at that time.

The *Annales* was met with a very favorable critical reception and was very successful in its early years. It was in such demand that it was able to increase the frequency of its publications in 1932. However, in 1938 the journal appeared to be running its course and the publishers ceased their support. https://en.wikipedia.org/wiki/Lucien_Febvre

SIR RODERICK CASTLE FLOUD, FBA (B. 1942)

Floud is an economic historian and a leader in the field of anthropometric history. He has been provost of the London Guildhall University, vice-chancellor and president of the London Metropolitan University, acting dean of the School of Advanced Study at the University of London, and provost of Gresham College (2008–14). He is the son of Bernard Floud, M.P.

As well as his professional academic career, Floud is a leading economic and social historian. He was one of the first people in

Britain to apply statistics and computing to the study of economic history, and he was also a leader in the field of anthropometric history, the study of changes in human heights and weights. His D.Phil. thesis, later published as *The British Machine Tool Industry, 1850–1914* made use of econometric analysis and he soon published *An Introduction to Quantitative Methods for Historians* and other books and articles on computing and statistics in history. He has recently taken up an entirely new field, the economic and social history of British gardening. His book on this topic was published by Allen Lane in November 2019.

Floud has been the editor of 4 editions of what is now *The Cambridge Economic History of Modern Britain*, the leading university textbook on the topic. He has also published books and articles on higher education, part-time students, access to university courses and the regulation of universities. https://en.wikipedia.org/wiki/Roderick_Floud

DAVID LLOYD GEORGE, 1ST EARL LLOYD-GEORGE OF DWYFOR, OM, PC (1863–1945)

Lloyd George was a Welsh statesman who served as Prime Minister of the United Kingdom from 1916 to 1922. He was the final Liberal to hold the post of Prime Minister, but his support increasingly came from the Conservatives who finally dropped him.

Lloyd George was a first language Welsh speaker, born on 17 January 1863 in Chorlton-on-Medlock, Manchester, to Welsh parents. He was raised in Wales from around 3 months old, first briefly in Pembrokeshire, and then in Llanystumdwy, Carnarvonshire. He is so far the only British Prime Minister to have been Welsh and to have spoken English as a second language. His father, a schoolmaster, died in 1864 and he was raised in Wales by his mother and her shoemaker brother, whose Liberal politics and Baptist faith strongly influenced Lloyd George; the same uncle helped the boy embark on a career as a solicitor after leaving school.

Lloyd George became active in local politics, gaining a reputation as an orator and a proponent of a Welsh blend of radical Liberalism which championed nonconformism and the disestablishment of the Anglican church in Wales, equality for labourers and tenant farmers, and reform of land ownership. In 1890, he narrowly won a by-election to become the Member of Parliament for Caernarvon Boroughs, in which seat he remained for 55 years. https:// en.wikipedia.org/wiki/David_Lloyd_George

EDWARD GIBBON, FRS (1737-94)

Gibbon was an English historian, writer and Member of Parliament. His most important work, *The History of the Decline and Fall of the Roman Empire*, was published in six volumes between 1776 and 1788 and is known for the quality and irony of its prose, its use of primary sources, and its polemical criticism of organised religion. https://en.wikipedia.org/wiki/Edward_Gibbon

FELIX GILBERT (1905-91)

Gilbert was a German-born American historian of early modern and modern Europe. Gilbert was born in Baden-Baden, Germany to a middle-class Jewish family, and part of the Mendelssohn Bartholdy clan. In the latter half of the 1920s, Gilbert studied under Friedrich Meinecke at the University of Berlin. Gilbert's area of expertise was the Renaissance, especially the diplomatic history of the period. He was a fellow of the Institute for Advanced Study in Princeton from 1962 to 1975, and maintained an active involvement as an emeritus faculty member until his death in 1991.

The main reading room of the German Historical Institute in Washington, D.C. is named in his honor. https://en.wikipedia.org/wiki/Felix_Gilbert

SIR HROTHGAR JOHN HABAKKUK (1915-2002)

Habakkuk was a British economic historian. Habakkuk was born in Barry, Vale of Glamorgan, Wales, the son of Evan and Anne Habakkuk. He was named 'Hrothgar' after Hroðgar in Beowulf, which his father was reading at the time of his birth. However, he came to be known as John when he started to travel to the United States, and when he was knighted he found it easier to call himself 'Sir John' than 'Sir Hrothgar'. His surname was assumed by a seventeenth-century forebear after the prophet Habakkuk, it being a Welsh custom at that time to take patronymics from the Bible.

He was educated at Barry County School and St John's College, Cambridge (scholar and Strathcona Student, starred first class degree in History 1936). (He was not, as sometimes erroneously stated, connected with Jesus College, Cambridge). He began to study for a PhD under John Clapham, but his progress was interrupted by the Second World War. In 1938, he was elected a Fellow of Pembroke College, Cambridge, a position he held until 1950. He worked in the Foreign Office 1939–42 and the Board of Trade 1942–46, during which period he still found time to carry out research at the Public Record Office and in the archives of country houses. After World War II, he was from 1946 until 1950 Director of Studies and Librarian of the college and Lecturer in the Faculty of Economics. In 1973, Pembroke College elected him to an Honorary Fellowship. From 1950 until 1960, he was editor, with Michael Postan, of *The Economic History Review*. https://en.wikipedia.org/wiki/John_Habakkuk

JOHN EDWARD CHRISTOPHER HILL (1912–2003)

Hill was an English Marxist historian and academic, specialising in 17th-century English history. From 1965 to 1978 he was Master of Balliol College, Oxford.

After graduating, he became a fellow of All Souls College. In 1935, he undertook a ten-month trip to Moscow, Soviet Union. There he became fluent in Russian and studied Soviet historical scholarship, particularly that relating to Britain.

Hill returned to Oxford University after the War to continue his academic work. In 1946, he and many other Marxist historians formed the Communist Party Historians Group. In 1949, he applied to be the chair of History at the newly created Keele University, but was turned down because of his Communist Party affiliations. He helped create the journal *Past and Present* in 1952, that focused on social history.

Many of Hill's most notable studies focused on 17th-century English history. His books include *Puritanism and Revolution* (1958), *Intellectual Origins of the English Revolution* (1965 and revised in 1996), *The Century of Revolution* (1961), *AntiChrist in 17th-century England* (1971), *The World Turned Upside Down* (1972) and many others.

He retired from Balliol in 1978 when he took up a full-time appointment for two years at the Open University. He continued to lecture thereafter from his home at Sibford Ferris, Oxfordshire. https://en.wikipedia.org/wiki/Christopher_Hill_(historian)

THOMAS HOBBES (1588–1679)

Hobbes's current reputation rests largely on his political philosophy, was a thinker with wide-ranging interests. In philosophy, he defended a range of materialist, nominalist, and empiricist views against Cartesian and Aristotelian alternatives. In physics, his work was influential on Leibniz, and led him into disputes with Boyle and the experimentalists of the early Royal Society. In history, he translated Thucydides' *History of the Peloponnesian War* into English, and later wrote his own history of the Long Parliament. In mathematics he was less successful, and is best remembered for his repeated unsuccessful attempts to square the circle. But despite that, Hobbes was a serious and prominent participant in the intellectual life of his time. https://plato.stanford.edu/entries/hobbes/

ERIC JOHN ERNEST HOBSBAWM, CH, FRSL, FBA (1917–2012)

Hobsbawm was a British historian of the rise of industrial capitalism, socialism and nationalism. A life-long Marxist, his socio-political convictions influenced the character of his work. His best-known works include his trilogy about what he called the 'long 19th century' (*The Age of Revolution: Europe 1789–1848*, *The Age of Capital: 1848–1875* and *The Age of Empire: 1875–1914*), *The Age of Extremes* on the short 20th century, and an edited volume that introduced the influential idea of 'invented traditions'. https://en.wikipedia.org/wiki/Eric_Hobsbawm

PATRICIA LESLEY HOLLIS, BARONESS HOLLIS OF HEIGHAM, PC, DL NÉE WELLS (1941–2018)

Hollis was a Labour member of the House of Lords of the United Kingdom. She was educated at Plympton Grammar School, at Girton College, Cambridge (BA), the University of California and Columbia University, New York (both where she was Harkness Fellow from 1962 to 1964), and at Nuffield College, Oxford (MA, DPhil). While in the United States, Hollis was active in the civil rights movement, picketing segregated restaurants and helping hold voter registration drives in Mississippi.

She was a lecturer in modern history, reader and Dean at the University of East Anglia in Norwich from 1967 until 1990. She served as a National Commissioner for English Heritage from 1988 until 1991. https://en.wikipedia.org/wiki/Patricia_Hollis,_Baroness_Hollis_of_Heigham

DAME OLWEN HUFTON, DBE, FBA, FRHISTS (B. 1938)

Hufton is a British historian of early modern Europe and a pioneer of social history and of women's history. She is an expert on early modern, western European comparative socio-cultural history with special emphasis on gender, poverty, social relations, religion and work. Since 2006 she has been a part-time Professorial Research Fellow at Royal Holloway, University of London.

Hufton's academic career began as a lecturer at the University of Leicester from 1963 to 1966. From Leicester she moved to the University of Reading, where she taught for more than twenty years; and then to Harvard, where from 1987 to 1991 she was the University's first Professor of Modern History and Women's Studies. After four years in America, she returned to Europe in 1991 to become Professor of History and Civilisation at the European University Institute in Florence. Six years later, in 1997, she returned to Britain to become Leverhulme Professor of History at Oxford. She retired in 2003, and is now Fellow Emeritus of Merton College. In 2006 she joined Royal Holloway as a part-time Professorial Research Fellow in the History Department. https://en.wikipedia.org/wiki/Olwen_Hufton

JAMES BYSSE JOLL, FBA (1918-94)

Joll was a British historian and university lecturer whose works included *The Origins of the First World War and Europe since 1870*. He also wrote on the history of anarchism and socialism.

was educated at Winchester, the University of Bordeaux and New College, Oxford. He left to join the British Army in 1940, eventually serving in the Special Operations Executive. He returned to Oxford after World War II, completed his studies, and became an instructor there. He was a Fellow and Tutor in Politics from 1947 until 1950. He then transferred to St Antony's College. In 1955 he met the painter and art historian John Golding; the two men formed a long relationship which lasted until Joll's death.

While at Oxford, Joll wrote a book on the *Second International* (1955) and a book on Léon Blum, Walter Rathenau, and Filippo Tommaso Marinetti, called *Intellectuals in Politics* (1960). In 1964 he published *The Anarchists*, which showed his intertwined interests in the culture, events, political philosophy, and individual personalities forming the history of a Leftist movement.

In 1967 Joll left St Antony's, Oxford to teach at the London School of Economics, as the Stevenson Professor of International History. His best known work was *Europe since 1870: An International History*, which appeared in 1973. He returned to biography in 1977, with his book on Italian Marxist intellectual Antonio Gramsci; he was elected a Fellow of the British Academy in the same year. Several prizes in the Department of International

History at the London School of Economics remain named in his honour. Later, he gave refuge to Anthony Blunt, Golding's colleague at the Courtauld Institute and former teacher, after Blunt's exposure as a former Soviet spy, for which Joll was attacked in the press.

Following his retirement in 1981, he became Emeritus Professor of the University of London. https://en.wikipedia.org/wiki/James_Joll

GARETH STEDMAN JONES, FBA (B. 1942)

Jones is an English academic and historian. As Professor of the History of Ideas at Queen Mary, University of London, he deals particularly with working-class history and Marxism.

Educated at St Paul's School and Lincoln College, Oxford, where he graduated in history in 1964, Stedman Jones went on to Nuffield College, Oxford to take a DPhil in 1970.

He moved to Cambridge in 1974, becoming a Fellow of King's College, Cambridge, and in 1979, a lecturer in history. He was a research fellow at Nuffield College, Oxford from 1967 to 1970, a senior associate member of St Antony's College, Oxford in 1971–72, and an Alexander von Humboldt Stiftung Fellow, Department of Philosophy, Goethe University, Frankfurt in 1973–74, before becoming a lecturer in history at Cambridge in 1979–86 and a reader in History of Social Thought there in 1986–97. He has served as co-director of the Centre for History and Economics at King's since 1991 and held the post of professor of political science since 1997.

From 1964 to 1981 Stedman Jones served on the editorial board of the *New Left Review*. He was a joint founder of the *History Workshop Journal* in 1976. https://en.wikipedia.org/wiki/Gareth_Stedman_Jones

MAURICE HUGH KEEN, OBE, FBA, FRHISTS, FSA (1933-2012)

Keen was a British historian specializing in the Middle Ages. His father had been the Oxford University head of finance ('Keeper of the University Chest') and a Fellow of Balliol College, Oxford, and after schooling at Winchester College, Maurice became an undergraduate there in 1954. He was a contemporary and lifelong friend of Tom Bingham, later the Senior Law Lord, as well as of the military historian, Sir John Keegan, whose sister Mary he married.

Keen's first success came with the writing of *The Outlaws of Medieval Legend* while still a Junior Research Fellow at The Queen's College, Oxford, 1957–61. He was elected a tutorial Fellow of Balliol in 1961, retaining his fellowship until his retirement in 2000, when he was elected a Fellow Emeritus. He also served as Junior Dean (1963–68), Tutor for Admissions (1974–78), and Vice-Master (1980–83).

In 1984, Keen won the Wolfson History Prize for his book *Chivalry*. The book redefined in several ways the concept of chivalry, underlining the military aspect of it.

Keen was elected a Fellow of the British Academy, a Fellow of the Royal Historical Society, and a Fellow of the Society of Antiquaries of London.

He appears in the 1989 fictional novel *The Negotiator* by Frederick Forsyth.

He was an enthusiastic governor of Blundell's School in Tiverton for many years, the school being linked to Balliol by a scholarship and fellowship foundation gift. https://en.wikipedia.org/wiki/Maurice_Keen

SIR DAVID LINDSAY KEIR (1895–1973)

Keir was an historian by training whose academic interests centred on legal and constitutional history, and whose career also took him into university administration, at University College, Oxford; Balliol College, Oxford where he was Master; a brief spell at Harvard; and for 10 years he was Vice Chancellor and President, Queen's University, Belfast, a highly significant time which covered the World War II and saw the University move into the post-War period. Keir received many honorary degrees including an that of DCL (Doctor of Civil Law) from Oxford University in 1960. https://bit.ly/2S3Thq6

LESZEK KOŁAKOWSKI (1927–2009)

Kołakowski was a Polish philosopher and historian of philosophy who became one of Marxism's greatest intellectual critics.

Kolakowski was educated privately and in the underground school system during the German occupation of Poland in World War II. In 1950 he received an M.A. in philosophy from the University of Łódź, and in 1953 he received a doctorate in philosophy from the University of Warsaw, where he taught and served as chair of the department of the history of philosophy until 1968. Kołakowski began his scholarly career as an orthodox Marxist. He was a member of the communist youth organization and joined the Polish United Workers' Party (PUWP; the communist party) in 1945. When he was sent to Moscow for a course for promising intellectuals, however, he began to become disenchanted with the Soviet Marxist system.

Upon his return to Poland, he became part of the movement for democratization that led to the Polish workers' uprising of 1956. His revisionist critique of *Joseph Stalin, What Is Socialism?* (1957), was officially banned in Poland but was widely circulated nonetheless. His 1959 essay 'The Priest and the Jester', in which Kołakowski explored the roles of dogmatism and skepticism in intellectual history, brought him to national prominence in Poland. In the 1950s and '60s he published a series of books on the history of Western philosophy and a study of religious consciousness and institutional religion, at the same time attempting to define a humanistic Marxism; the latter effort resulted in *Towards a Marxist Humanism* (1967). https://www.britannica.com/biography/Leszek-Kolakowski

THOMAS SAMUEL KUHN (1922–1996)

Kuhn was one of the most influential philosophers of science of the 20th century, perhaps the most influential. His 1962 book *The Structure of Scientific Revolutions* is one of the most cited academic books of all time. Kuhn's contribution to the philosophy of science marked not only a break with several key positivist doctrines, but also inaugurated a new style of philosophy of science that brought it closer to the history of science.

His account of the development of science held that science enjoys periods of stable growth punctuated by revisionary revolutions. To this thesis, Kuhn added the controversial 'incommensurability thesis', that theories from differing periods suffer from certain deep kinds of failure of comparability. https://plato.stanford.edu/entries/thomas-kuhn/

EMMANUEL BERNARD LE ROY LADURIE (B. 1929)

Le Roy Ladurie is a French historian whose work is mainly focused upon Languedoc in the Ancien Régime, particularly the history of the peasantry. One of the leading historians of France, Le Roy Ladurie has been called the 'standard-bearer' of the third generation of the Annales school and the 'rock star of the medievalists', noted for his work in social history.

Montaillou is a book by Emmanuel Le Roy Ladurie that was first published in 1975. It was first translated into English in 1978 by Barbara Bray, and has been subtitled 'The Promised Land of Error and Cathars and Catholics in a French Village'.

Montaillou was Ladurie's 'most important and popular work'. Ladurie used the inquisitorial records of Jacques Fournier to reconstruct the lives of the inhabitants of Montaillou in the Ariège (at the time, the county of Foix). The work was part of the historical anthropology of the Annales school. https://en.w_kipedia.org/wiki/Emmanuel_Le_Roy_Ladurie. https://en.wikipedia.org/wiki/Montaillou_(book)

FIONA MACCARTHY, OBE (1940–2020)

MacCarthy was a British biographer and cultural historian best known for her studies of 19th- and 20th-century art and design.

After graduation MacCarthy's first job was as a merchandise editor and then journalist on *House & Garden* magazine. MacCarthy joined *The Guardian* in 1963 initially as an assistant to the women's editor Mary Stott. She was then appointed the newspaper's design correspondent, working as a features writer and columnist, sometimes using a pseudonymous byline to avoid two articles appearing in the same issue. In this role she interviewed David Hockney, Betty Friedan and John Lennon among others. She left *The Guardian* in 1969, briefly becoming women's editor of the *London Evening Standard* before settling in Sheffield.

In Sheffield MacCarthy became a biographer and critic. After writing a biography of the arts and crafts designer C.R. Ashbee, she came to wider attention as a biographer with a once-controversial study of the Roman Catholic craftsman and sculptor Eric Gill, first published in 1989. Subsequent biographies of Stanley Spencer in 1997 and of Byron in 2002 enhanced her reputation for undertaking detailed research into her subjects. MacCarthy was also known for her arts essays and reviews, which appeared in *The Guardian*, *The Times Literary Supplement* and *The New York Review of Books*. She contributed to TV and radio arts programmes. https://en.wikipedia.org/wiki/Fiona_MacCarthy

FREDERIC WILLIAM MAITLAND (1850–1906)

Maitland was an English jurist and historian of English law whose special contribution was to bring historical and comparative methods to bear on the study of English institutions.

Educated at Eton and at Trinity College, Cambridge, Maitland studied law at Lincoln's Inn, London, and was called to the bar in 1876. After practicing in London, he became reader in English law (1884) and professor (1888) at Cambridge. His best-known work, *The History of English Law Before the Time of Edward I*, 2 vol. (1895), was written with Sir Frederick Pollock.

He also edited several volumes published by the Selden Society for the study of English law, which he and others founded in 1887. His work helped to trace the influence of Roman law in English legal history. https://www.britannica.com/biography/Frederic-William-Maitland

BRONISŁAW KASPER MALINOWSKI (1884–1942)

Malinowski was one of the most important anthropologists of the 20th century who is widely recognized as a founder of social anthropology and principally associated with field studies of the peoples of Oceania. A prolific writer, he soon published reinterpretations of Australian Aboriginal data from literature then very popular in anthropological circles. These gained him a reputation and promoted his plans for field research, and in 1914 he was able to go to New Guinea. Six months' work among the Mailu on the south coast produced a monograph that, while lacking theoretical development, was sufficient—along with his study of the Australian family—to earn him a doctor of science (D.Sc.) degree from the University of London in 1916.

When he moved to the nearby Trobriand Islands, where he worked for two years in 1915–16 and 1917–18, Malinowski's talents flowered. Living in a tent among the people, speaking the vernacular fluently, recording 'texts' freely on the scene of action as well as in set interviews, and observing reactions with an acute clinical eye, Malinowski was able to present a dynamic picture of social institutions that clearly distinguished ideal norms from actual behaviour. In later publications on ceremonial exchange; on agricultural economics; on sex, marriage, and family life; on primitive law and custom; and on magic and myth, he drew heavily on his Trobriand data in putting forward theoretical propositions of significance in the development of social anthropology. Yet, while very rewarding, his field experience had its strains. Writing in Polish for his own private record, Malinowski kept field diaries in which he exposed very frankly his problems of isolation and of his relations with New Guinea people. https://www.britannica.com/biography/Bronislaw-Malinowski

DAVID MCLELLAN (B. 1940)

McLellan is an English scholar of Karl Marx and Marxism. He was educated at Merchant Taylors' School and St John's College, Oxford University.

McLellan is currently visiting Professor of Political Theory at Goldsmiths' College, University of London. He was previously Professor of Political Theory at the Department of Politics and International Relations at the University of Kent. McLellan has also been Visiting Professor at the State University of New York, Guest Fellow in Politics at the Indian Institute of Advanced Study, Simla, and has lectured widely in North America and Europe. https:// en.wikipedia.org/wiki/David_McLellan_(political_scientist)

JOHN DAVID MABBOTT (1898–1988)

Mabbott was President of St John's College, Oxford from 1963 from to 1969. He was educated at Berwickshire High School; the University of Edinburgh; and St John's. He was a Lecturer in Classics at the University of Reading from 1922 to 1923; and then a Lecturer at the University College of North Wales from 1923 to 1924. He was Fellow of St John's from 1924 to 1963; Tutor from 1930 to 1956; and Senior Tutor from 1956 to 1963. He wrote: *The State and the Citizen* (1948); *An Introduction to Ethics* (1966); *John Locke* (1973); and *Oxford Memories* (1986). https://en.wikipedia.org/wiki/John_David_Mabbott

PETER MATHIAS, CBE, FRHISTS, FBA, MAE (1928–2016)

Mathias was a British economic historian and the former Chichele Professor of Economic History at the University of Oxford. His research focused on the history of industry, business, and technology, both in Britain and Europe. He is most well known for his publication of *The First Industrial Nation: an Economic History of Britain 1700–1914* (1969), which discussed not only the multiple factors that made industrialisation possible, but also how it was sustained. https://en.wikipedia.org/wiki/Peter_Mathias

ARNALDO DANTE MOMIGLIANO (1908–87)

Momigliano was an Italian historian known for his work in historiography, characterised by Donald Kagan as 'the world's leading student of the writing of history in the ancient world'.

In the 1930s, Momigliano joined the National Fascist Party, swore loyalty to Benito Mussolini, and sought exemption from antisemitic Italian racial laws as a party member. Momigliano believed that several classical works of European literature had contributed to the nationalism and warfare in Europe, and considered works such as *Germania* and the *Iliad* as 'among the most dangerous books ever written'. Momigliano considered it wasteful and 'comical' to spend much efforts at identifying and explaining the forces held responsible for the gradual disintegration of the Roman Empire.

After 1930, Momigliano contributed a number of biographies to the *Enciclopedia Italiana*; in the 1940s and 1950s he contributed biographies to the *Oxford Classical Dictionary* and *Encyclopædia Britannica*. In 1974, he was made an honorary Knight Commander of the Order of the British Empire (KBE). https://en.wikipedia.org/wiki/Arnaldo_Momigliano

MICHEL EYQUEM DE MONTAIGNE (1533-92)

Also known as Lord of Montaigne, he was one of the most significant philosophers of the French Renaissance, known for popularizing the essay as a literary genre. His work is noted for its merging of casual anecdotes and autobiography with intellectual insight. His massive volume Essais contains some of the most influential essays ever written.

Montaigne had a direct influence on Western writers including Francis Bacon, René Descartes, Blaise Pascal, Voltaire, Jean-Jacques Rousseau, David Hume, Edward Gibbon, Virginia Woolf, Albert Hirschman, William Hazlitt, Ralph Waldo Emerson, John Henry Newman, Karl Marx, Sigmund Freud, Charles Darwin, Friedrich Nietzsche, Stefan Zweig, Eric Hoffer, Isaac Asimov, and possibly, on the later works of William Shakespeare.

During his lifetime, Montaigne was admired more as a statesman than as an author. https://en.wikipedia.org/wiki/Michel_de_Montaigne

CHARLES-LOUIS DE SECONDAT, BARON DE LA BRÈDE ET DE MONTESQUIEU (1689–1755)

Generally referred to as Montesquieu, he was a French judge, man of letters, and political philosopher.

He is the principal source of the theory of separation of powers, which is implemented in many constitutions throughout the world. He is also known for doing more than any other author to secure the place of the word 'despotism' in the political lexicon. His anonymously-published *The Spirit of Law* in 1748, which was received well in both Great Britain and the American colonies, influenced the Founding Fathers in drafting the United States Constitution. https://en.wikipedia.org/wiki/Montesquieu

PRYS MORGAN, FRHISTS, FSA, FLSW (B. 1937)

Morgan is a Welsh historian. Prys Morgan was born in Britain at Cardiff in 1937, the son of academic T.J. Morgan. His parents first met at the National Eisteddfod of Wales in 1926. Like his brother, Rhodri Morgan, Prys Morgan was educated at Whitchurch Grammar School and St John's College, Oxford.

From 1964 he taught history at Swansea University, where his father had been a professor. He is now an Emeritus Professor of the university.

Following his retirement from academic life, he became President of the National Eisteddfod of Wales at Swansea, President of the Honourable Society of Cymmrodorion, and is joint director of the Iolo Morganwg project at the Centre for Welsh and Celtic Studies in Aberystwyth. He is also a Founding Fellow of the Learned Society of Wales and is a Member of its inaugural Council. https://en.wikipedia.org/wiki/Prys_Morgan

SIR LEWIS BERNSTEIN NAMIER (1880–1962)

Namier was a British historian, who was most noted for his work on 18th- and 19th-century Europe. He immigrated to England in 1906 and studied at Balliol College, Oxford. He took British nationality and legally adopted an Anglicized name before World War I, in which he served first in the army and then in the Foreign Office, where he remained until 1920. Namier failed to get a teaching post at Oxford, went into business, and later devoted his time to research.

The appearance of Namier's *The Structure of Politics at the Accession of George III* in 1929 revolutionized 18th-century historiography and remains his most considerable work. By intensive research over a brief period, he aimed to show why men entered politics, and he rejected the simple classification of Whig and Tory in favour of personal, family, or regional interests. He was professor of modern history (1931–53) at the Victoria University of Manchester and produced various books of essays and two important works: *1848: The Revolution of the Intellectuals* (1946) and *Diplomatic Prelude, 1938–39* (1948). Of an official *History of Parliament*, begun under his editorship, part I, *The House of Commons, 1745–90*, in three volumes, appeared in 1964.

Namier was made an honorary fellow of Balliol in 1948 and was knighted in 1952. His approach to history attracted many followers but also created opposition among historians who felt that he ignored irrational elements in history in favour of a preoccupation with the mechanism of politics. https://www.britannica.com/biography/Lewis-Bernstein-Namier

ERWIN PANOFSKY (1892–1968)

Panofsky was a German-Jewish art historian, whose academic career was pursued mostly in the U.S. after the rise of the Nazi regime.

Panofsky's work represents a high point in the modern academic study of iconography, which he used in hugely influential works like his 'little book' *Renaissance and Renascences in Western Art* and his masterpiece, *Early Netherlandish Painting*.

Many of his works are still in print, including *Studies in Iconology: Humanist Themes in the Art of the Renaissance* (1939), *Meaning in the Visual Arts* (1955), and his 1943 study *The Life and Art of Albrecht Dürer*. Panofsky's ideas were also highly influential in intellectual history in general, particularly in his use of historical ideas to interpret artworks and vice versa. https://en.wikipedia.org/wiki/Erwin_Panofsky

TEIFION PHILLIPS (1917–2002)

Phillips was a British academic and historian. He arrived in 1946 to teach History at the Barry Boys' County School for one term – and retired as Headmaster (of Barry Comprehensive School) in 1981. Over that 35-year period Teifion Phillips would prove to be one of the most extraordinary teachers of 20th-century Wales.

The grammar school was already in the habit of producing shooting stars for the academic firmament: through its redbrick late Victorian buildings in the 1930s had passed the archaeologist Glyn Daniel, the Cambridge economic historian David Joslin and a future Vice-Chancellor of Oxford University, Sir John Habakkuk.

Phillips now set about creating a conveyor belt of 'Barry historians'. Within a decade boys began to arrive in clutches at Balliol College, Oxford, to read History. The talent spotter became a mythical figure in pedagogic circles. His hit rate, at Oxford and then elsewhere, started early with the second pupil he sent to Balliol in 1952 after National Service, the future President of Corpus Christi and the greatest cultural historian of the early modern world, Sir Keith Thomas. http://bit.ly/3rK0kVw

DAVID BEERS QUINN (1909–2002)

Quinn was an Irish historian who wrote extensively on the voyages of discovery and colonisation of America. Many of his publications appeared as volumes of the Hakluyt Society. He played a major role in assisting the presentation of the historical aspects during the quadricentennial celebrations (1984–87) of the first establishment a colony at Roanoke Island.

He became interested in the voyages of discovery made by Humphrey Gilbert. At that time historians relied uncritically on the works of Richard Hakluyt published around 1600. Quinn's work and the new sources he discovered resulted in his first volume for the Hakluyt Society, and marked the beginning of his seminal work on voyages of exploration, which he developed from 1944 at University College, Swansea. In 1957 he moved to Liverpool University. https:// en.wikipedia.org/wiki/David_Beers_Quinn

KEITH GILBERT ROBBINS, FRSE, FRHISTS, FLSW (1940-2019)

Robbins was a British historian and Vice-Chancellor of the University of Wales, Lampeter. Professor Robbins was educated at Bristol Grammar School, and Magdalen and St Antony's Colleges, Oxford.

His academic career began in 1963 as Assistant Lecturer in History at the University of York where he subsequently became Lecturer. He moved to the University College of North Wales, Bangor, in 1971, as Professor of History and was later appointed Dean of the Faculty of Arts. In 1980 he moved to the University of Glasgow as Professor of Modern History. https://en.wikipedia.org/ wiki/Keith_Robbins

JEAN-JACQUES ROUSSEAU (1712-78)

Rousseau was a Genevan philosopher, writer, and composer. His political philosophy influenced the progress of the Enlightenment throughout Europe, as well as aspects of the French Revolution and the development of modern political, economic and educational thought.

His *Discourse on Inequality* and *The Social Contract* are cornerstones in modern political and social thought. Rousseau's sentimental novel *Julie*, or the *New Heloise* (1761) was important to the development of preromanticism and romanticism in fiction. His *Emile*, or *On Education* (1762) is an educational treatise on the place of the individual in society. Rousseau's autobiographical writings— the posthumously published *Confessions* (composed in 1769), which initiated the modern autobiography, and the unfinished *Reveries of the Solitary Walker* (composed 1776–78)—exemplified the late-18th-century 'Age of Sensibility', and featured an increased focus on subjectivity and introspection that later characterized modern writing. https://en.wikipedia.org/wiki/Jean-Jacques_Rousseau

RAPHAEL ELKAN SAMUEL (1934–96)

Samuel was a British Marxist historian, described by Stuart Hall as 'one of the most outstanding, original intellectuals of his generation'. He was professor of history at the University of East London at the time of his death and also taught at Ruskin College from 1962 until his death. He founded the History Workshop movement at trade union connected Ruskin College, Oxford. Samuel and the History Workshop movement powerfully influenced the development of the approach to historical research and writing commonly called 'history from below'.

In 1987 Samuel married the writer and critic Alison Light. Samuel's archive is held at Bishopsgate Library. https://en.wikipedia.org/wiki/Raphael_Samuel

PAOLO SARPI (1552–1623)

Sarpi was an Italian patriot, scholar, and state theologian during Venice's struggle with Pope Paul V. Between 1610 and 1618 he wrote his *History of the Council of Trent*, an important work decrying papal absolutism. Among Italians, he was an early advocate of the separation of church and state. https://www.britannica.com/biography/Paolo-Sarpi

PAUL ALEXANDER SLACK, FBA (B. 1943)

Slack is a British historian. He is a former Principal of Linacre College, Oxford, Pro-Vice-Chancellor of the University of Oxford, and Professor of Early Modern Social History in the University of Oxford.

Slack was educated at Bradford Grammar School, the University of Oxford (BA, DPhil). He was a Fellow of Exeter College, Oxford from 1973 until 1996. He served as Junior Proctor during the academic year 1986/7 and Chairman of the General Board 1995/6.

On 1 October 1996 he took office as Principal of Linacre College. He retired in September 2010. He was appointed Pro-Vice-Chancellor in 1997, becoming in 2000 Pro-Vice-Chancellor (Academic Services and University Collections). In 1999 he was appointed Professor of Early Modern Social History. He is also a member of the Environmental Change Institute Advisory Board and a former Chairman of the Curators of the University Libraries. Slack was elected a Fellow of the British Academy in 1990. https://en.wikipedia.org/wiki/Paul_Slack

QUENTIN ROBERT DUTHIE SKINNER, FBA (B. 1940)

Skinner is a British intellectual historian. He is regarded as one of the founders of the Cambridge School of the history of political thought. He has won numerous prizes for his work, including the Wolfson History Prize in 1979 and the Balzan Prize in 2006. Between 1996 and 2008 he was Regius Professor of History at the University of Cambridge. He is currently the Barber Beaumont Professor of the Humanities and Co-director of The Centre for the Study of the History of Political Thought at Queen Mary University of London.

Skinner is regarded as one of the founders of the Cambridge School of the history of political thought, best known for its attention to what J.G.A. Pocock has described as the 'languages' in which moral and political philosophy has been written. Skinner's contribution has been to articulate a theory of interpretation in which leading texts in the history of political theory are treated essentially as interventions in on-going political debates, and in which the main focus is on what individual writers may be said to have been doing in what they wrote. https://en.wikipedia.org/wiki/Quentin_Skinner

SIR RICHARD WILLIAM SOUTHERN, FBA, FRSL (1912-2001)

Southern who published under the name R.W. Southern, was a noted English medieval historian, based at the University of Oxford. He was a fellow of Balliol from 1937 to 1961 (where he lectured alongside Christopher Hill), Chichele Professor of Modern

History at Oxford from 1961 to 1969, and president of St John's College, Oxford, from 1969 to 1981. He was president of the Royal Historical Society from 1969 to 1973. Southern was awarded the Balzan Prize for Medieval History in 1987. He was knighted in 1974.

Southern's *The Making of the Middle Ages* (1953) was a seminal work, and established Southern's reputation as a medievalist. This pioneering work, sketching the main personalities and cultural influences that shaped the character of Western Europe from the late 10th to the early 13th century and describing the development of social, political, and religious institutions, opened up new vistas in medieval history, and has been translated into many languages. https://en.wikipedia.org/wiki/R._W._Southern

JONATHAN DERMOT SPENCE (B. 1936)

Spence is an English-born American historian and public intellectual specialising in Chinese history. He was Sterling Professor of History at Yale University from 1993 to 2008. His most widely read book is The Search for Modern China, a survey of the last several hundred years of Chinese history based on his popular course at Yale. A prolific author, reviewer, and essayist, he has published more than a dozen books on China. He retired from Yale in 2008.

Spence's major interest is modern China, especially the Qing Dynasty, and relations between China and the West. Spence frequently uses biographies to examine cultural and political history. Another common theme is the efforts of both Westerners and Chinese 'to change China', and how such efforts were frustrated. https://en.wikipedia.org/wiki/Jonathan_Spence

JOHN BARRY STEANE (1928–2011)

Steane was an English music critic, musicologist, literary scholar and teacher, with a particular interest in singing and the human voice. His 36-year career as a schoolmaster overlapped with his career as a music critic and author of books on Elizabethan drama, and opera and concert singers.

Among Steane's works are critical studies of Christopher Marlowe and Alfred Tennyson, and a series of books on music, concentrating on singing and singers. He contributed to a range of musical journals, including *Gramophone* and *The Musical Times*, and wrote articles for the *Grove Dictionary of Music and Musicians* and the *Oxford Dictionary of National Biography*. https://en.wikipedia.org/wiki/J._B._Steane

LAWRENCE STONE (1919-99)

Stone was an English historian of early modern Britain, after a start to his career as an art historian of English medieval art. He is noted for his work on the English Civil War and the history of marriage, families and the aristocracy.

Stone began as a medievalist, and his first book was the volume on medieval sculpture in Britain for what is now the *Yale History of Art* series (then the *Pelican History of Art*). He was a bold choice by the series editor, Nicholas Pevsner, but the book was well received.

According to Stone, narrative is the main rhetorical device traditionally used by historians. In 1979, at a time when Social History of the previous generation was demanding a social-science model of analysis, Stone detected a revival in historiography of the narrative. https://en.wikipedia.org/wiki/Lawrence_Stone

HUGH STRETTON, AC (1924-2015)

Stretton was an Australian historian who wrote books on politics, urban planning and economics, and a Rhodes Scholar. He was a key figure in the development and implementation of government policies affecting cities, particularly during the Whitlam Government. https://en.wikipedia.org/wiki/Hugh_Stretton

TACITUS (AD 56-C. 120)

Tacitus was a Roman orator and public official, probably the greatest historian and one of the greatest prose stylists who wrote in the

Latin language. Among his works are the *Germania*, describing the Germanic tribes, the *Historiae* (Histories), concerning the Roman Empire from AD 69 to 96, and the later *Annals*, dealing with the empire in the period from AD 14 to 68. https://www.britannica.com/biography/Tacitus-Roman-historian

RICHARD HENRY TAWNEY (1880–1962)

Tawney was an English economic historian and one of the most influential social critics and reformers of his time. He was also noted for his scholarly contributions to the economic history of England from 1540 to 1640.

Tawney was educated at Rugby School and at Balliol College, Oxford. After doing social work in London at Toynbee Hall, he became an active member of the Workers' Educational Association in Rochdale, Lancashire, serving as its president from 1928 to 1944. He taught tutorial classes (for working-class students) at Oxford, where he wrote his first major work, *The Agrarian Problem in the Sixteenth Century* (1912). That study of the use of land in an underdeveloped economy that was simultaneously in the midst of a population explosion and a price revolution (caused by the influx of New World gold and silver) opened a new avenue of research for historians. The next year he began teaching at the London School of Economics, becoming professor of economic history in 1931 and professor emeritus in 1949.

Tawney was an ardent socialist who helped formulate the economic and moral viewpoint of Britain's Labour Party in the 1920s and '30s by his influential publications. https://www.britannica.com/biography/Richard-Henry-Tawney

ALAN JOHN PERCIVALE TAYLOR, FBA (1906–90)

Taylor was a British historian who specialised in 19th- and 20th-century European diplomacy. Both a journalist and a broadcaster, he became well known to millions through his television lectures. His combination of academic rigour and popular appeal led the historian Richard Overy to describe him as 'the Macaulay of our age'. In a 2011 poll by *History Today* magazine, he was named the fourth most important historian of the previous 60 years. https://en.wikipedia.org/wiki/A._J._P._Taylor

EDWARD PALMER THOMPSON (1924–93)

Thompson was a British historian, writer, socialist and peace campaigner. He is probably best known today for his historical work on the British radical movements in the late 18th and early 19th centuries, in particular *The Making of the English Working Class* (1963).

His work is considered by some to have been among the most important contributions to labour history and social history in the latter twentieth-century, with a global impact, including on scholarship in Asia and Africa. In a 2011 poll by *History Today* magazine, he was named the second most important historian of the previous 60 years, behind only Fernand Braudel. https://en.wikipedia.org/wiki/E._P._Thompson

PAUL THOMPSON (B. 1935)

Thompson is a British sociologist and oral historian. Prior to his recent retirement, he held the position of Research Professor of Sociology at the University of Essex. Thompson is regarded as a pioneer in social science research, particularly due to the development of life stories and oral history within sociology and social history.

Thompson is regarded as one of the pioneers of oral history as a research methodology in the social sciences. In 1971 he founded the Oral History Society and the journal *Oral History*. Between 1970 and 1973 he carried out a project titled 'Family Life and Work Experience before 1918' which was the first national oral history interview study to be carried out in Britain. The project resulted in a number of publications, including Thompson's *The Edwardians: The Remaking of British Society*, which was published in 1975 and again in revised form in 1992. https://en.wikipedia.org/wiki/Paul_Thompson_(oral_historian)

ALEXIS CHARLES HENRI CLÉREL, COMTE DE TOCQUEVILLE (1805-59)

Colloquially known as Tocqueville, he was a French aristocrat, diplomat, political scientist, political philosopher and historian. He is best known for his works *Democracy in America* (appearing in two volumes, 1835 and 1840) and *The Old Regime and the Revolution* (1856). In both, he analysed the improved living standards and social conditions of individuals as well as their relationship to the market and state in Western societies. *Democracy in America* was published after Tocqueville's travels in the United States and is today considered an early work of sociology and political science. https://en.wikipedia.org/wiki/Alexis_de_Tocqueville

ARNOLD JOSEPH TOYNBEE, CH, FBA (1889-1975)

Toynbee was a British historian, a philosopher of history, an author of numerous books and a research professor of international history at the London School of Economics and King's College London. Toynbee in the 1918–50 period was a leading specialist on international affairs.

He is best known for his 12-volume *A Study of History (1934–1961)*. With his prodigious output of papers, articles, speeches and presentations, and numerous books translated into many languages, Toynbee was a widely read and discussed scholar in the 1940s and 1950s. However, by the 1960s his magnum opus had fallen out of favour among mainstream historians and his vast readership had faded. https://en.wikipedia.org/wiki/Arnold_J._Toynbee

HUGH REDWALD TREVOR-ROPER, BARON DACRE OF GLANTON, FBA (1914-2003)

Trevor-Roper was an English historian. He was Regius Professor of Modern History at the University of Oxford. He was a polemicist and essayist on a range of historical topics, but particularly England in the 16th and 17th centuries and Nazi Germany.

Trevor-Roper's most widely read and financially rewarding book was titled *The Last Days of Hitler* (1947). It emerged from his assignment as a British intelligence officer in 1945 to discover what happened in the last days of Hitler's bunker.

From his interviews with a range of witnesses and study of surviving documents he demonstrated that Hitler was dead and had not escaped from Berlin. He also showed that Hitler's dictatorship was not an efficient unified machine but a hodge-podge of overlapping rivalries. His reputation was 'severely damaged' in 1983 when he authenticated the *Hitler Diaries* shortly before they were shown to be forgeries. https://en.wikipedia.org/wiki/Hugh_Trevor-Roper

THUCYDIDES (C. 460–C. 400 BC)

Thucydides was an Athenian historian and general. His History of the Peloponnesian War recounts the fifth-century BC war between Sparta and Athens until the year 411 BC. Thucydides has been dubbed the father of 'scientific history' by those who accept his claims to have applied strict standards of impartiality and evidence-gathering and analysis of cause and effect, without reference to intervention by the deities, as outlined in his introduction to his work.

He also has been called the father of the school of political realism, which views the political behavior of individuals and the subsequent outcomes of relations between states as ultimately mediated by, and constructed upon, the emotions of fear and self-interest. His text is still studied at universities and military colleges worldwide. The Melian dialogue is regarded as a seminal work of international relations theory, while his version of Pericles' Funeral Oration is widely studied by political theorists, historians, and students of the classics.

More generally, Thucydides developed an understanding of human nature to explain behaviour in such crises as plagues, massacres, and civil war. https://en.wikipedia.org/wiki/Thucydides

ALEXIS CHARLES HENRI CLÉREL, COMTE DE TOCQUEVILLE (1805–59)

Colloquially known as Tocqueville, he was a French aristocrat, diplomat, political scientist, political philosopher and historian. He is best known for his works *Democracy in America* (appearing in two volumes, 1835 and 1840) and *The Old Regime and the Revolution* (1856). In both, he analysed the improved living standards and social conditions of individuals as well as their relationship to the market and state in Western societies. *Democracy in America* was published after Tocqueville's travels in the United States and is today considered an early work of sociology and political science. https://en.wikipedia.org/wiki/Alexis_de_Tocqueville

GEORGE MACAULAY TREVELYAN, OM, CBE, FRS, FBA (1876–1962)

Trevelyan was a British historian and academic. He was a Fellow of Trinity College, Cambridge, from 1898 to 1903. He then spent more than twenty years as a full-time author. He returned to the University of Cambridge and was Regius Professor of History from 1927 to 1943. He served as Master of Trinity College from 1940 to 1951. In retirement, he was Chancellor of Durham University.

The noted historian E. H. Carr considered Trevelyan to be one of the last historians of the Whig tradition.

Many of his writings promoted the Whig Party, an important aspect of British politics from the 17th century to the mid-19th century, and its successor, the Liberal Party. Whigs and Liberals believed the common people had a more positive effect on history than did royalty and that democratic government would bring about steady social progress. https://en.wikipedia.org/wiki/G._M._Trevelyan

'VOLTAIRE' FRANÇOIS-MARIE AROUET (1694–1778)

Known by his nom de plume Voltaire, he was a French Enlightenment writer, historian, and philosopher famous for his wit, his criticism of

Christianity—especially the Roman Catholic Church—as well as his advocacy of freedom of speech, freedom of religion, and separation of church and state.

Voltaire was a versatile and prolific writer, producing works in almost every literary form, including plays, poems, novels, essays, histories, and scientific expositions. He wrote more than 20,000 letters and 2,000 books and pamphlets. He was one of the first authors to become renowned and commercially successful internationally. He was an outspoken advocate of civil liberties, and he was at constant risk from the strict censorship laws of the Catholic French monarchy. His polemics witheringly satirized intolerance, religious dogma, and the French institutions of his day. https://en.wikipedia.org/wiki/Voltaire

MARTHA BEATRICE WEBB, BARONESS PASSFIELD, FBA NÉE POTTER (1858–1943)

Webb was an English sociologist, economist, socialist, labour historian and social reformer. It was Webb who coined the term collective bargaining. She was among the founders of the London School of Economics and played a crucial role in forming the Fabian Society. https://en.wikipedia.org/wiki/Beatrice_Webb

MAXIMILIAN KARL EMIL WEBER (1864–1920)

Weber was a German historian, sociologist, jurist, and political economist, who is regarded today as one of the most important theorists on the development of modern Western society. His ideas would profoundly influence social theory and social research. Despite being recognized as one of the fathers of sociology, along with Karl Marx, Auguste Comte and Émile Durkheim, Weber never saw himself as a sociologist, but as a historian.

Unlike Émile Durkheim, Weber did not believe in monocausal explanations, proposing instead that for any outcome there can be multiple causes. As such, he was a key proponent of methodological anti-positivism, arguing for the study of social action through interpretive (rather than empiricist) methods, based on understanding the purpose and meanings that individuals attach to their own actions. Weber's main intellectual concern was in understanding the processes of rationalisation, secularisation, and 'disenchantment', which he took to be the result of a new way of thinking about the world, associating such processes with the rise of capitalism and modernity.

Weber is best known for his thesis combining economic sociology and the sociology of religion, emphasising the importance of cultural influences embedded in religion as a means for understanding the genesis of capitalism (contrasting Marx's historical materialism). Weber would first elaborate his theory in his seminal work, *The Protestant Ethic and the Spirit of Capitalism* (1905), where he attributed ascetic Protestantism as one of the major 'elective affinities' involved in the rise of market-driven capitalism and the rational-legal nation-state in the Western world. https://en.wikipedia.org/wiki/Max_Weber

LUDWIG WITTGENSTEIN (1889–1951)

Considered by some to be the greatest philosopher of the 20th century, Ludwig Wittgenstein played a central, if controversial, role in 20th-century analytic philosophy. He continues to influence current philosophical thought in topics as diverse as logic and language, perception and intention, ethics and religion, aesthetics and culture. Originally, there were two commonly recognized stages of Wittgenstein's thought—the early and the later—both of which were taken to be pivotal in their respective periods. In more recent scholarship, this division has been questioned: some interpreters have claimed a unity between all stages of his thought, while others talk of a more nuanced division, adding stages such as the middle Wittgenstein and the third Wittgenstein. Still, it is commonly acknowledged that the early Wittgenstein is epitomized in his Tractatus Logico-Philosophicus. By showing the application of modern logic to metaphysics, via language, he provided new insights into the relations between world, thought and language and thereby into the nature of philosophy. It is the later Wittgenstein, mostly recognized in the Philosophical Investigations, who took the more revolutionary step in critiquing all of traditional philosophy including its climax in his own early work. The nature of his new philosophy is heralded as anti-systematic through and through, yet still conducive to genuine philosophical understanding of traditional problems. https://plato.stanford.edu/entries/wittgenstein/

ANTHONY WOOD (1923-87)

Wood was a British school teacher and historian. He was an expert on 19th and 20th century European history and was head of history at Winchester College. He was the author of the popular The Russian Revolution in the Seminar Studies in History series, which has not been out of print since it was first published in 1979. https://en.wikipedia.org/wiki/Anthony_Wood_(historian)

SIR (ERNEST) LLEWELLYN WOODWARD (1890-1971)

Woodward was a British historian. He was educated at Merchant Taylors' School and Corpus Christi College, Oxford, and after the First World War became a lecturer in Modern History and fellow of All Souls College from 1919 to 1944 and a fellow at New College from 1922 to 1939. Later he was Montague Burton Professor of International Relations (1944–47) and then Professor of Modern History at Oxford. He later taught at Princeton University in the United States (1951–62). His scope was impressively wide, his first publication being on the late Roman Empire whilst on sick leave from service in the First World War but his most famous works being on the First World War. He wrote *The Age of Reform* in the Oxford History of England. https://en.wikipedia.org/wiki/Llewellyn_Woodward

WILLIAM WORDSWORTH (1770-1850)

Wordsworth was an English Romantic poet who, with Samuel Taylor Coleridge, helped to launch the Romantic Age in English literature with their joint publication *Lyrical Ballads* (1798). Wordsworth's magnum opus is generally considered to be *The Prelude*, a semi-autobiographical poem of his early years that he revised and expanded a number of times. It was posthumously titled and published by his wife in the year of his death, before which it was generally known as 'the poem to Coleridge'. Wordsworth was Poet Laureate from 1843 until his death from pleurisy on 23 April 1850. https://en.wikipedia.org/wiki/William_Wordsworth

THEODORE ZELDIN, CBE (B. 1933)

Zeldin is an Oxford scholar and thinker whose books have searched for answers to three questions. Where can a person look to find more inspiring ways of spending each day and each year? What ambitions remain unexplored, beyond happiness, prosperity, faith, love, technology or therapy? What role could there be for individuals with independent minds, or who feel isolated or different, or misfits? Each of Zeldin's books illuminates from a different angle what people can do today that they could not in previous centuries. https://en.wikipedia.org/wiki/Theodore_Zeldin

Social Science Press is grateful and therefore acknowledges the various websites from which information was drawn to create the endnotes and Appendix. All the websites have been duly cited, but a special thanks is owed to Wikipedia, Britannica and Stanford Encyclopedia of Philosophy.